#WWE

THE YEAR'S WORK: STUDIES IN FAN CULTURE AND CULTURAL THEORY

Edward P. Comentale and Aaron Jaffe, editors

#WWE

Professional Wrestling in the Digital Age

EDITED BY DRU JEFFRIES

INDIANA UNIVERSITY PRESS

This book is a publication of

Indiana University Press
Office of Scholarly Publishing
Herman B Wells Library 350
1320 East 10th Street
Bloomington, Indiana 47405 USA

iupress.indiana.edu

© 2019 by Indiana University Press

Manufactured in the United States of America

Cataloging information is available from the Library of Congress.

ISBN 978-0-253-04490-7 (hardback)
ISBN 978-0-253-04491-4 (paperback)
ISBN 978-0-253-04494-5 (ebook)

1 2 3 4 5   24 23 22 21 20 19

*This book is dedicated to Charlotte Kannegiesser,
the real highlight of the 2013 Elimination Chamber
pay-per-view. Stay baby, pony girl.*

CONTENTS

Introduction: Storyworld, Wrestling,
Entertainment / Dru Jeffries   1

PART I: CORPORATE KAYFABE: WWE AS MEDIA EMPIRE

one   World Building in the WWE Universe / Eero Laine   25

two   The Work of Wrestling: Struggles for
         Creative and Industrial Power in
         WWE Labor / Andrew Zolides   47

three Mapping the WWE Universe:
         Territory, Media, Capitalism / Dru Jeffries
         and Andrew Kannegiesser   65

four   Narrative Smarts: Negotiations of Creative
         Authority in Wrestling's Reality Era / Christian Norman   83

PART II: MARKS AND SMARTS: WWE'S UNRULY FANDOMS

five   Sport vs. Spectacle: Fan Discontent and the
         Rise of Sports Entertainment / Shane Toepfer   103

six   The Marks Have Gone Off-Script:
         Rogue Actors in WWE's Stands / Sam Ford   120

seven Botchamania and the Acoustics of Professional
         Wrestling / Christian B. Long   138

**PART III: THEN, NOW, FOREVER: WRESTLING WITH WWE'S
PAST AND TRANSMEDIA FUTURE**

eight "Tout It Out": WWE's Experimentation and
         Failure with Social TV / Cory Barker   159

nine   "We're Not Just Cheerleaders": Reading the
         Postfeminist Polysemy of *Total Divas* / Anna F. Peppard   177

ten   Daniel's Specter: Daniel Bryan, Chris Benoit,
and the Work of Mourning / Sean Desilets   198

Index   217

Contents

#WWE

INTRODUCTION

Storyworld, Wrestling, Entertainment

Dru Jeffries

Professional wrestling has long been defined by *kayfabe,* a concept that directly connects today's multimillion-dollar global industry with its humble roots in carnival tents and local gymnasiums. Kayfabe signifies the central premise underlying every professional wrestling performance: that the outsize and colorful characters, the spectacular athletic contests in which they compete, and the ongoing serialized narratives in which these physical conflicts appear are "authentic, spontaneous, unscripted."[1] In the days of the traveling carnival, kayfabe represented the knowledge gap between the conman and his mark, and maintaining this gap was necessary to "protect the business."[2] The term thus refers not just to the creation of a fictional storyworld but also to the power dynamic between creators and audiences that it engenders. As Eero Laine describes it, "kayfabe is the truth those in power tell you. It is the storylines and corporate narrative presented to the public. It is also an acknowledgement that even as you try to break through the web of kayfabe, you are still probably being duped one way or another."[3] In the context of contemporary professional wrestling, however, the knowledge gap between creators and audiences has narrowed considerably. In a world where fans enjoy unprecedented access to backstage rumors and even the performers themselves via social media and other online platforms, "the game" has evolved from a con perpetrated upon an unwitting victim to a televised (or otherwise mediated) fiction that is both mutually agreed upon and collaboratively constituted.[4] To break kayfabe today is merely to acknowledge what every wrestling fan already knows: that professional wrestlers are theatrical performers rather than competitive athletes, that the outcomes of matches are predetermined to facilitate ongoing serialized narratives, and that a corporate enterprise like World Wrestling Entertainment (WWE) is much more directly comparable to media industry giants like Disney and Netflix than to professional sporting leagues like the National Football League (NFL) or Major League Baseball (MLB).

#WWE: Professional Wrestling in the Digital Age is particularly interested in this last point of comparison. Under the corporate leadership of its founder, chair, and principal shareholder, Vince McMahon, and his immediate family—including wife Linda, daughter Stephanie, son Shane, and son-in-law Paul "Triple H" Levesque—WWE has developed, refined, and transformed the performance genre historically known as professional wrestling into the televisual (and increasingly transmedia) genre of "sports entertainment."[5] Through its presence on broadcast television and live shows around the world, as well as its aggressive expansion into non-wrestling-related entertainment media, WWE has established itself as a dominant force not only in the professional wrestling industry but also in global popular culture more broadly. The ten chapters in this book view and analyze WWE through the lens of television and media studies, treating the company not strictly as a professional wrestling promotion or federation but rather as a brand, an employer, a publicly traded company, a content producer and distributor, a sprawling transmedia storyworld, and an object of fandom that contributes to the contemporary mediasphere in unique and instructive ways. Such an approach is also consistent with WWE's front-facing corporate identity: tellingly, the company no longer defines itself as a professional wrestling federation but rather as "an integrated media organization and recognized leader in global entertainment" devoted to "creat[ing] and deliver[ing] original content 52 weeks a year to a global audience."[6]

To date, academic analyses of professional wrestling have largely focused on sociological/ethnographic studies of wrestling culture and content analyses of wrestling narratives, resulting in a discourse primarily interested in issues of representation, particularly with respect to race, gender, class, and nationalism. While such research is obviously valuable, the effects of mediation on the presentation and content of professional wrestling have been more or less neglected in the existing discourse. In a recent piece exploring the interdisciplinary possibilities of professional wrestling scholarship, Garrett L. Castleberry suggests that a "method conjoining the disciplines of media studies, communication studies, and television studies" would be particularly useful for understanding the narrative complexity, transmedia synergy, and modes of audience engagement that define the genre in the present day.[7] The essays in this volume answer Castleberry's call, drawing connections between WWE's business practices and the increasingly diversified media and narrative content they create and distribute.

Since becoming a publicly traded corporation in 1999, WWE has consistently increased its efforts toward developing ancillary products and business ventures, each seeking to broaden the appeal of their brand beyond the traditional confines of the professional wrestling genre. In so doing, they have also exploded the concept of kayfabe, creating multiple overlapping storyworlds, each of which bears its own unique relationship to the main storyworld (as constructed in WWE's weekly television shows and monthly pay-per-view "supercard" events). To date, these ancillary products have included reality television series (in both competition and *Real Housewives*–style "catfights and confessionals" modes), documentaries modeled after ESPN's *30 for 30* series, roundtable discussion shows, animated television series (for both children and adult audiences), prank and sketch comedy shows, and films (both theatrical and direct-to-video) featuring WWE performers in lead or supporting roles. Observing the contradictions that arise between these various access points to what has become known as the "WWE Universe," Brian Jansen notes that the company's content diversification strategy "might foreclose the possibility of total immersion in WWE's [main] on-screen product, but if it limits audience's suspension of disbelief, it opens, in its blurring of fact and fiction, new storytelling possibilities."[8] Far from causing audiences to lose interest, these authorized, controlled, and always-mediated peeks behind the proverbial curtain explicitly encourage fans to view the main product intertextually and to understand WWE's kayfabe storyworld as a narrative construct—to dig deeper rather than take the larger-than-life storytelling at face value.[9]

Indeed, WWE's core product—serialized wrestling events, staged before live audiences in arenas around the world and broadcast either on traditional television networks or on the company's own subscription-based streaming service—holds strong despite (or perhaps because of) the loosening of kayfabe. Their weekly flagship television series, *Monday Night Raw* (1993–), holds the record as the longest-running weekly episodic American television program of all time, boasting more than 1,300 episodes to date; its sister show, *SmackDown Live* (1999–), surpassed the 1,000-episode milestone in October 2018. In May 2018, WWE signed lucrative deals to keep both shows on the air through 2024, with *Raw* remaining on the USA Network (for $265 million) while *SmackDown Live* will move to Fox (for an astounding $1.025 *billion*). While the cultural and financial impact of *SmackDown*'s migration from the USA Network to Fox remains to be seen, WWE's stock rose to record heights in response to the announcement.[10] WWE's integration of social networking into their televised programming encourages fan engagement with their media content across a variety of platforms, while the 2014 launch of the WWE Network—a Netflix-style subscription service that combines 24-7 programmed content with an extensive on-demand streaming archive—represents a massive step toward the company's actualization as not merely a content producer but a powerful distributor as well.

It is *this* WWE that *#WWE* interrogates: not merely a television show, but a complex media empire worthy of extensive and multifaceted analysis. Situating the company both as the industry leader in professional wrestling and as a media conglomerate operating within contemporary convergence culture, the following ten chapters construct a rich and complex portrait of WWE as it exists and operates today—or, more precisely, from about 2011 to the present. In contemporary WWE programming, the content (i.e., what is seen on television screens and across a variety of transmedia channels) and the business (i.e., what transpires backstage, in writer's rooms and corporate offices) are deliberately intertwined and confused; kayfabe is flexible enough that performers and announcers can acknowledge realities external to WWE's serialized storyworld (e.g., Brock Lesnar's participation in UFC events or performers' histories with other promotions prior to signing with WWE); and viewers are sophisticated enough not just to integrate these various threads into a coherent entertainment experience but also to participate in the creation of the serialized storyworld themselves.[11] WWE thereby presents itself as an ideal case study for research related to issues as diverse as world building and transmedia storytelling, labor and production culture in the media industries, sports geography, rhetorical narratology, fan discontent, audience participation and performativity, online fan productivity, social media and convergence culture, reality television, and collective mourning. While the connections between these ten seemingly disparate topics may not be immediately apparent, the essays in this collection tackle each of these subjects and more while also coalescing to form a cogent vision of WWE as a media empire. In the concluding section of this introduction, I will provide more details about these individual chapters and the way they fit together. First, however, I will provide more detail on WWE's contemporary period and the reasons it is worthy of such extended and specific attention.

THREE ENCOUNTERS WITH REALITY: 1997, 2011, 2018

As professional wrestling gradually evolved from a mode of ephemeral live performance to live events that are filmed for worldwide distribution and disseminated, both live and in perpetuity, via an increasing number of media channels and platforms, the governing logic of kayfabe has become increasingly untenable and, arguably, unnecessary. WWE first acknowledged this new reality more than two decades ago, when Vince McMahon opened the December 15, 1997, episode of *Monday Night Raw* with an unprecedented direct address to the at-home viewing audience.[12] In this scripted announcement, McMahon speaks openly about "sports entertainment" as a form of creative production comparable to "soap operas like the *Days of Our Lives*, or music videos such as those on MTV, daytime talk shows like *Jerry Springer* and others, cartoons like the *King of the Hill* on Fox, sitcoms like *Seinfeld*, and other widely accepted forms of television entertainment."[13] The short segment served two main functions, both of which became increasingly salient to the company's evolution over the following years. First, it functioned as an obvious bid for mainstream recognition and legitimacy. While McMahon's desire for WWE to be considered "beyond the confines of sports presentation into the wide-open environment of broad-based entertainment" could always be felt in the company's programming, it became more and more apparent over the following years, manifesting, for instance, in the company's decision to expand its viewership and sponsorship opportunities by mandating a TV-PG rating on all televised WWE programming starting in 2008, and culminating most recently in the company's first serious bid for Emmy consideration in 2018.[14] As Alfred Konuwa writes for *Forbes* with respect to the latter: "While an Emmy victory, let alone a nomination, remains highly unlikely, WWE's obvious push to become Emmy material appears to be yet another strategic branding move with an end game of WWE being accepted as a mainstream property. . . . As the market leader, WWE's once-ludicrous ambitions to win an Emmy demonstrates a potential long-term plan to revamp its product as more than only niche entertainment."[15]

Second, McMahon's monologue represents a formal and explicit acknowledgment of professional wrestling's status as *fictional* entertainment. "We in the WWF think that you the audience are, quite frankly, tired of having your intelligence insulted," McMahon says, acknowledging the incompatibility of kayfabe with the increased savviness of contemporaneous television audiences. With McMahon's address clearly situated outside the diegesis of *Monday Night Raw*, however, the storyworld collectively constituted by *Raw* and other WWE programs and events proceeded more or less unchanged in terms of its narrative address.[16] While the line separating "good guys" from "bad guys" became blurrier during the late 1990s, performers were nevertheless still expected to stay on script and in character before the cameras. *Kayfabe is dead, long live kayfabe!*

At the time, this segment served as a kind of unofficial inauguration of a period of WWE programming widely known as the "attitude era," so-called for its edgy content defined by crotch-chopping factions like D-Generation X and beer-swilling badasses like "Stone Cold" Steve Austin.[17] It would be nearly fifteen years later, however, before *Raw* featured a segment that would finally make good on McMahon's promise to respect audiences' intelligence and truly incorporate their extratextual knowledge of the business into an onscreen narrative. Wrestling fans and historians often cite the closing segment of the June 27, 2011, episode of *Raw* as almost single-handedly inaugurating a new era of WWE storytelling—one that would become widely known as the "reality era," so-called for its looser adherence to kayfabe and increased willingness to acknowledge and incorporate selected aspects of the external world into the WWE diegesis.[18]

At the time, CM Punk, a "heel" (wrestling parlance for bad guy), was in a main event feud with perennial "babyface" (good guy) John Cena over the WWE Championship. Punk's WWE contract was set to expire the day after his scheduled bout with Cena at the forthcoming *Money in the Bank* pay-per-view event, and he had previously made his intentions known: to win Cena's title and then leave the company while holding it, humiliating WWE's top star and robbing the company of their brass ring. To this point, the animosity between these two characters had played out in mostly typical ways, so when Punk interrupted *Raw*'s main event—a "tables" match between Cena and R-Truth—to cost Cena the victory, it was merely business as usual. But eagle-eyed viewers may have sensed that something stranger was going on: instead of wearing a T-shirt with his own logo, as he had during his appearance earlier in the program, Punk now wore a shirt emblazoned with "Stone Cold" Steve Austin's logo.[19] With Cena still writhing in performed pain amid the splintered fibers of a halved wooden table, Punk grabs a microphone and begins to walk away from the ring. Instead of continuing to the backstage area, however, Punk turns around to face the ring, sits down cross-legged on the ramp, and launches into what would prove to be a historic monologue.

The line between reality and kayfabe in professional wrestling can be slippery, and in this case, deliberately so; it should therefore be emphasized up front that Punk's monologue should not be understood as a true, spontaneous, unscripted event (a shoot, in the parlance of the industry), nor as an entirely fictional event (a work), but rather as a blend of the two (a worked shoot). Worked shoots are meant to give viewers the impression that performers are going off-script and transgressing kayfabe—even while they do so with WWE's express permission. (Recall Laine: "Even as

Fig. 0.1. CM Punk throws a verbal pipe bomb on *Monday Night Raw*. Screenshot from *Monday Night Raw*, June 27, 2011.

you try to break through the web of kayfabe, you are still probably being duped one way or another."[20]) Was the renewal of Punk's WWE contract truly up in the air, or was this merely a narrative contrivance to elevate the stakes of the upcoming championship match, thereby driving pay-per-view buys? Online gossip sites reported at the time that the status of Punk's contract negotiations was unknown—a fact that WWE exploited to increase audiences' investment in the narrative they were telling—but it seems unlikely that McMahon and his creative team would build their main-event storyline around a performer whose future with the company was legitimately uncertain.[21]

Punk begins his monologue in typical fashion, complaining that while Cena is viewed as the best in the company, Punk is more deserving of recognition as "the best in the world." From here, however, things take a turn. "There's one thing you're better at than I am," Punk intones, "and that's *kissing Vince McMahon's ass*."[22] On the face of it, Punk's invocation of the WWE chairman and authority figure isn't particularly strange, as McMahon has always had a significant onscreen presence in WWE, both as a play-by-play announcer and as a hyperbolically villainous version of himself in storylines. What makes Punk's callout unusual is that he is referring not to "Mr. McMahon," the character McMahon plays in WWE programming, but to the *real* McMahon, the booker who calls the shots and thereby controls the destiny of every performer in his company. Punk proceeds to historicize Cena—the performer rather than the character—as part of a lineage of babyface champions handpicked by McMahon for superstardom, reframing the history of WWE in terms of sycophancy rather than meritocracy: "You're as good at kissing Vince's ass as Hulk Hogan was! I don't know if you're as good as *Dwayne*, though—he's a really good ass-kisser. Always was and still is." By disparaging three of WWE's top stars of all time—Hulk Hogan, Dwayne "The Rock" Johnson, and John Cena, each of whom has achieved some measure of Hollywood stardom beyond the niche of sports entertainment—Punk also exposes the personal and corporate machinations that underlie what viewing audiences experience as, in Roland Barthes's words, "a sort of mythological fight between Good and Evil."[23]

After Punk's speech, heel-face dynamics—that is, the relative moral alignments that determine which characters crowds are meant to cheer or boo in a given storyline—became much thornier. For one segment of the audience, Cena's credo of "Hustle, Loyalty, Respect" would continue to reflect a staunch morality worth cheering for. But for an increasingly vocal segment of that same viewership, Cena's babyface shtick would ring increasingly hollow as his extratextual complicity with McMahon suddenly became textual. According to the zero-sum logic of professional wrestling, where winners only emerge at the expense of losers, every push for an established wrestler like Cena—or, worse yet, a retired one like The Rock—means another equally or more deserving performer gets buried. Punk's monologue explicitly posits a fictional world authored by the whims of a single man, wherein the success or failure of individual characters (and, by direct extension, the financial security of the performers who embody these characters) is determined by favoritism rather than pure athletic ability, determination, or charisma. Punk offers himself to WWE viewers as a martyr of this rigged system: "The only thing that's *real* [in WWE] is *me*, and the fact that day in and day out, for almost six years I've proved to everybody in the world that I'm the best on this microphone, in that ring—even at commentary! Nobody can touch me!" With a face increasingly flushed with seemingly genuine anger, Punk's diatribe builds to its damning crescendo: "The fact that Dwayne is in the main event of *WrestleMania* next year and I'm not makes me sick!" As Jansen expertly summarizes: "These are not the usual talking points of a wrestling showdown. Punk does not want to be champion. He does not want revenge. He does not feel slighted by his opponent, nor is there any backdrop of shifting personal alliances. Rather, Punk wants the status often associated with a worker of his talents: top-billing, a place of prominence in promotional materials, the chance to star in films and television."[24] As Punk pivots to tell a story that would surely illustrate his complaints about WWE management in even more vivid detail, his microphone is cut, and *Raw* goes off the air with an inaudible Punk yelling at the camera.

Although Punk's speech was improvised, he had been given permission to "air his grievances" with the company during the segment.[25] As a worked shoot, it was particularly effective in disarming viewers, not just because it transgressed so many of WWE's established storytelling protocols but also because Punk calls attention to each transgression as such: he acknowledges and looks directly into the camera ("Oops! I'm breaking the fourth wall!"); he refers to WWE Superstars by their legal names rather than their character names (*"Dwayne,"* not The Rock); he mentions rival professional wrestling promotions by name, positioning WWE as part of a global industry rather than a self-contained narrative universe ("I'm leaving with the WWE Championship on July 17th and hell, who knows, maybe I'll go defend it in New Japan Pro Wrestling. Maybe I'll go back to Ring of Honor"); he calls out an ex-WWE wrestler who has found success on the independent circuit, acknowledging that performers continue to exist after parting ways with the company ("Hey Colt Cabana, how you doing?"); and, most obviously, he directly insults McMahon's management of WWE ("He's a millionaire that should be a billionaire") and WWE's "first family" in general ("I'd like to think that maybe this company will be better after Vince McMahon is dead, but the fact is it's going to get taken over by his idiotic daughter and his doofus son-in-law and the rest of his stupid family"). Punk's choice of accoutrement—the aforementioned "Stone Cold" Steve Austin T-shirt—may be the only clue that the segment is really a work after all: by aligning himself with Mr. McMahon's most famous antagonist in storylines throughout the attitude era, Punk implicitly challenges viewers to decide whether his metafictional barbs at McMahon are legitimate or, like similar insults lobbed at McMahon by Austin, merely part and parcel of the WWE storyworld.[26]

Two weeks later on *Raw*, Punk cemented his legacy in WWE with a single phrase: "In anybody else's hands, this is just a microphone. In my hands, it's a pipe bomb." His fourth-wall-breaking monologue thus became retroactively known as the "pipe bomb" promo, and it has since been widely credited with inaugurating what eventually became known as the reality era. Writing in the late 1990s, Henry Jenkins described the relationship between WWE and reality thus: "The programs' formats mimic the structures and visual styles of non-fiction television, of sports coverage, news broadcasts, and talk shows. . . . The WWF narrative preserves the illusion at all costs. There is no stepping outside the fiction, no acknowledgment of the production process or the act of authorship. When the performers are featured in *WWF Magazine,* they are profiled in character. Story segments are told in the form of late-breaking news reports or framed as interviews. The commentators are taken by surprise, interrupted by seemingly unplanned occurrences."[27] As Jenkins notes, WWE storytelling had largely been defined by its attempt to create a hermetically sealed, self-contained fictional world—to maintain kayfabe both on and off television. McMahon's 1997 monologue represented an initial (albeit extradiegetic) acknowledgment that professional wrestling is (and always has been) a fictional entertainment genre rather than a legitimate sport; Punk, however, brought this same logic to bear upon the WWE storyworld itself. While this pipe bomb didn't fully or permanently explode professional wrestling's reliance on kayfabe, it was certainly powerful enough to blow a hole in the concept—just enough for a sliver of light from an external reality to shine in.

Wrestling journalist David Shoemaker immediately recognized the impact of Punk's promo, hailing it as the beginning of what he dubbed, perhaps prematurely, the worked-shoot era.[28] The genius of Punk's venomous monologue, and worked shoots in general, is that they exploit the tenuousness of the fictional construct upon which professional wrestling narratives depend, driving viewer interest by manufacturing uncertainty about where kayfabe ends and reality begins. Devoted fans are thereby tantalized with precisely that which the product has, for most of the industry's history, been expressly designed to conceal: the real backstage machinations, production processes, and locker-room hostilities that are obscured by cartoonish exaggerations of the same, by fictional storytelling and character work, and by amazing feats of athleticism, all of which take place in full view of the crowds and the cameras. It is this insatiable desire to know the backstage realities of the business—to reveal that which has been hidden—that separates the hardcore wrestling fan (the "smart") from the casual or naive viewer (the "mark") who can more readily accept the pleasures of the fictional world as fantasy.[29] As Jansen argues, engaging with WWE programming involves a complex negotiation of real and fake as viewers read *through* the fiction to glean these hidden truths: "To refer to the 'real' of wrestling today is to refer to backstage politics, writers' rooms, booking decisions, and corporate judgments about who has star potential, who is popular in the locker room, or who is unpopular with management. It is a kind of real that, strangely, even contradictorily, embraces the fake. When a WWE crowd boos a performer today, it is likely they are booing the writers responsible for that performer's character rather than the actual performer."[30]

While the worked-shoot era is a perfectly apt designation for the mode of storytelling and viewership initiated by Punk's pipe bomb, Shoemaker quickly dropped it, referring to WWE's new phase in his next column and thenceforth as the reality era.[31] This more inclusive term has caught on with fans and industry insiders alike for how well it articulates the increasingly metafictional storytelling wrought not just by worked shoots such as Punk's but, even more significantly, by the rise of new media and WWE's transformation from a professional wrestling promotion to an American media empire in the age of convergence.[32] Worked shoots, after all, are merely one site where fiction and reality brush against each other in the contemporary WWE; since 2011, the company has consistently emphasized nonkayfabe, reality-based content in their media portfolio, and such content has become ever more prominent since the launch of the WWE Network in 2014. As Shoemaker wrote in 2011: "If the history of wrestling were itself a storyline, the central conflict would be the tension between the real world and wrestling's peculiar unreality. . . . Times have changed, but the question now is how WWE will address its on-screen product while acknowledging a broader world. No one's going to watch a wrestling show when the best stuff is happening on Twitter and YouTube. But a wrestling reality that acknowledges that the real world exists? Well, that makes some sense."[33] As Shoemaker suggests here, the online interactivity and ability for fans to share, spread, and accumulate backstage knowledge on platforms like Twitter and YouTube catalyzed the reality era. Increasingly, the reality era and the narratives that constitute it are fundamentally inseparable from their transmedia context—that is, from the multiple media channels across which these narratives are distributed and within which they are dissected.

The tantalizing and ambiguous blend of real and fake in Punk's pipe bomb has since been exploited by other performers, including some who possess considerable institutional power within WWE and, thus, a larger stake in the company's long-term success. In the seven years since Punk's speech, for instance, McMahon's "idiotic daughter" Stephanie and "doofus son-in-law" Paul "Triple H" Levesque—WWE's actual chief brand officer and executive vice president of talent, live events, and creative, respectively—have repeatedly broken character on *Raw* and elsewhere to make "historic" announcements, most often revolving around new initiatives involving WWE's female Superstars. On the July 23, 2018, episode of *Raw*, for instance, Vince, Stephanie, and Triple H appeared in the ring together to announce WWE's first all-women's pay-per-view event, *Evolution*.[34] With much of the WWE roster gathered together on the entrance ramp, Triple H describes these performers not as individuals in competition with each other but rather as "a giant team" that puts their "ultimate trust in [each other's] hands" every time they enter the squared circle—an explicit recognition that professional wrestling is, at its heart, a collaborative performance that "demands skilled coordination, control, trust, and empathy."[35] Triple H's voice quavers with (worked? shoot?) emotion as he applauds the women on the roster specifically: "We have stood in awe watching you, some of us—some of us with a tear in our eye as you have stolen the show again and again."[36] As this and other similar segments demonstrate, the facts of external reality are increasingly viewed not as hostile to or incompatible with the WWE storyworld but rather as enriching it, deepening audience engagement by encouraging viewers to invest emotionally not just in the characters and their fictional exploits but also in the performers themselves.[37]

With regard to the line between fiction and reality—between "fake" sport and "real" performance—WWE is presently in a period of expansion and experimentation, making it an ideal case study for media and television research. Beginning in 2011 and continuing to the present day, this period is defined by three central qualities, each of which expands WWE's storyworld in distinct but complementary ways: (1) self-reflexive narratives that deliberately trouble the relationship between fiction and reality (e.g., via worked shoots, or by blurring the line between performers' fictional and nonfictional personae); (2) a fandom that hungers to know the reality of the business and that has unprecedented access to resources for gathering and spreading such information (e.g., message boards, online dirt sheets, podcasts, shoot interviews with industry insiders, and performers' social media accounts); and (3) the company's own attempts at content diversification and expansion into a variety of media platforms beyond broadcast television (e.g., the WWE Network and its glut of original programming). While it is possible to consider these three aspects in isolation, they also operate synergistically. For instance, content created and curated for the WWE Network may be designed to satiate fandom's desire for behind-the-scenes/shoot narratives, while also allowing WWE to reassert control over those narratives by folding them into its corporate history; likewise, storytelling in the main televised product draws upon fans' high levels of backstage and historical knowledgeability, rewarding deeper levels of engagement and even incorporating fans into the narratives being told in various ways. The ten chapters that follow are organized

Fig. o.2. The WWE roster stands atop the entrance ramp as Stephanie McMahon announces WWE's first all-women's pay-per-view event, *Evolution*. Screenshot from *Monday Night Raw*, July 23, 2018.

into three sections that roughly correspond to these subject areas. As in most edited collections, these chapters can be read as standalone pieces in whatever order the reader chooses; however, great care has been taken to ensure that these individual chapters fit and flow together in such a way that reading the entire book in sequence will be a uniquely satisfying and coherent experience.

UNDERSTANDING WWE IN THE DIGITAL AGE

The first section, "Corporate Kayfabe: WWE as Media Empire," considers McMahon's media empire as a business first and foremost, placing it within its historical, industrial, and cultural contexts while also articulating its role in contemporary convergence culture specifically. Eero Laine's opening chapter makes WWE's relevance to the latter explicit, beginning with a comparison between WWE's approach to world building and that seen in the Marvel Cinematic Universe. Laine presents a compelling account of how the various "worlds" that compose the WWE Universe often come into conflict with other parts of the company's business initiatives and partnerships. Paying attention to how WWE's philanthropic endeavors—including their annual *Tribute to the Troops* show and their ongoing partnership with the Susan G. Komen For the Cure Foundation for breast cancer awareness—uneasily interact with the content of the company's storytelling, Laine masterfully articulates the difficulties of narrative world building for publicly traded, for-profit corporations such as WWE. Andrew Zolides then turns his attention to how WWE treats its performers, which has become more salient than ever in the wake of Linda McMahon's appointment as the head of President Donald Trump's Small Business Administration.[38] By defining WWE Superstars as independent contractors rather than employees, the company systematically denies them job security, health care, and the powers of collective bargaining while also using restrictive noncompete clauses to prevent them from seeking opportunities outside of the company.[39] In this essential work, Zolides considers how these laborers—whose very *names* are often trademarked by WWE, preventing them from being used elsewhere without the company's express permission—navigate this difficult situation, drawing upon celebrity studies research to reveal the various kinds of labor and exploitation involved in being a WWE Superstar in the transmedia era.

Next, Dru Jeffries and Andrew Kannegiesser expand upon Laine's interest in the WWE Universe as a fictional construct, using the company's preferred nomenclature for their fandom and storyworld as a jumping-off point for a historical analysis of the company's evolution from regional wrestling promotion to global media empire. Informed by sports geography and the spatial turn in the humanities, Jeffries and Kannegiesser argue that the wrestling industry's "territory system"—whereby discrete local wrestling promotions operated only within mutually agreed-upon geographical boundaries—remains central to how WWE conceives of itself to this day, despite having single-handedly dismantled the territory system decades ago by taking their business national and, later, global. The designation "WWE Universe" thereby articulates more than just the company's fandom and diegesis; it also reflects WWE's efforts at total media and geographical domination. Finally, Christian Norman closes the section by exploring how WWE addresses its audience differently in the reality era compared to earlier epochs. Using a rhetorical narratology approach, Norman theorizes the new power dynamic between the company and its consumers and the ways this interactive and conflictual relationship manifests in WWE's storytelling, building on the preceding chapters by explicating the effects of the company's corporate ethos on its narrative products.

Norman's essay also provides a natural pivot point into the book's second section, "Marks and Smarts: WWE's Unruly Fandoms," which turns its attention to the fan cultures that have emerged around WWE. While Norman is interested in how WWE chooses to address its fandom—either as marks, the rare viewers that guilelessly believe in the reality of the narrative universe, or as smarts, the kind of fan that accepts the fiction as such while also integrating behind-the-scenes or insider knowledge into the viewing experience—the three chapters in this second section focus on the attitudes, practices, and labor that fans perform in (and in response to) WWE content. Fan discontent is a recurring theme throughout, as loyal WWE viewers are often openly disparaging of the company's bombastic approach to storytelling and insufficiently sports-like presentation. In this vein, Shane Toepfer's contribution draws upon primary research conducted on the ground at *WrestleMania XXX* to assess the attitudes of wrestling fans toward WWE's product. His findings reveal a profound ambivalence about the contemporary state of professional wrestling, as the kind of fan most eager to witness the company's grandest spectacle of the year also expresses a fundamental sense of dissatisfaction with WWE's emphasis on pageantry over wrestling. As in previous chapters, the conflict between WWE's classification of its product as sports entertainment rather than professional wrestling is crucial to these viewers.

Sam Ford then explores the ways that WWE fans mobilize their dissatisfaction with the company's storytelling by becoming "rogue actors" intent on sabotaging live performances. Ford argues that fans can collectively resist fulfilling the roles that have been scripted for them; in fact, they can actively—and sometimes successfully—change the direction of the serialized story in ways that are oppositional to (what they surmise to be) WWE's narrative intent. This section concludes with Christian B. Long's examination of Botchamania, a popular series of online fan videos that put moments of spectacular in-ring failure on display. Considering the videos in the tradition of online fan productivity known as vidding, Long argues that these videos function as a critical reading practice that has the potential to unearth the underexplored acoustics of professional wrestling. Botchamania thereby celebrates and analyzes wrestling performances across multiple registers simultaneously: as a fictional narrative centered on personal conflict, certainly, but also as a craft based on collaboration, communication, and improvisatory skill.

The three chapters that compose the volume's third and final section, "Then, Now, Forever: Wrestling with WWE's Past and Transmedia Future," investigate some of the ways that WWE uses different media to exert control over narratives concerning the company's past, present, and future. The first two essays in this section explore the company's attempts to diversify their media portfolio through short-form online video and reality television, respectively. Analyzing the former, Cory Barker's chapter excavates WWE's attempt to integrate the fledgling social media platform Tout into their televised programming. Even though the company's experiment with Tout was ultimately short-lived, Barker argues that it has shaped their social media strategy (spanning platforms such as YouTube, Twitter, and Instagram) to this day. By contrast, WWE's forays into reality television, which is the subject of Anna F. Peppard's contribution, have been more successful and long-lived. *Total Divas* (2013–), a reality program that combines the popular "catfights and confessionals" format with a behind-the-scenes look at women in the professional wrestling industry, functions simultaneously as an extension of WWE's kayfabe storyworld and as a kayfabe-breaking peek behind the curtain. It is thus a rich and often contradictory text, promising unprecedented access to the "real lives" of female WWE performers, but only through the highly codified pleasures of reality TV. Synthesizing the bodies of scholarship concerning the construction of gender in both (feminine-coded) reality television and (masculine-coded) professional wrestling, Peppard argues that *Total Divas'* treatment of femininity speaks not just to WWE's historical and ongoing ambivalence regarding its female performers but also to the polysemy that is characteristic of contemporary postfeminist culture more generally.

The book's final chapter grapples with WWE's often clumsy attempts to control problematic narratives in real time through the systematic denial and erasure of the past. Specifically, Sean Desilets explores what is arguably the most notorious incident in professional wrestling history: celebrated WWE Superstar Chris Benoit's double murder-suicide, in which he killed his wife and son using variations on his signature in-ring holds before hanging himself from a piece of weightlifting equipment. Because of the obvious connections between the grisly specifics of these heinous acts and Benoit's profession, WWE's response to this tragedy was to simply erase Benoit from its historical record, removing his name from their official website and banning his archival trace from all future programming. What is repressed, however, inevitably returns: Desilets therefore looks to the affective resonances between the careers of Benoit and Daniel Bryan, a WWE Superstar whose look and wrestling style recalls Benoit to many fans, effectively turning Bryan into a living citation to the verboten figure. Through a Derridean "hauntology" of Benoit and Bryan, Desilets movingly uncovers the ways in which Bryan has allowed fans to perform the mourning work that WWE actively denied them through their erasure of Benoit.

Ultimately, the essays in this collection all seek to identify and understand the central features that characterize WWE as a holistic enterprise, encompassing not just a particular genre of television programming and weekly serialized narrative storytelling but also an approach to labor and business practices, a series of transmedia strategies, multiple social media presences, a diverse and productive set of fan communities, a carefully controlled public image meant to appeal to shareholders, and so on. Crucially, the contributors recognize that none of these practices or qualities exists in isolation from the others; the essays in this volume are therefore particularly interested in exploring points of intersection between the various facets that define WWE as a media empire today. Just as the company's forays into reality television will influence how viewers engage with the core product, direct interactions with Superstars on Twitter can affect how fans understand WWE's treatment of its workers; similarly, the company's attempts to prescribe fans' behavior and to shape the narrative of professional wrestling history in its favor will ultimately lead to new forms of fan productivity and grassroots efforts to preserve cultural memory—and all of these interactions will inevitably be recuperated into WWE's own storytelling, where they will in turn produce new narratives and engender new effects. At this point, WWE is undoubtedly among the most popular, enduring, relevant, and interesting narrative entertainments in contemporary American culture, and it is also among the most complex manifestations of media convergence in the postmillennial era. Taken collectively, the essays in *#WWE: Professional Wrestling in the Digital Age* capture this complexity, delivering a coherent and cogent analysis of World Wrestling Entertainment as a media empire.

NOTES

1. Jenkins, "'Never Trust a Snake,'" 51.

2. As *The Professional Wrestlers' Workout & Instructional Guide* states, "The *carny* spoken among performers dates back to the time when wrestling matches were held at carnivals. Grapplers learned a secret way to communicate amongst themselves to protect the inner workings of the business, especially from inquiring fans. Wrestlers would use a variation of Pig Latin combined with terms unique to the industry, which is a practice still done by some performers today. The term *kay fabe* is used to describe that exclusionary process" (Race et al., 125).

3. Laine, "Professional Wrestling Scholarship," 90.

4. Jansen, "'Yes! No!,'" 639.

5. For more on the origins of sports entertainment, see Jeffries and Kannegiesser's chapter in this volume.

6. WWE, "Company Overview," http://corporate.wwe.com/who-we-are/company -overview. In 2002, a lawsuit from the World Wildlife Fund prompted McMahon to rebrand his World Wrestling Federation (WWF) as World Wrestling Entertainment (WWE), a change that better reflected the company's long-standing approach to professional wrestling as an entertainment genre rather than a legitimate sport.

7. Castleberry, "Squared Circle Intentionalities," 100. Castleberry uses *television studies* in the sense proposed by Jonathan Gray and Amanda D. Lotz. As they write, television studies "conceives of television as a repository for meanings and a site where cultural values are articulated. It assumes television is a key part of lived, everyday culture in contemporary society and

one which may allow us to understand large parts of that culture. It is also an industrial entity produced under specific conditions that require analysis precisely because it is one of our society's prime storytellers, a resource and tool for learning, deliberation, debate, and persuasion, and a site wherein power and ideology operate" (Gray and Lotz, *Television Studies*, 22).

8. Jansen, "'Yes! No!,'" 640.

9. See Christian B. Long's chapter in this volume for one case study of contemporary wrestling fans' sophisticated, multilayered viewing practices and the role of mediation therein.

10. Konuwa, "How Billion-Dollar SmackDown Live-To-Fox Deal Could Legitimize WWE Brand Split In 2019"; Guthrie, "Wrestle Mania!," 46. Interestingly, Fox's acquisition of *Smack-Down* has been framed as part of a larger initiative by the network to double down on live sports coverage in the era of cord-cutting, and the network intends to cross promote its WWE programming alongside NFL's *Thursday Night Football* and Ultimate Fighting Championship (UFC) events. See Otterson, "WWE's 'SmackDown Live' Moves to Fox."

11. As Castleberry puts it, "performers have histories that sometimes involve multiple personae across several companies. These storylines often linger, either directly or as a kind of spectral presence that haunts the performer's career" ("Squared Circle Intentionalities," 110).

12. Though WWE was still known as WWF at the time, I will refer to the company as WWE for ease of readability. Direct quotations including references to the WWF will remain unchanged. Similarly, *Raw* and *SmackDown* have gone through naming variations over the years, but they will be referred to throughout this book as *Monday Night Raw* (or *Raw* for short) and *SmackDown Live* (or *SmackDown* for short).

13. WWE, "Mr. McMahon."

14. As Jim Parsons detailed for *The Sportster*, "WWE presented shows like *Raw 25*, the *WWE 24: Empowered* special on the Women's Revolution and some *Mixed Match Challenge* episodes. And they succeeded in getting several shows on the preliminary ballots. *Raw* and *Mixed Match Challenge* were slotted for Best Structured Reality Program, *Total Bellas* and *Total Divas* for Outstanding Unstructured Reality Program, *WrestleMania 34* for Outstanding Variety Special and *WWE 24: Empowered* and *Andre the Giant* for Best Documentary or Nonfiction Special. Unfortunately, it did not result in any actual nominations" ("WWE's Emmy Consideration").

15. Konuwa, "WWE Campaigning For 2018 Emmy Nod."

16. For a more detailed discussion of the evolution of WWE's narrative address over time, see Christian Norman's chapter in this volume.

17. WWE and its fans seem to be deeply invested in dividing the history of the company and its storytelling into distinct phases, or eras. The Wikipedia page for "History of WWE," for instance, currently lists nine individual eras, spanning the company's inception as the World Wide Wrestling Federation in 1963 to the "new" era beginning in 2016. See Wikipedia, "History of WWE."

18. Fans continue to debate when the reality era truly began. See, for instance, https://www.wrestlingforum.com/general-wwe/1202353-your-opinion-when-did-reality-era-officially-begin.html and https://www.reddit.com/r/SquaredCircle/comments/65qn15/when_did_the_reality_era_end_and_the_new_era/. The Wikipedia entry mentioned in the previous footnote states that the "PG era" lasted from 2008 to 2013, citing the 2014 *Royal Rumble* as the beginning of the reality era.

19. Punk spoke of his decision to wear an Austin tee for this particular segment in an interview with *GQ*: "The idea of being on television is to wear your T-shirt so people see it and maybe buy it. I had gone out previously in the night and wrestled. You throw your T-shirt on the ground, and I don't know what the hell happens to it after that. I came to the back, and I was looking for another T-shirt. I sent somebody to go and get one, and they came back with a XXL. I was like, 'I'm going to be swimming in this thing.' And it's always creepy when you're wearing wrestling trunks with a shirt because it doesn't look like you're wearing any pants. I had a Stone Cold Steve Austin shirt in my bag, and it fit me. I chuckled to myself and put it on. Am I planting seeds? I don't know." Breihan, "GQ&A."

20. Laine, "Professional Wrestling Scholarship," 90.

21. See, for instance, Paglino, "Exclusive."

22. WWE's official YouTube channel doesn't have this clip in full, but rather has only a (heavily edited) recap video. See WWE, "Raw: A Special Look."

23. Barthes, "World of Wrestling," 30. That WWE's fourth major success, "Stone Cold" Steve Austin, would not only escape Punk's scrutiny in this speech but be the subject of a seemingly loving homage is an irony that undermines the sincerity of Punk's anger.

24. Jansen, "'Yes! No!,'" 638.

25. Gomez, "Interview." By allowing Punk to air his grievances with WWE on television and from within the company's storyworld—rather than, say, on his personal Twitter account—WWE successfully co-opted what might otherwise have become a legitimate rebellion. If interviews with Punk are to be believed, he was perfectly willing, if not eager, to walk away from WWE: "At that point, I was so out the door. . . . I was counting down the days" (Gomez, "Interview"). In the immediate aftermath of this segment, however, Punk was booked to win the WWE Championship from Cena at *Money in the Bank* and ultimately kept the title for a record-breaking 434 days. If nothing else, this testifies to McMahon's confidence in Punk as a performer and as a representative of WWE on the cultural stage, not in spite of but rather *as a direct result* of this promo.

26. For a view on what such debates look like, see https://www.reddit.com/r/SquaredCircle/comments/287ut6/i_have_a_few_questions_about_cm_punks_original/.

27. Jenkins, "'Never Trust a Snake,'" 51.

28. Shoemaker, "Brief History of Wrestling Fakery."

29. The three chapters that compose the middle section of this book explore these concepts in detail.

30. Jansen, "'Yes! No!,'" 637.

31. Shoemaker, "Back to Unreality."

32. Triple H, for instance, used fans' understanding of the reality era to generate "heat" (a negative crowd reaction) for his heel character in an in-ring interview segment with announcer Michael Cole on the March 24, 2014, episode of *Raw*. See WWE, "Triple H Vows."

33. Shoemaker, "Introducing the Worked-Shoot Era."

34. While the company still refers to such events as pay-per-views, since the launch of the WWE Network they would be more accurately described as WWE Network exclusives. Part of the incentive for WWE to launch the network was to control the distribution (and become the sole financial beneficiary) of these monthly pay-per-view supercard events.

35. Smith, "Passion Work," 162.

36. The phrase "with a tear in [my] eye" is likely a deliberate allusion to a famous promo given by Ric Flair—a sixteen-time world champion and the father of Charlotte Flair, one of the top female Superstars on the current WWE roster—at the 1992 *Royal Rumble*. Similarly to CM Punk wearing a "Stone Cold" T-shirt during the pipe bomb, referencing a worked promo in the context of what seems to be a shoot serves to gently undermine the reality seemingly on display.

37. WWE, "Stephanie McMahon." WWE has also developed a knack for exploiting their own previous shortcomings by issuing (and then endlessly congratulating themselves for) long-overdue correctives that are probably driven as much by audience demand as by any genuine progressivity on behalf of WWE. The *Evolution* pay-per-view and the Women's Evolution more generally are perhaps the best example of this tendency. See Anna F. Peppard's chapter in this volume for more detail.

38. As many have pointed out, Trump himself has a storied history with WWE, dating back to 1988. For a reading of this history, see Mazer, "Donald Trump Shoots the Match." As an aside, it's also worth noting that Vince and Linda McMahon donated significantly to Trump's pseudocharity, the Trump Foundation (in the amount of $5 million), and to his presidential campaign ($7.5 million) (Berman and Fahrenthold, "Donald Trump").

39. As this book was going to press, the HBO series *Last Week Tonight with John Oliver* devoted an episode to this very issue. See LastWeekTonight, "WWE."

Barthes, Roland. "The World of Wrestling." In *Steel Chair to the Head: The Pleasure and Pain of Professional Wrestling*, edited by Nicholas Sammond, 23–32. Durham, NC: Duke University Press, 2005.

Berman, Mark, and David A. Fahrenthold. "Donald Trump Plans to Shut Down His Charitable Foundation, Which Has Been Under Scrutiny for Months." *Washington Post*, December 24, 2016. Accessed June 27, 2017. https://www.washingtonpost.com/news/post-politics /wp/2016/12/24/donald-trump-plans-to-shut-down-his-charitable-foundation-which-has -been-under-scrutiny-for-months/.

Breihan, Tom. "The GQ&A: C.M. Punk." *GQ*. July 13, 2011. Accessed June 27, 2017. http://www .gq.com/story/cm-punk-wwe-wrestling-interview.

Castleberry, Garrett L. "Squared Circle Intentionalities: What a Framework for 'Wrestling Studies' Can Look Like." *The Popular Culture Studies Journal* 6, no. 1 (2018): 100–120.

Gomez, Luis. "Interview: Behind the Snarl of CM Punk." *Chicago Tribune*, March 26, 2012. Accessed August 23, 2018. http://articles.chicagotribune.com/2012-03-26/entertainment /chi-interview-wwe-cm-punk-20120326_1_cm-punk-wwe-championship-john-cena/2.

Gray, Jonathan, and Amanda D. Lotz. *Television Studies*. Cambridge: Polity Press, 2012.

Guthrie, Marisa. "Wrestle Mania! Behind Two TV Body Slams." *Hollywood Reporter*. May 30, 2018: 46.

Jansen, Brian. "'Yes! No! . . . Maybe?': Reading the Real in Professional Wrestling's Unreality." *Journal of Popular Culture* 51, no. 3 (2018): 635–56.

Jenkins, Henry. "'Never Trust a Snake': WWF Wrestling as Masculine Melodrama." In *Steel Chair to the Head: The Pleasure and Pain of Professional Wrestling*, edited by Nicholas Sammond, 33–66. Durham, NC: Duke University Press, 2005.

Konuwa, Alfred. "How Billion-Dollar SmackDown Live-To-Fox Deal Could Legitimize WWE Brand Split In 2019." *Forbes*. May 21, 2018. Accessed August 16, 2018. https://www.forbes .com/sites/alfredkonuwa/2018/05/21/how-massive-smackdown-live-to-fox-deal-could -legitimize-wwe-brand-split-in-2019/#16954b0047d8.

———. "WWE Campaigning for 2018 Emmy Nod: What This Could Mean for Overlooked Genre." *Forbes*. June 4, 2018. Accessed August 16, 2018. https://www.forbes.com/sites /alfredkonuwa/2018/06/04/wwe-campaigning-for-2018-emmy-nod-what-this-could -mean-for-overlooked-genre/#4623b8f9370a.

Laine, Eero. "Professional Wrestling Scholarship: Legitimacy and Kayfabe." *Popular Culture Studies Journal* 6, no. 1 (2018): 82–99.

Last Week Tonight. "WWE: Last Week Tonight with John Oliver (HBO)." YouTube video, 23:06. Posted March 31, 2019. Accessed May 5, 2019. https://www.youtube.com/watch?v= m8UQ4O7UiDs.

Mazer, Sharon. "Donald Trump Shoots the Match." *TDR: The Drama Review* 62, no. 2 (Summer 2018): 175–200.

Otterson, Joe. "WWE's 'SmackDown Live' Moves to Fox Broadcasting in 2019." *Variety*. June 26, 2018. Accessed August 16, 2018. https://variety.com/2018/tv/news/wwe-smackdown-live -fox-2019-1202858691/.

Paglino, Nick. "Exclusive: Last Minute CM Punk/WWE Contract Status Update." *Wrestle Zone*. July 17, 2011. Accessed August 23, 2018. http://www.mandatory.com/wrestlezone/news /238727-exclusive-last-minute-cm-punkwwe-contract-status-update.

Parsons, Jim. "WWE's Emmy Consideration Bid Fails." *Sportster*. July 14, 2018. Accessed August 22, 2018. https://www.thesportster.com/news/wwe-emmy-nomination-fail/.

Race, Harley, Ricky Steamboat, and Les Thatcher, with Alex Marvez. *The Professional Wrestlers' Workout & Instructional Guide*. Champaign, IL: Sports Publishing, 2005.

Shoemaker, David. "Back to Unreality." *Grantland*. August 30, 2011. Accessed August 15, 2018. http://grantland.com/features/introducing-worked-shoot-era/.

———. "A Brief History of Wrestling Fakery." *Grantland*. June 15, 2012. Accessed June 27, 2017. http://grantland.com/features/john-cena-big-show-how-century-pretend-fighting-led-wwe-reality-era/.

———. "Introducing the Worked-Shoot Era." *Grantland*. August 1, 2011. Accessed August 16, 2018. http://grantland.com/features/introducing-worked-shoot-era/.

Smith, R. Tyson. "Passion Work: The Joint Production of Emotional Labor in Professional Wrestling." *Social Psychology Quarterly* 71, no. 2 (June 2008): 157–76.

Wikipedia. "History of WWE." *Wikipedia: The Free Encyclopedia*. August 20, 2018. Accessed August 23, 2018. https://en.wikipedia.org/wiki/History_of_WWE.

WWE. "Mr. McMahon Ushers in the Attitude Era." YouTube video, 2:17. Posted January 6, 2014. Accessed August 16, 2018. https://www.youtube.com/watch?v=PjBeCwz2fXg&t=30s.

———. "Raw: A Special Look at CM Punk's Controversy-Ridden Tirade at the Conclusion of Raw Roulette." YouTube video, 2:31. Posted July 4, 2011. Accessed August 26, 2018. https://www.youtube.com/watch?v=ZUvxtlpvd3s.

———. "Stephanie McMahon Announces WWE Evolution: Raw, July 23, 2018." YouTube video, 4:27. Posted July 23, 2018. Accessed August 16, 2018. https://www.youtube.com/watch?v=E_HMfe1Rfi4.

———. "Triple H Vows to End the 'Yes!' Movement at WrestleMania: Raw, March 24, 2014." YouTube video, 3:53. Posted March 24, 2014. Accessed August 23, 2018. https://www.youtube.com/watch?v=hemBUIEc1uo.

DRU JEFFRIES teaches in the Cultural Studies Department at Wilfrid Laurier University. He is author of *Comic Book Film Style: Cinema at 24 Panels Per Second*.

PART I

CORPORATE KAYFABE: WWE AS MEDIA EMPIRE

chapter one

WORLD BUILDING IN THE WWE UNIVERSE

Eero Laine

Just before the 2015 Academy Awards, WWE.com featured a number of parody movie posters containing WWE Superstars in made-up film roles under the banner "WWE Invades the Oscars."[1] One of the imitation film posters was for *Guardians of the WWE Universe,* featuring wrestlers Stardust, Paige, Erick Rowan, El Torito, and, notably, Batista, who also starred as the character Drax in the Marvel film that the poster parodies, *Guardians of the Galaxy* (2014). In this simple doubling—Batista/Drax and WWE Universe/Marvel Cinematic Universe—WWE deftly underlined the collision of two fictional narrative worlds that occurred when Dave Bautista (known simply as Batista in WWE and described in the blurb of the faux poster as "a tattooed powerhouse") painted over his heavily muscled, tattooed body to play an alien with a heavily muscled, tattooed body.[2] The poster, as it hinges on Bautista's body, highlights a real and physical overlap between fictional universes. This chapter examines such moments when the fictional WWE Universe spills out of its diegetic bounds, focusing in particular on how WWE's built media universe is shaped by its interactions with so-called real life in both deliberate and unintentional ways.

It might go without saying that many, many media universes exist—think *Star Wars, Star Trek, Lord of the Rings,* DC Comics, Marvel, Disney—wherein multitudes of smaller worlds, realities, timelines, and variations on characters shape narrative webs that stretch from print to screen and back again.[3] Fictional characters reappear across multiple media (e.g., film, television, novels, comic books, video games) and are carefully protected, critiqued, and re-created by creators and fans alike. Such fictional universes, which are at times also referred to as worlds, are intentionally flexible, are changed over time, and are often adopted as cultural touchstones across generations of fans and consumers.

Increasingly, these fictional worlds pass through various media and offer multiple opportunities for fan engagement. Henry Jenkins refers to the phenomenon as "convergence culture," which he describes as "a moment when fans are central to how culture operates."[4] Fictional worlds, previously considered to be created and owned by a central author or creative team, are now in part shaped and produced by those who consume them, and they quickly spiral beyond their original medium and genre. Matt Hills productively shifts the conversation to the many incongruent aspects of fandom, putting forward the idea that "fandom is not simply a 'thing' that can be picked over analytically. It is also always performative; by which I mean that it is an identity which is (dis-)claimed, and which performs cultural work."[5] That is, fans do not act as isolated groups but rather operate within culture and through the fictional worlds they are so passionate about.

While Derek Johnson offers a corrective away from world building to "the significance of world *sharing*, where multiple communities of production share that process of construction in collaborative, but also ambivalently competitive ways," he ultimately insists on his own model of franchising.[6] He suggests that "there are limitations to a theory of franchise creativity based in world-building. Any storyteller arguably builds a world in establishing narrative settings, which suggests that world-building would not be a creative phenomenon exclusive to franchising. Furthermore, not all franchise exchanges occur within the production of fictional narratives, so theories of franchised creativity should not overestimate the significance of these narrative frames."[7] Johnson thus offers an expansive view that extends beyond the confines of discrete fictional worlds, instead emphasizing franchise creation, exchange, and marketing as the primary creative endeavors within convergence culture.

Jonathan Gray takes many of these insights further by situating the corporate owners that lie behind the creative teams within the same world as the fans and the narrative content itself. In his book *Show Sold Separately*, Gray writes that "as film and television viewers, we are all part-time residents of the highly populated cities of Time-Warner, DirecTV, AMC, Sky, Comcast, ABC, Odeon, and so forth, and yet none of these cities' architecture is televisual or cinematic by nature."[8] He suggests that any "extended presence" of the filmic or televisual material must be read through their myriad ads, trailers, video games, and other paratextual material.[9] That is, according to Gray, media and advertising work by "not simply telling us to buy such products or services, but by creating a life, character, and *meaning* for all manner of products and services."[10] Each of these perspectives examines the building of fictional worlds and the ways they begin to intervene into our own lived reality, whether through technological convergence, fan labor, the ability to spin off franchises, or the development of worlds through toys, promos, spoilers, and so on.

The WWE Universe should fit neatly into such academic narratives, and it often does—but not perfectly. This chapter thus takes up the matter of building the WWE Universe through particular worlds that often serve both a charitable function and a means of expanding the WWE brand. After an overview of the importance of the live event in profes- sional wrestling, I will examine WWE's military outreach and annual *Tribute to the Troops* show as a primary example of the WWE Universe rubbing against the real world. I use this example to explain the ways that the WWE Universe extends its presence on a global scale through charitable events. However, these separate worlds do not always add up to a coherent universe. In the final section of this chapter, I examine those moments when worlds collide—for instance, when a performer is punished for their character's unpatriotic actions, when outreach to one group conflicts with other business interests, or when heel characters support an altruistic charity awareness campaign. Rather than disrupt the continuity of the fiction, I argue that such moments actually serve to further ground the WWE Universe in our own world. To a greater extent than with comparable fictional worlds that exist only on screens and paper, rather than as a series of live performances, spillages between the WWE Universe and the real world effectively blur the lines between story and business, fiction and life, thereby reinforcing rather than undermining the credibility of the WWE storyworld.

Body Building/World Building

Though often associated with new media and technologies that readily support sharing, modification, and duplication, the roots of the now seemingly ubiquitous concept of sprawling fictional universes can actually be traced back much further. The *Oxford English Dictionary* suggests that the term *world building* was used as early as 1900 in reference to theatrical entertainment: "Those great epochal dramas . . . appeared to our fathers to be majestic monitors and memorials of world-building and fate-defying individualities."[11] The "great epochal dramas" referenced in this context are classics of the stage presented "as if history had come down to us on stupendous stepping-stones—Caesar, Cleopatra, Charlemagne, Macbeth, Richard, Napoleon"—and those who created the dramatic worlds for them to rule.[12] We can look to theatrical performance—especially in the nineteenth century with its serial dramas and melodramas, popular characters that appear in different plays, and recurring motifs—as a sort of world building that might prefigure contemporary discussions of integrated media properties. Indeed, Marvin Carlson describes the ghostly aspects of theater as a way of reading the entire theatrical apparatus as a sort of continuous creative machinery—or "memory machine," as he puts it—that builds, adapts, and adopts fictional worlds with each performance.[13]

In many ways, then, professional wrestling in general and the WWE Universe in particular are merely embracing their origins in late nineteenth-century carnivals and athletic shows, where the fictive world of apparently competitive sport was created and re-created in each new performance site. That is to say, WWE builds on this long history, but with a twist: WWE creates hybrid entertainment that is based in live, popular theater and is circulated globally by other media. While camera tricks, special effects, and computer-generated graphics are employed to augment and insulate the filmed performer's body, the bodies of wrestlers very clearly exist, and their performances occur without any mediated safety net: there are no retakes, stunt doubles, or postproduction effects.[14] As I have argued elsewhere with Broderick Chow, this real-life danger grounds the wrestlers in our world (and is also affirmed by the rigorous and often exhausting work and travel schedule of professional wrestlers, as well as by fans through applause and admiration for high-risk maneuvers) as wrestlers "labour through a performance of pain, which is frequently made apparent in their bruised, bloody and broken bodies."[15] The performance of professional wrestling is literally imprinted on the wrestlers' bodies insofar as the actions of their characters have material effects on the wrestlers themselves.[16]

This relationship works in the other direction as well, as the bodies of the wrestlers very clearly also inhabit a sprawling narrative universe—the WWE Universe—that manifests in various mediated forms, including cartoons, television shows, media interviews, comic books, social media accounts, commercials, merchandise, and movies. To return to the example that opened this chapter, Dave Bautista can be Drax from *Guardians of the Galaxy* (the comic book, film series, etc.) and can take part in the Marvel Cinematic Universe, but as an actor, Bautista stops inhabiting the character of Drax when the cameras stop rolling. There is much less, however, that separates Bautista, the actor, from Batista, the WWE Superstar. Through wrestlers' bodies and their necessarily live performances, the fictional WWE Universe is—strangely yet necessarily—also our own universe.

THE WWE UNIVERSE

The concept of the WWE Universe is quite simple: it refers to anything that is connected to WWE performances, including both fans and physical spaces. Announcers frequently mention it during televised matches when they prompt "the WWE Universe" to discuss the matches on social media. Similarly, when wrestlers find themselves on the other side of the barricades that surround the ring, announcers exclaim that the fight has made its way "into the WWE Universe." The WWE Universe therefore encompasses the ring and all of the space surrounding the ring, including the fans who actively support and create the WWE brand by interacting with it on social media, television, films, and advertising, as well as by chanting at live shows, holding signs, and even booing Superstars they don't like.

Such a wide reading is expanded upon by WWE. Their corporate website's Frequently Asked Questions page asks, "How can I join the WWE Universe?" The response is incredibly straightforward: "In addition to watching WWE programming on television, millions of people are joining WWE's many social media outlets including the following below or catching all the action online at wwe.com."[17] Essentially, if people tune in or otherwise participate in discussions about WWE in any online or public forum, they are considered part of the WWE Universe. Given WWE's vast reading and the deliberate porousness of the WWE Universe, this book might even be folded into it. This expansiveness and ease of entry is one of the reasons WWE is frequently touted as an exemplary model for corporate branding and business partnerships. As noted earlier, however, such marketing is really just a new twist on an old idea. WWE has taken the show business machinery from the roots of professional wrestling and extended its reach from the fictional ring into the rest of the world using mediated distribution and social media. As Garret L. Castleberry and Carrielynn D. Reinhard, with Matt Foy and Christopher J. Olson, note, the internet and social media work for wrestling both spatially and temporally, with WWE now streaming its historic video archives on their own streaming service.[18] Together, the WWE Network and the company's use of social media connect viewers and fans around the world with the company's content from the past and present. Of course, these forms of advertising and synergistic promotion are nearly ubiquitous today with lifestyle brands and immersive shopping experiences, but for professional wrestling this sort of world building is actually a return to sports entertainment's origins in carnival and the concept of kayfabe.[19]

WWE has adapted to the changing face of the internet, which is ruled by a handful of sites, including Facebook, Twitter, Instagram, and other social networking interfaces.[20] WWE creates a massive amount of content to push to these and other social media sites, culled from recordings from live shows, WWE's archive of footage, and unique content created to respond to current events, such as the Oscars parody mentioned earlier. Social media feeds are also used to continue and advance storylines between live performances. Mark Keyes, WWE's vice president of web production, describes this process:

> Our form of content is really entertainment, it's not sports. So, a lot of "news," if you will, is really an extension of the storyline that you're seeing on TV. . . . One of the things that WWE can do as a program that runs 52 weeks a year that is literally scripted week by week, is that we can augment our storylines with simple feeds to these social networks on a weekly basis. So, with a two-hour show that runs on Monday, we have the ability to, two or three times a week, prompt that something else is happening and that [fans] should see it. [We can] continue the story that ended on Monday night and carry it through to the next Monday night.[21]

In this way, the storylines from the kayfabe world of the ring are pushed outward through social media. As Benjamin Litherland notes, "The presentation of online kayfabe collapses the notion of a contained diegesis, and Twitter becomes an extension of the fictional and performed world."[22] Of course, this process further integrates the fictional world into the lived reality of fans and others in the WWE Universe. It also means that the performance never really ends: the performers are always performing, the producers are always producing, and consumers are constantly consuming.

The plots and characters move seamlessly between live televised productions and social media feeds, where they appear alongside one's friends and family. Superstars are all trademarked extensions of the WWE brand, but many also post their own material, which frequently blurs the lines between kayfabe and the actual opinions of the wrestlers. These posts increase brand awareness among WWE fans and are intended to closely tie consumers to WWE's living products: as Erica Swallow puts it in an article on Mashable.com, "You get to see what they're feeling and what they're thinking as they travel around the country and world."[23] Independent wrestler Colt Cabana claims that "social media has made wrestlers three-dimensional. Fans can now not only decide who their favorite wrestlers are from their performance, but they can also see if they like who they are as people."[24] Indeed, because fans have their favorite wrestlers and those that they simply like to hate, WWE maintains separate social media accounts for most wrestlers, who are treated as separate brands. WWE can select which wrestlers to promote through merchandise, storylines, and other corporate pushes by gauging each wrestler's success as an individual brand. In this way, WWE uses Twitter and Facebook to perform market research in real time.[25] This development also has a corollary in the live professional wrestling event, where audible crowd support (or a lack thereof) has always been a factor in future booking and storyline decisions, up to and including the determination of the next champion.[26]

WWE's use of social media should serve to highlight how information flows and is monetized through the WWE Universe to the profit of the publicly traded corporation. While ostensibly a laterally organized collection of fans and detractors—and there are *many* detractors within wrestling fandom—the WWE Universe thrives on the old carnival tradition of just getting people inside the tent. Once inside, viewers are a captive audience: marks to be tempted, cajoled, and given the hard sell. What's different today, however, is the size of the carnival tent, which has expanded to encompass the entire world.

WWE WORLDS: MULTIPLE AUDIENCES

Especially since its initial stock offering in 1999, WWE has attempted to establish itself as a reputable company, a process that involved, among other things, transitioning all of its televised content to a TV-PG rating. The company's executive vice president of talent, live events, and creative, Paul "Triple H" Levesque, has described the violence in wrestling as being similar to that of Wile E. Coyote, which seems to appease some parents and quite a few advertisers.[27] While the offering allowed WWE to raise capital quickly, the company's basic business model was frequently called into question by academics, traders, and business writers.[28] As Ted Butryn suggests, such changes are driven by "WWE's desire to penetrate and settle into new global markets" with programming "that can be consumed more comfortably by more people globally."[29]

This is not to reduce the arrangement to simple economism but rather to consider the very real political and economic changes that have affected WWE as a burgeoning global performance company. Driven by an attempt to present a brand and company that are in line with prevailing business practices, WWE has engaged a number of initiatives designed to bolster its reputation as a civic leader. WWE proudly maintains a considerable program of corporate charity, which allows the company to target specific groups and appeal to a diverse array of consumers while expanding their global brand. Alicia Jessop makes the connection explicit in an article in the *Huffington Post*: "Throughout his tenure as WWE CEO, Vince McMahon has made charitable giving and philanthropic projects cornerstones of the WWE business model."[30] Michelle Wilson, WWE's chief marketing officer, goes one step further and explains the scope of their charity work: "Giving back to the community has always been part of the company's

DNA. Since we're in different cities 52 weeks out of the year, Vince wanted to give back. We see it not just about giving back, but about making our fans feel stronger about causes that matter to them."[31] Such charity work may come as a surprise to some who do not actively follow professional wrestling—and perhaps not without reason, as there are very few companies where upper management routinely and publicly assault (and are assaulted by) their employees.

WWE's "Commitment to Community and Family" states that the company "is committed to leveraging the power of its brand and platforms to help address important social issues worldwide including diversity and inclusion, education, military support and providing hope to those in need."[32] Unlike other companies that might donate a portion of their profits to a particular cause or incorporate the logo of a nonprofit into their product packaging, WWE is a live performance company, and it leverages its live content throughout its charity work. The WWE product is, like many other live performance companies, intricately tied to the workers who create it (i.e., the performers). In its diversity of charitable causes, WWE is able to provide something for everyone who might be interested in its product.

CASE STUDY: MILITARY OUTREACH

"Welcome everyone to the most patriotic show on television!" ring announcer Michael Cole bellowed to home viewers of WWE's eleventh annual *Tribute to the Troops* event, which was held at Joint Base Lewis-McChord near Tacoma, Washington, in December 2013.[33] Since 2010, the annual event has been performed and taped on military bases in the United States, but from 2003 through 2009, the event was held on active US military bases in either Iraq or Afghanistan. The general format of the hour-long taped event includes a welcome from announcers or a WWE executive, a performance of the national anthem, and then a series of video clips and wrestling matches that generally eschew any ongoing storylines and that are largely based on a traditional face/heel (good guy/bad guy) wrestling dynamic. The video clips involve celebrities thanking the troops for their service and wrestlers meeting with the troops—shaking hands, giving high fives, working out together, and signing autographs.

Such linkages between militarism and professional wrestling are perhaps indicative of a recent shift in the patriotic logic of professional wrestling. Up until the mid-1990s, many wrestling narratives revolved around attempts by the "all-American" good guy (such as Hulk Hogan or Sgt. Slaughter) to defeat the foreign bad guy (such as Yokozuna or the

Iron Sheik). As these conventions were increasingly deemphasized, a process that accelerated after 2001, wrestling began to present a general mythologized reflection of the military instead of allegorical individuals. Rather than pinning all patriotic duties on individual wrestlers who enact a fantasy of US supremacy within a scripted storyline, in light of the *SmackDown* episode that aired shortly after September 11, 2001, wrestling's new narrative made live theatrical wrestling violence itself into an act of patriotism.[34] As a publicly traded multinational corporation, WWE stages these patriotic reflections within the system of a rapidly expanding corporate ring.

Most corporate charity that involves the military maintains a tight focus on the troops, explicitly depoliticizing any military campaigns that the troops themselves might be participating in at any given time. Taking up the troops (as well as veterans) as objects of adoration allows the charitable corporation to brand *itself* as patriotic—that is, to take on the mythos of the military and to avoid explicitly partisan politics.[35] The connection between troops and corporations performs theatrical myths that pervade narratives surrounding both professional wrestling and the US military. Central to this mythology is the melodramatic idea of fighting the good fight against an evil opponent.

For such marketing connections between a corporation and the military to succeed, Stephanie M. Yeung suggests that "the combination of the product and the veteran must not only portray the company as socially responsible but it must also mark the purchaser as patriotic, while simultaneously speaking to their unique identity as a savvy consumer."[36] Such a move has larger implications beyond its use in attracting customers and suggests the ways that even charitable activity elides the larger issues and conversations. As Yeung writes, "Thus, what begins to occur when the veteran is at the center of these campaigns is that the larger issues of the wars, such as the grand stakes of waging war or the high rates of bodily and psychic trauma it produces, for which veterans are meant to serve as proxy, evanesce. While veterans and veteran causes have become pervasive, paradoxically the wars in which they have served, along with their provocations and aftermath, elude examination."[37] Of course, it might not be that WWE is inherently militaristic but that it benefits from its association with the military; it shapes its narrative world within and through its work with the US military.

From the video available, when WWE visited Iraq and Afghanistan for earlier iterations of *Tribute to the Troops*, the audience was primarily made up of active-duty soldiers. Similar to the lively crowds before which

WWE regularly performs, the soldiers carried signs, camcorders, and pieces of wrestling fan ephemera, including replica belts, T-shirts, and bandanas. The ring, flanked with military personnel and military vehicles, integrated itself into the military landscape surrounded by soldiers carrying guns while perched atop tanks and personnel carriers. At one point in the second *Tribute to the Troops* in 2004, wrestler Rey Mysterio led a group of troops cheering "Feliz Navidad!" while holding an M16 in one hand and a pistol in the other. The ring announcers frequently emphasize the military vehicles and hardware around the ring, excitedly exclaiming the names of the machines that make up the set for the event: an A-10 Warthog, Apache helicopters, Humvees, various tanks, and transport vehicles. The announcers thus call attention to the set and normalize it within both the military context *and* WWE's fictional wrestling universe. The live event, as the cornerstone of WWE's business model, fits neatly into the US military base and blends the real military base into the fictional WWE Universe for a national television audience.[38]

The event has featured sitting US presidents, including both George W. Bush and Barack Obama. The 2008 *Tribute to the Troops* was the first time Bush gave a recorded message.[39] He returned in 2010, which (perhaps not incidentally) coincided with Republican (and former WWE chief executive officer) Linda McMahon's US Senate campaign. Obama appeared in 2011 and again in 2012. It is worth noting that the flexible nature of wrestling promotions allows for presidents from both parties to appear on the show; WWE is careful to maintain a nonpartisan stance while establishing itself as patriotic and supportive of the US commander in chief.[40]

In addition to the hour-long television special, WWE Superstars make many appearances surrounding the actual wrestling event. In 2013, wrestlers John Cena, Big Show, and Kaitlyn participated in military small-arms training and received a tour of a Stryker armored attack vehicle.[41] The wrestlers basically play as soldiers for the day, performing the roles of new recruits while smiling for cameras. To stage wrestling matches in Iraq, in Afghanistan, and on military bases in the United States is to insert WWE into the real world of military training and deployment.

In 2009, like other sporting and media companies, WWE gained the sponsorship of the National Guard, and they emphasized the partnership at the annual *WrestleMania* event.[42] The National Guard issued a press release on the events leading up to *WrestleMania 25*, which included a "Show Us Your Guns" competition and an obstacle course.[43] It was promoted as a way of "tapping into" millions of WWE fans: "Senior Guardmembers are excited to tap into the WWE's 15 million fans to build interest in the

National Guard and meet recruiting goals for 2009. 'We are extremely thrilled to work with WWE and tap into the millions of loyal and passionate fans,' said Lt. Col. Joseph Day, chief of Army National Guard Marketing and Advertising. 'This is a great opportunity for our recruitment and activation outreach.'"[44] WWE was compensated for its work with the military through ongoing contracts worth millions of dollars.[45] Such sports sponsorships were controversial as they basically funneled tax dollars into WWE, NASCAR driving teams, and other for-profit corporate entities. WWE received more than $5 million in sponsorship for each year of the agreement.[46] The National Guard sponsorships with WWE engaged current and future military personnel and veterans on a number of levels:

> The Army National Guard sponsors to build visibility and generate leads for enlistments. The Guard aligns with properties that reach high school students and 18-to-24-year-olds, with a secondary target of military veterans and parents, teachers and other centers of influence. The National Guard has inked several new deals over the past six months including the NFL Buffalo Bills, USA Luge and US Youth Soccer, with additional deals in the works. Uses USA Luge to support three athletes enrolled in the National Guard World Class Athlete Program, an initiative that allows athletes/soldiers to train in sport as part of their military duties. Activates WWE by hosting WWE superstars at recruitment and retention events around the world; Kofi Kingston serves as spokesperson for the National Guard Youth Challenge Program.[47]

Although the company is certainly guided by the patriotism of its corporate leaders, as a publicly traded company, its primary motive is to turn a profit. To understand WWE's support of the US military as crude patriotism, as many liberal detractors have, is to miss a larger critique that recognizes the socioeconomic benefits of overlapping the world of staged wrestling with real military operations.

Indeed, for WWE corporate outreach, a change in programming and in public relations "has cleared the way for more blue-chip advertisers to come aboard, including PepsiCo, AT&T and Procter & Gamble."[48] It is a performance that is highly portable; the images from military bases are strikingly similar to the other charity work performed by the wrestlers. From visiting hospitalized children to building playgrounds, WWE has done its best to appeal to new shareholders in this way.

The cover of WWE's 2004 annual report features a picture of John Cena reaching toward the camera while held in Kurt Angle's "Patriot Lock." In large letters, the cover reads, "Reach." In a text box overlaying this image from *WrestleMania XX*, it is made clear who precisely WWE hopes to reach: ". . . current fans . . . fans that were . . . fans that will be . . . new friends and supporters . . . investors."[49] Shortly after WWE's initial public offering, *Businessweek* suggested through interviews with financial consultants that the stock was sure to go up "once buyers realize that the WWF is such a potent brand" because "the average Wall Street investor is not exactly the demo[graphic]" that watches wrestling.[50] WWE quickly appointed Linda McMahon as CEO, which some financial analysts conceded had "convinced investors that WWF leadership is very professional. That's right, professional. And anyone who's got a problem with that should go talk to Vince."[51] Interestingly, that is exactly what sponsors tend to do.

The same aspects of live performance that allow WWE and its fictional universe to bleed so easily into other realities also make it difficult for some to understand where its theatricality begins and ends. As a publicly traded live entertainment company, however, WWE arguably finds itself under more scrutiny than other wrestling promotions and even media companies. Where a film or television producer usually does not have to apologize for fictional characters' misbehavior, the lines between character, actor, and company are not as clearly delineated for WWE or its sponsors. In 2011, segment producer and former wrestler David "Fit" Finlay was fired for producing a segment in which Dolph Ziggler, then a heel, interrupted "The Star-Spangled Banner" at a live event. Allegedly a member of the National Guard attended the live show and reported the incident, which resulted in Finlay's firing. Finlay intended the event to be viewed as theater: "It wasn't intended to insult anybody in that way—it was just part of an entertaining show. That's what we do, we entertain—it's about cheers and boos."[52] However, the National Guard—at the time a major sponsor and corporate partner—had more difficulty separating the heel's politics from the company's. As one self-described "angry fan" notes: "After becoming a publicly traded company, the only way the WWE would be able to stay in business is if they got big money from big companies to continue doing the big things they've been doing for years."[53] It is perhaps not surprising that a corporate entertainment company would want to keep its sponsors happy. However, problems with the content are not limited to sponsors' complaints, especially when the various worlds that WWE curates for different subsets of fans come into direct conflict.

When WWE Worlds Collide

Because professional wrestling blurs the lines between performer and character, reality and fiction, the matter with Finley and the National Guard is not unique. Indeed, WWE's support of the military is just one aspect of its public outreach campaigns, which fall under the banner of "WWE Community." This so-called community is split into four main areas—Diversity, Education, Hope, and Military—each of which involves partnerships with other national organizations.[54] Diversity includes antibullying campaigns and partnerships with the Special Olympics and GLAAD; Education focuses on reading initiatives and facility improvements in grade schools; Hope generally focuses on terminal diseases and partners with the Susan G. Komen Foundation and Make-A-Wish; and Military focuses on the US military through nonprofits that provide training and job placement for veterans and through various entertainment tours, such as *Tribute to the Troops*. While it is an undoubtedly peculiar, if not occasionally paradoxical, combination of campaigns for a company that derives its profits from staging theatrical brawls, it is indicative of WWE's intentionally flexible brand identity.

WWE is particularly effective across these various spheres because it has a stable of charismatic and camera-ready spokespeople. For instance, Fred Rosser (a former WWE Superstar known within the company's programming as Darren Young), who became the first openly gay active wrestler when he came out in 2013, regularly made appearances representing WWE at GLAAD-sponsored events.[55] The wrestlers represent WWE as both brand ambassadors and products. To see John Cena participating in live-fire exercises or Darren Young marching in the New York and San Francisco Pride Parades is, in a sense, to see WWE doing the same.

However, such outreach can be fraught, as was seen in 2015 when WWE embarked upon a Middle East tour and Rosser "was intentionally left off the card, according to WWE, because of his sexuality."[56] The *Washington Post* reported that "the UAE has a poor track record when it comes to the lesbian, gay, bisexual and transgender populations, which is why, according to WWE, Young's been left off the card."[57] In response, WWE issued the following statement: "WWE does not discriminate against individuals regardless of age, race, religion or sexual orientation, and we continue to proudly support Fred Rosser (aka WWE Superstar Darren Young) for being open about his sexuality. Unfortunately, WWE cannot change cultures and laws around the world, and thus we did not send Fred Rosser to the United Arab Emirates for our upcoming events for his own protection. WWE also fully supports Fred Rosser's right to express his views on personal social media accounts rather than WWE's corporate platforms."[58]

Rosser was very active on social media in response, saying, "I feel like no none [sic] has my back and it upsets me. The struggle is real. I'm human," and "My freedom of speech is gone. Gone but not forgotten."[59] Rosser also questioned why the company would even travel to a place that apparently prohibited him and women performers, answering his question in the same tweet: "I get it! #MillionsofDollars."[60] The following year, when former WWE announcer and Hall of Famer Jim Ross was pressed on whether promoting a show in Saudi Arabia might conflict with WWE's corporate diversity policies, he suggested "that the questioner was 'overthinking' the matter. He continued 'Of course it's all about the money. When was it not all about the money? Diversification has zero to do with a country's laws or customs.'"[61] It is an illuminating admission and turn of phrase. It is also clear that in parts of the Middle East, governments (and the laws and customs they enforce) are actively involved in shaping local WWE events. Justin D. Martin explains: "The Qatari government's Tourism Authority was the primary sponsor of the WWE event, part of the country's strategy to promote economic growth through sports and entertainment. That strategy, in part, hinges on attracting viewers from more abstemious parts of the Persian Gulf. One such viewer, a 25-year-old Saudi named Emad Allari, told me he flew in from Riyadh, where WWE shows, like movie theaters, are banned. 'I'm a big fan,' he said. 'Watching WWE is the reason why I love to do bodybuilding now.' Last year, he flew to Abu Dhabi for a three-day WWE show there."[62]

Indeed, WWE has indicated that it wants to continue to expand globally through its roster and its touring locations.[63] Further expanding the fictional world of wrestling into heretofore-untapped markets within the real world will inevitably result in more clashes between WWE's roster and local customs. For instance, in an echo of Rosser's deliberate omission from the Middle East tour, 2018's *Greatest Royal Rumble* event in Saudi Arabia excluded WWE Superstar Sami Zayn from the card because of the Canadian performer's Syrian heritage.[64]

Such gestures at times border on the absurd as the world of corporate charity clashes with the fictional world in the ring. For instance, in October 2014, WWE, like other media and sports companies, teamed up with Komen for the Cure to raise money for breast cancer awareness. For WWE, this effort involved sending wrestlers out for photo opportunities and "raising awareness" through their live and televised content. The middle rope of the ring was pink for the whole month, all of the wrestlers incorporated pink into their gear, and the branded T-shirts many wrestlers wore on the way to the ring were available for sale on the WWE website.

Every wrestler participated in the Komen for the Cure promotion, including a heel faction called the Real Americans. Originally a parody of the Tea Party, the gimmick found an audience among WWE fans, who quickly embraced the two wrestlers who would begin their matches by holding their hands over their hearts and bellowing, "We the people!" These comedic impressions of conspiracy-theorist-real-patriots enraged conservative political commentator Glenn Beck enough that he complained about them on his radio show: "'The WWE now has put a new character out that is demonizing the TEA [sic] Party,' Beck said. 'You know Linda McMahon, I'm sorry you didn't win. We should have seen how [sic] your true colors early on, and I think we did. She's just one of these progressive Republicans that we worry about.'"[65]

WWE's response to Beck encapsulates the basic logic of wrestling storytelling: "'WWE is creating a rivalry centered on a topical subject that has varying points of view,' The WWE said. 'This storyline was developed to build the Mexican American character [Alberto] Del Rio into a hero given WWE's large Latino base, which represents 20 percent of our audience.'"[66] Put plainly, WWE deliberately creates inflammatory racist products or characters that are designed to offend and infuriate its audience because people will pay money to see such characters get beaten up.[67] Monetary motivations aside, and despite WWE's intentions to create heels out of the Real Americans, many fans cheered them on as they continued to do battle with various nonwhite wrestlers on the roster.

When WWE partnered with Komen for the Cure, the Real Americans entered the ring wearing pink "We The People" T-shirts that encouraged everyone to "Rise Above Cancer." The Real Americans then had a match in which they defeated Santino Marella and the Great Khali, thereby linking Susan G. Komen's breast cancer awareness campaign with the familiar nationalist narrative of white American wrestlers fighting threatening foreigners that can be found throughout wrestling history.[68] The clash between WWE's world of corporate charity and the kayfabe world of the WWE Universe was noted by many fans, but, in the end, the WWE Universe is so intentionally flexible that it can withstand such criticisms. In fact, such attention can be leveraged for further promotion, generating additional heat for the heel team as the serialized storyline evolves.

Conclusion

WWE, like many performance and media companies, has actively curated and built a fictional universe of characters and plots that actively engages with and is cocreated by its fans and audience members. Yet, the worlds that WWE creates within that larger universe frequently clash with and contradict each other. Two articles on *Kayfabe News*, a parody website devoted to fake wrestling news, highlight such apparent discrepancies in the WWE Universe. Comedy is useful here, as it quickly cuts to the absurd logic of such fantastic creations, which are otherwise treated very seriously (or at least earnestly) by marketers and consumers alike. The first plays up the contrived nature of branded narrative networks like the WWE Universe with the headline "Stephen Hawking Struggles to Explain WWE Universe." Sarcastically emphasizing the company's attempt to brand its own fandom, the article explains: "The WWE Universe seems to have been created from nothing—*ex nihilo*—about two years ago. Before then, no one had even heard of the WWE Universe—just WWE. Now it's ubiquitous."[69] Indeed, the fact that one need only be aware of WWE content to be considered a part of the WWE Universe is particularly noteworthy here. The other article pokes fun at the idea that members of the WWE Universe actually have little say over the content of WWE programming, with the headline "WWE Universe Goes on Strike."[70] Calling attention to the fact that fans labor in their roles as they shape WWE content across the various worlds that constitute the WWE Universe, the article states that "frustrated fans of World Wrestling Entertainment, branded collectively as the WWE Universe, have walked out on strike against the company."[71] The conclusion of the article reflects the cynicism felt by many wrestling fans: "Members of the WWE Universe insist they will not watch WWE programming again until their grievances are addressed. It is more likely, however, that they will continue watching as usual but complain extra-loud about it."[72] The struggles of professional wrestling extend beyond the in-ring action for fans, wrestlers, and promoters alike. Even knowing that the only real way to show disgust or to hurt WWE is to stop consuming their products, fans nevertheless continue to watch—channeling their criticism into the narratives designed and sold by WWE. In the WWE Universe, as in many popular forms, fan discontent becomes content.

NOTES

1. WWE, "WWE Invades the 2015 Oscars."
2. Ibid.
3. Indeed, many of these fictional universes overlap and are owned by the same or related parent companies.
4. Jenkins, *Fans, Bloggers, and Gamers*, 1.
5. Hills, *Fan Cultures*, xi.
6. Johnson, *Media Franchising*, 22.
7. Ibid., 108.
8. Gray, *Show Sold Separately*, 1.

9. Ibid., 2.

10. Ibid., 3.

11. The quote is pulled from a misogynistic *Harper's Weekly* article decrying the feminizing effect that Alexandre Dumas fils' *Camille* had on the theater. See Wheeler, "The Unseemly Drama," 280.

12. Ibid.

13. See Carlson, *Haunted Stage*.

14. For a more comprehensive argument about the centrality of live performance in professional wrestling, see Laine, "Stadium Sized Theatre."

15. Chow and Laine, "Audience Affirmation," 44.

16. Also see Broderick Chow's work on strongmen and bodybuilding: Chow, "Muscle Memory" and "Work and Shoot." In addition, Nell Haynes provides an important intervention on mediated and globally circulated bodies and identities through her fieldwork with *luchadoras* in Bolivia: see Haynes, "Global Cholas."

17. WWE, "WWE Fan Questions and Services."

18. Castleberry and Reinhard, with Foy and Olson, "Introduction," 72.

19. Kayfabe is taken up here, as I have defined it elsewhere, as "the visible and observable theatrical presentation of a fictional or predetermined world and timeline, which, not incidentally, co-exists neatly with our own. That is, kayfabe might be seen as the theatricality that overlays performance—the storyline surrounding the clothesline." See Laine, "Professional Wrestling Scholarship," 90–91. For more on the theatricality and performance of professional wrestling see Chow, Laine, and Warden, "Introduction."

20. See Swallow, "How WWE Conquered."

21. Ibid.

22. Litherland, "Breaking Kayfabe Is Easy," 532.

23. Swallow, "How WWE Conquered."

24. Olson, "Twitter, Facebook, and Professional Wrestling," 309.

25. Swallow, "How WWE Conquered."

26. See, for instance, the analysis of Daniel Bryan's rise to the championship through a turbulent mix of interest from investors, fans, and creatives at WWE in Laine, "Stadium Sized Theatre," as well as Christian Norman's essay in this volume.

27. Flint, "WWE Is Showing a Flipside."

28. For an analysis of such discourse, see Battema and Sewell, "Trading in Masculinity."

29. Butryn, "Global Smackdown," 285.

30. Jessop, "WWE Work to End Bullying."

31. Ibid.

32. Ibid.

33. WWEwrestling4all, "WWE 12/13/11." For more on WWE's global expansion, with attention to community and military outreach, see: Butryn, "Global Smackdown"; Laine, "Professional Wrestling"; and Nevitt, "'Spirit of America Lives Here.'"

34. These shifts in character and programming are discussed at length in Nevitt, "'Spirit of America Lives Here.'"

35. See Yeung, "Framing the Fight."

36. Ibid., 106–7.

37. Ibid., 106.

38. For a more detailed analysis of how WWE transforms locations such as these into branded spaces, see Dru Jeffries and Andrew Kannegiesser's chapter in this volume.

39. Bedard, "Bush's Tribute to the Troops and WWE."

40. This stance is particularly notable in light of the 2016 presidential election, in which neither of the major party candidates appeared on WWE programming during the election. This is perhaps due to the fact that the nomination and election of Donald Trump, who has himself been

a recurring figure in WWE storylines, sparked numerous comparisons between and debates about electoral politics and professional wrestling. See Mazer, "Donald Trump Shoots the Match"; Warden, Chow, and Laine, "Working Loose"; and Mazer, "Sharon Mazer Responds to Warden, Chow, and Laine."

41. WWE, "WWE Superstars Get Stryker and Small Arms Training."

42. WWE, "Army National Guard to Roll With WWE."

43. McCollum, "Army Guard Joins WWE."

44. Ibid.

45. Betty McCollum, "290 House Republicans and Democrats Defeat McCollum Amendment to Prohibit Wasteful Pentagon Spending on Pro Wrestling and NASCAR," press release, June 14, 2013, accessed September 23, 2016, http://mccollum.house.gov/press-release/290-house-republicans-and-democrats-defeat-mccollum-amendment-prohibit-wasteful.

46. Caldwell, "WWE News."

47. IEGSR, "Despite Budget Cutbacks."

48. Flint, "WWE Is Showing a Flipside."

49. WWE, "World Wrestling Entertainment, Inc. 2004 Annual Report."

50. Brady, "WWF."

51. Ibid.

52. Gargiulo, "Fit Finlay Breaks His Silence."

53. Morris, "One Fan's Frustration."

54. WWE, "WWE Community."

55. While WWE did not call attention to Rosser's coming out in any of its broadcast programming, he was featured prominently on the WWE website, and the company issued statements of support and directed others to social media related to the announcement. See WWE, "WWE Releases Statement in Support of Darren Young." Rosser was released from WWE in 2017; see Esnaashari, "Fred Rosser Drives Forward." At the 2018 *WrestleMania* event in New Orleans, WWE staged an entrance for Finn Bálor featuring local LGBTQ fans wearing shirts with his rainbow-colored logo and donated 20 percent of the T-shirt sales to GLAAD. The event also featured the first openly gay woman wrestler, Sonya Deville, who wrestled in the first-ever Women's Royal Rumble match. See Marr, "WWE's Finn Bálor Celebrated LGBTQ People."

56. Payne, "Fans Stand with Gay WWE Star Darren Young."

57. Ibid.

58. Middleton, "WWE Issues Statement on Darren Young."

59. Stroud, "Darren Young Has Lost His 'Freedom of Speech.'"

60. Ibid.

61. EWrestlingNews Staff, "Royal Ramblings."

62. Martin, "Why Pro Wrestling Is Perfect."

63. "Annual Report," Form 10-k, WWE World Wrestling Entertainment Inc., *Morningstar*, April 30, 2001, 4–5, accessed September 23, 2016, http://quote.morningstar.com/stock-filing/Annual-Report/2001/4/30/t.aspx?t=XNYS:WWE&ft=10-K&d=498a2b58b94c536c.

64. Martinez, "Latest on Sami Zayn's Absence."

65. Sulla-Heffinger, "Glenn Beck Slams WWE Stars."

66. Ibid.

67. This is not significantly different from many melodramatic Hollywood films where the audience is meant to cheer the demise of the bad guys, but in wrestling the audience sometimes cheers for the bad guys. For more on the role of live audiences in WWE performances, see Sam Ford's essay in this volume.

68. Medalis, "Real Americans def. Santino Marella and the Great Khali."

69. Kayfabe Staff, "Stephen Hawking Struggles."

70. Kayfabe Staff, "WWE Universe Goes on Strike."

71. Ibid.

72. Ibid.

Bibliography

Bateman, Oliver. "Wrestling, Politics, and the Violent Realities of 2016." *Pacific Standard.* December 22, 2016. Accessed December 23, 2016. https://psmag.com/wrestling-politics -and-the-violent-realities-of-2016-475d90d4438#.dw1c75x2q.

Battema, Douglas, and Philip Sewell. "Trading in Masculinity: Muscles, Money, and Market Discourse in the WWF." In *Steel Chair to the Head: The Pleasure and Pain of Professional Wrestling,* edited by Nicholas Sammond, 260–94. Durham, NC: Duke University Press, 2005.

Bedard, Paul. "Bush's Tribute to the Troops and WWE." *US News & World Report.* December 16, 2008. Accessed August 16, 2016. http://www.usnews.com/news/blogs/washington -whispers/2008/12/16/bushs-tribute-to-the-troops-and-wwe.

Brady, Diane. "The WWF: Blood, Sweat, and a Lady Named Linda." *Bloomberg Businessweek.* January 23, 2000. Accessed August 5, 2016. http://www.businessweek.com/stories/2000 -01-23/the-wwf-blood-sweat-and-a-lady-named-linda.

Butryn, Ted. "Global Smackdown: Vince McMahon, World Wrestling Entertainment, and Neoliberalism." In *Sport and Neoliberalism: Politics, Consumption, and Culture,* edited by David L. Andrews and Michael L. Silk, 280–93. Philadelphia: Temple University Press, 2012.

Caldwell, James. "WWE News: Ntl. Guard Sponsorship Money Revealed, Stock Hits Benchmark for First Time Since 2011, Storyline Carries Over to 'Daily Show,' Austin on 'Corolla,' Stasiak, NBA/WWE Parody." *Pro Wrestling Torch.* June 19, 2013. Accessed September 23, 2016. http://www.pwtorch.com/artman2/publish/WWE_News_3/article _71396.shtml#.VD_5UOdRETk.

Carlson, Marvin. *The Haunted Stage: Theatre as Memory Machine.* Ann Arbor: University of Michigan Press, 2003.

Castleberry, Garrett L., and Carrielynn D. Reinhard, with Matt Foy and Christopher J. Olson. "Introduction: Why Professional Wrestling Studies Now? Legitimizing a Field of Interdisciplinary Study." *Popular Culture Studies Journal* 6, no. 1 (2018): 65–81.

Chow, Broderick D. V. "Muscle Memory: Re-enacting the fin-de-siècle Strongman in Pro Wrestling." In *Performance and Professional Wrestling,* edited by Broderick Chow, Eero Laine, and Claire Warden, 143–53. London: Routledge, 2017.

———. "Work and Shoot: Professional Wrestling and Embodied Politics." *TDR: The Drama Review* 58, no. 2 (2014): 72–86.

Chow, Broderick, and Eero Laine. "Audience Affirmation and the Labour of Professional Wrestling." *Performance Research* 19, no. 2 (June 2014): 44–53.

Chow, Broderick, Eero Laine, and Claire Warden. "Introduction: Hamlet Doesn't Blade: Professional Wrestling, Theatre, and Performance." In *Performance and Professional Wrestling,* edited by Broderick Chow, Eero Laine, and Claire Warden, 1–6. London and New York: Routledge, 2017.

Esnaashari, Farbod. "Fred Rosser Drives Forward, Continues Outreach despite Leaving Darren Young and WWE Behind." *ESPN.* March 9, 2018. Accessed August 14, 2018. http://www .espn.com/wwe/story/_/id/22702163/even-darren-young-wwe-fred-rosser-continues -lgbtq-anti-bullying-outreach.

EWrestlingNews Staff. "Royal Ramblings: Saudi Arabia, Women, and WWE." *EWrestlingNews.* April 22, 2016. Accessed September 25, 2016. http://www.ewrestlingnews.com/articles /royal-ramblings-saudi-arabia-women-and-wwe.

Flint, Joe. "WWE Is Showing a Flipside." *LA Times.* August 24, 2009. Accessed September 23, 2016. http://articles.latimes.com/2009/aug/24/entertainment/et-wwe24.

Haynes, Nell. "Global Cholas: Reworking Tradition and Modernity in Bolivian Lucha Libre." *Journal of Latin American and Caribbean Anthropology* 18, no. 3 (2013): 432–36.

Hills, Matt. *Fan Cultures*. London: Routledge, 2002.

Gargiulo, Eric. "Fit Finlay Breaks His Silence on WWE Firing." *Camel Clutch Blog*. July 11, 2011. Accessed September 3, 2016. http://camelclutchblog.com/fit-finlay-breaks-his-silence-on -wwe-firing/.

Gray, Jonathan. *Show Sold Separately*. New York: New York University Press, 2010.

IEGSR. "Despite Budget Cutbacks, US Armed Forces Remain a Formidable Player in Sponsorship." *IEGSR*. February 21, 2012. Accessed September 23, 2016. http:// www.sponsorship.com/iegsr/2012/02/21/Despite-Budget-Cutbacks,-U-S--Armed -Forces-Remain-.aspx.

Jenkins, Henry. *Fans, Bloggers, and Gamers: Exploring Participatory Culture*. New York: New York University Press, 2006.

Jessop, Alicia. "WWE Work to End Bullying at Wrestlemania 29." *Huffington Post*. April 7, 2013. Accessed July 5, 2016. http://www.huffingtonpost.com/alicia-jessop/wrestlemania-29 _b_3029746.html.

Johnson, Derek. *Media Franchising: Creative License and Collaboration in the Culture Industries*. New York: New York University Press, 2013.

Kayfabe Staff. "Stephen Hawking Struggles to Explain WWE Universe." *Kayfabe News*. March 5, 2012. Accessed September 15, 2016. http://www.kayfabenews.com/stephen-hawking -struggles-to-explain-wwe-universe/.

———. "WWE Universe Goes on Strike." *Kayfabe News*. January 27, 2014. Accessed September 15, 2016. http://www.kayfabenews.com/wwe-universe-goes-on-strike/.

Laine, Eero. "Professional Wrestling: Creating America's Fight Culture." In *Sports at the Center of Popular Culture: The Television Age*. Vol. 2 of *American History through American Sports: From Colonial Lacrosse to Extreme Sports*, edited by Daniel Coombs and Bob Batchelor, 219–36. Santa Barbara: Praeger, 2012.

———. "Professional Wrestling Scholarship: Legitimacy and Kayfabe." *Popular Culture Studies Journal* 6, no. 1 (2018): 82–99.

———. "Stadium Sized Theatre: WWE and the World of Professional Wrestling." In *Performance and Professional Wrestling*, edited by Broderick Chow, Eero Laine, and Claire Warden, 39–47. London: Routledge, 2016.

Litherland, Benjamin. "Breaking Kayfabe Is Easy, Cheap and Never Entertaining: Twitter Rivalries in Professional Wrestling." *Celebrity Studies* 5, no. 4 (2014): 531–33.

Marr, Rhuaridh. "WWE's Finn Bálor Celebrated LGBTQ People at Wrestlemania 34." *Metro Weekly*. April 9, 2018. Accessed August 14, 2018. https://www.metroweekly.com/2018/04 /wwes-finn-balor-celebrated-lgbtq-people-at-wrestlemania-34/.

Martin, Justin D. "Why Pro Wrestling Is Perfect for the Modern Middle East." *Foreign Policy*. March 22, 2013. Accessed September 25, 2016. http://www.foreignpolicy.com/articles /2013/03/22/pro_wrestling_modern_middle_east_qatar.

Martinez, Phillip. "The Latest on Sami Zayn's Absence from WWE's 'Greatest Royal Rumble' in Saudi Arabia." Player.One. *Newsweek*. May 3, 2018. Accessed July 20, 2018. https://www .newsweek.com/wwe-sami-zayn-greatest-royal-rumble-update-910177.

Mazer, Sharon. "Donald Trump Shoots the Match." *TDR: The Drama Review* 62, no. 2 (Summer 2018): 175–200.

———. "Sharon Mazer Responds to Warden, Chow, and Laine." *TDR: The Drama Review* 62, no. 2 (Summer 2018): 216–19.

McCollum, S. Patrick. "Army Guard Joins WWE for Tag Team Event." National Guard. April 1, 2009. Accessed September 23, 2016. http://www.nationalguard.mil/News/Article/574134 /army-guard-joins-wwe-for-tag-team-event/.

Medalis, Kara A. "The Real Americans def. Santino Marella and the Great Khali." WWE. October 6, 2013. Accessed August 16, 2016. http://www.wwe.com/shows/wwebattleground /2013/santino-marella-the-great-khali-vs-the-real-americans-26153269.

Middleton, Marc. "WWE Issues Statement on Darren Young." *Wrestling Inc.* February 1, 2015. Accessed August 4, 2016. http://www.wrestlinginc.com/wi/news/2015/0210/589348/wwe -issues-statement-on-darren-young/.

Morris, Ashley. "One Fan's Frustration with Fit Finlay's Release." *Bleacher Report.* June 29, 2011. Accessed September 3, 2016. http://bleacherreport.com/articles/753123-wwe-one-fans -frustration-with-fit-finlays-release.

Nevitt, Lucy. "'The Spirit of America Lives Here': US Pro-Wrestling and the Post-9/11 'War on Terror.'" *Journal of War and Culture Studies* 3, no. 3 (2010): 319–34.

Olson, Christopher J. "Twitter, Facebook, and Professional Wrestling: Indie Wrestler Perspectives on the Importance of Social Media." *Popular Culture Studies Journal* 6, no. 1 (2018): 306–16.

Payne, Marissa. "Fans Stand with Gay WWE Star Darren Young after He's Barred from UAE Tour." *Washington Post.* February 11, 2015. Accessed August 4, 2016. https://www .washingtonpost.com/news/early-lead/wp/2015/02/11/fans-stand-with-gay-wwe-star -darren-young-after-hes-barred-from-uae-tour/.

Stroud, Brandon. "Darren Young Has Lost His 'Freedom of Speech' over WWE's Tour of the United Arab Emirates." *Uproxx.* February 11, 2015. Accessed August 4, 2016. http://uproxx .com/prowrestling/darren-young-has-lost-his-freedom-of-speech-over-wwes-tour-of-the -united-arab-emirates/.

Sulla-Heffinger, Anthony. "Glenn Beck Slams WWE Stars as 'Stupid Wrestling People'— Whines Characters 'Demonizing' Tea Party." *New York Post.* February 24, 2013. Accessed August 6, 2016, http://nypost.com/2013/02/24/glenn-beck-slams-wwe-stars-as-stupid -wrestling-people-whines-characters-demonizing-tea-party/.

Swallow, Erica. "How WWE Conquered the Social Media Arena." *Mashable.* January 28, 2011. Accessed September 2, 2016. http://mashable.com/2011/01/28/wwe-social-media/.

Warden, Claire, Broderick Chow, and Eero Laine. "Working Loose: A Response to 'Donald Trump Shoots the Match' by Sharon Mazer." *TDR: The Drama Review* 62, no. 2, T238 (Summer 2018): 201–15.

Wheeler, A. C. "The Unseemly Drama." *Harper's Weekly.* March 24, 1900.

WWE. "Army National Guard to Roll With WWE." WWE. March 16, 2009. Accessed September 23, 2016. http://www.wwe.com/inside/news/armynatlguardwithwwe.

———. "World Wrestling Entertainment, Inc. 2004 Annual Report." WWE. Accessed September 29, 2016. http://ir.corporate.wwe.com/Cache/2784553.PDF?Y=&O=PDF&D=&FID= 2784553&T=&IID=4121687.

———. "WWE Community." WWE. Accessed August 15, 2016. https://community.wwe.com/.

———. "WWE Fan Questions and Services." WWE. Accessed February 13, 2015. http:// corporate.wwe.com/faq/wwe-fan-questions-and-services.

———. "WWE Invades the 2015 Oscars." WWE. Accessed August 4, 2016. http://www.wwe .com/inside/movie-posters-2015-oscars.

———. "WWE Releases Statement in Support of Darren Young." WWE. August 15, 2013. Accessed August 16, 2016. http://www.wwe.com/inside/wwe-releases-statement-on -darren-young-26140515.

———. "WWE Superstars Get Stryker and Small Arms Training: 2013 Tribute to the Troops (1:56)." WWE. December 17, 2013. Accessed September 17, 2016. http://www.wwe.com /videos/wwe-superstars-get-stryker-and-small-arms-training-2013-tribute-the-troops -26171091.

WWEwrestling4all. "WWE 12/13/11—Tribute to the Troops—Full Show." YouTube video, 1:51:08. Posted December 14, 2011. https://www.youtube.com/watch?v=GJFv2qz5K7I.

Yeung, Stephanie M. "Framing the Fight: Post-9/11 Warfare and the Logistics of Representation." PhD diss., University of Southern California, 2014. http://digitallibrary.usc.edu /cdm/compoundobject/collection/p15799coll3/id/443930/rec/.

EERO LAINE is Assistant Professor of Theatre at the University at Buffalo. He is coeditor of *Performance and Professional Wrestling*.

chapter two

THE WORK OF WRESTLING: STRUGGLES FOR CREATIVE AND INDUSTRIAL POWER IN WWE LABOR

Andrew Zolides

In the parlance of carnivals and circuses, *work* refers to anything that is scripted to occur or is planned in advance. Traditionally the word has referred to grifters or conmen *working* unwitting victims into parting ways with their money, but the culture of professional wrestling has also adopted the concept. Indeed, it is the work that distinguishes professional wrestling from both competitive sports and other kinds of fictional narratives. In many ways, however, this particular understanding of *work* also obscures the word's more traditional meaning, referring to labor, which is also central to the industry of professional wrestling. Therefore, this chapter seeks to interrogate the work of wrestling: that is, wrestling as a site of industry, labor, and the various social dynamics that combine to make it "just the weirdest fucking business in the world."[1]

By analyzing the industrial history and corporate culture of WWE, this chapter seeks to question where the work of wrestling is performed, and by whom. More specifically, I will address the unique positioning of professional wrestlers in WWE by analyzing the company's labor practices in relation to other cultural industries and critical discourses surrounding unionization. I will primarily be using the case study of former WWE performer Phil Brooks, who performed as a WWE Superstar under the name CM Punk. Brooks's high-profile exit from WWE in 2014, followed by his public denouncement of the company's health and wellness policies and WWE's varied responses to those claims, perfectly encapsulates the industrial and cultural politics that define the *work* world of the professional wrestling industry and of WWE in particular. I also explore the discourse surrounding unionization in the world of professional wrestling, comparing the aims and methods used by Brooks and other wrestlers against similar cases in which the creative or industrial agency of performers has been challenged. Lastly, I consider the creative struggles generated by this unique labor status, as wrestlers are tasked with fulfilling creative demands from management while also maintaining opportunities for individual expression and exploitation of their labor outside the company. In this regard, WWE's legal categorization of wrestlers as "independent contractors" is crucial to understanding how the company defers its liabilities and responsibilities regarding worker health and job stability while still denying its performers the freedom to pursue certain outside interests and creative endeavors—precisely the kind of opportunities this status is meant to allow.

Most academic research into professional wrestling addresses the topic of work as a mode of performance, as a mode of representation, or as a unique (sub)culture. Of course, these understandings are interrelated in various ways, but each draws upon a different disciplinary discourse, a different methodological approach, and a different set of research questions. Professional wrestling's categorization as a genre of performance is a natural approach to its study, given its inherently theatrical nature.[2] Even research that takes a more sports-based approach acknowledges the central role of performance in the genre. The leading expert on this front is Sharon Mazer, whose training as a theater and performance scholar informs her take on wrestling. Taking an ethnographic approach, she focuses on the people who perform in this culture: that is, the wrestlers themselves. While she invests heavily in the idea of how this culture is taught and performed as a skill, she gives no consideration to the fact that this performance is not merely a cultural expression but also a *profession*.[3]

It is into this body of work that I wish to intervene with a more focused consideration of the professional wrestler's labor beyond the physical training and the exploits seen within the confines of individual performances. Despite being part of larger industries of media production, distribution, theatrical performance, and merchandising, the professional wrestling industry as a distinct entity has not often been considered. Although some ethnographic accounts position their subjects within a larger industrial structure, wrestling is almost always seen through the lens of a culture, rather than a commercial industry that makes millions of dollars every year. This chapter intervenes by injecting the spirit of production-culture work into the study of professional wrestling, revealing the specificity of the wrestler's labor by identifying similarities and differences compared to other modes of performance within the culture industries. Professional wrestling is a particularly rich site for cultural labor analysis; indeed, the professional wrestler is primarily a character-performer, but one whose work and performance are physically tied to his or her body and personal image. For wrestlers, then, struggles with management over the direction and presentation of their character can have a considerable impact on performers' livelihoods.

Drawing upon the work of Timothy Havens, Amanda Lotz, and Serra Tinic, I will apply a critical media industries study approach to the question of labor in WWE. Similarly to middle-range industry-focused studies, critical media industries studies is placed between micro-level studies of ethnography and cultural sociology and more macro-level approaches, like political economic studies.[4] Key features of this approach that prove particularly useful in the examination of professional wrestling industry culture include "a 'helicopter' level view of industry operations, a focus on agency within industry operations, a Gramscian theory of power that does not lead to complete domination, and a view of society and culture grounded in structuration and articulation."[5] In other words, I aim to examine issues of agency and power within the professional wrestling industry from the perspective of individual performers and the organizations they work for and through. These elements will come out in the negotiation over the creation of cultural texts within the industry, including (but not limited to) ticketed live performances and merchandise. As will be discussed in the second half of this chapter, the site of this struggle over agency and autonomy is the wrestling *character*, ostensibly a fictional persona but one that is fundamentally inseparable from its deployment by both performer and industry.

This is where an understanding of celebrity studies research proves useful. Like the wrestling industry, the celebrity industry is ultimately concerned with the commodification, promotion, and monetization of individual public personae. While celebrity studies has evolved beyond its focus on celebrities-as-texts research to encompass more culturally and industry-focused questions, there is still a long way to go when it comes to studying celebrities' labor. Texts from Joshua Gamson, Graeme Turner, Frances Bonner, P. David Marshall, and others have helped shift the focus from Richard Dyer–style textual analyses to the construction of celebrities from an industrial standpoint. Gamson provides a starting point for much of this work. He notes that when "celebrity itself is . . . commodified[,] notoriety becomes a type of capital," emphasizing that celebrity texts are sites of negotiation between the various players involved, including managers, agents, publicists, studios, and more.[6] Surprisingly, however, he barely considers the actual celebrity's role as a laborer in this negotiation. A similar blind spot can be found in Turner, Bonner, and Marshall's look into the Australian celebrity industry in *Fame Games*. They follow the rise of "promotional culture" through the lenses of the agent, manager, and publicist, again obscuring the labor of the person being "constructed."[7] In sum, celebrity studies has grown to account for the ways celebrity is constructed *upon* an individual but not for the ways a person may construct celebrity upon oneself, often through conflict with the other agents involved. This emphasis on personal branding and self-publicity is crucial in the context of professional wrestlers since their status as independent contractors constantly puts them at odds with other agents while also making them personally responsible for their own profitability.

Despite the fact that WWE performers use skills like acting, stunt work, choreography, and others associated with the larger cultural industries, they are not part of any union. Indeed, previous attempts at unionization have been met with resistance, both from the company and sometimes from the performers themselves. John Caldwell and other production culture scholars have spoken at length about these sites of professional struggle, particularly noting how issues of creativity, compensation, and adjustments to new technologies drive most of the conflicts, resulting in self-reflexive pronouncements of one's professional identity.[8] Unions become sites of industrial reflexivity in the same way across the industry more broadly, albeit with an increased investment in political labor identity and struggle. While the lack of a professional wrestling union means these workers don't have access to this crucial site for the construction of professional identity, social media has arguably come to fulfill that role.

One of the industrial factors that distinguishes contemporary professional wrestling from other creative industries when it comes to employer-employee relations is the independent contractor status of nearly all wrestling performers. WWE performers designated as independent contractors can have long-term contracts that cover payment and residuals but do not include health insurance; they are also not considered full-time WWE employees, unlike those who serve in executive roles or at the company proper. This arrangement has positives and negatives for both parties. For example, performers listed as independent contractors are typically free to pursue other moneymaking ventures independent of the company, most often in the form of personal appearances. This works better in theory than in practice, at least with WWE, which is notoriously wary of its performers participating in non-WWE events.

A major issue of these independent contracts is the no-compete clause, which generally states that performers are not allowed to work for a competitor for a set amount of time (often several months) after the termination of their affiliation with WWE. These contracts more closely resemble studio-system-era Hollywood star contracts than contemporary entertainment relationships. The history of these clauses can be traced back to the idea of trade secrets and the fear that former employees could benefit a competitor by quickly switching between promotions. WWE, however, is not worried about trade secrets; rather, these restrictions are meant to ensure that their performers have a harder time making a living if they leave WWE, by signing with either an independent wrestling promotion or some nonwrestling venture. Independent contractors are thereby strong-armed into relying on WWE as their primary source of employment. David Shoemaker sums up this disconnect thus:

> Pro wrestlers are independent contractors because of tradition, but in the modern era the designation is sometimes closer to indentured servitude. They have to provide their own health insurance. They accept the contracts they're offered because there's almost nowhere else to work, and they're prohibited from doing any work outside of WWE or accepting sponsorships without WWE's express permission. They get paid according to an arcane system of base salary plus merchandise royalties plus pay-per-view bonuses; the last two categories are heavily influenced by the mercurial whims of WWE matchmaking, and since WWE Network came into existence and subscribers have been allowed to watch PPVs at no additional charge, the bonuses have largely dried up.[9]

WWE has doubled down on the independent contractor designation and the no-compete clause, with the *Wrestling Observer Newsletter* claiming that WWE's recent contracts feature even longer no-compete periods.[10] With the rise of new independent promotions in the United States and abroad, talent management and security continues to be a crucial part of the business as performers are slowly gaining more opportunities outside the WWE structure.

From WWE's perspective, however, the benefits of independently contracting their wrestlers are obvious. Any possible downsides, such as needing to renegotiate contracts more often or having performers show up where they are not wanted, are counteracted by WWE's virtual-monopoly status within the industry, their ability to offer much higher pay rates than independent wrestling promotions, and the lack of long-term stability in the freelance market. Perhaps the greatest benefit to WWE is also the one that brings them the most controversy: the lack of liability in providing employee health insurance.

WWE has certainly been criticized for these potentially exploitative contractual practices, as Ted Butryn notes in his chapter on WWE and neoliberalism. As he summarizes, "Numerous articles in the popular press, including the *New York Times* and *Wall Street Journal* . . . have either taken [Linda] McMahon's treatment of wrestlers to task or praises her keen sense of business acumen, depending on the perspective."[11] Because WWE is the most profitable wrestling company in the world by a wide margin, their business practices extend beyond their own corporate domain and influence how the rest of the industry functions. In some ways, the independent contractor status can be seen as an extension of professional wrestling's precorporate history as a sideshow attraction, a context in which an itinerant, transient workforce was commonplace and operated largely on handshake deals.[12] WWE has maintained that mentality, becoming a publicly traded company in which their most visible and highly paid workers are also on the hook for their own medical expenses. Add to this the fact that those very workers perform a physically demanding job that makes them significantly more prone to injury and health risk, and one can easily see the inherent danger to the way WWE does business.

This description makes WWE out to be something of an idealized neoliberal entity wherein the individual laborer, on the surface, is granted a great deal of freedom and doesn't represent a significant burden on the corporation. At the same time, however, this arrangement greatly reduces the autonomy of the individual wrestling performer by limiting their options for employment. As Butryn summarizes, "The laws of the free market and the morphing of the company's particular neoliberal agenda allowed McMahon to create his growing global multimedia empire, and yet it also essentially removed what might be termed the occupational subculture of wrestling in the process."[13] Like that of any good neoliberal entity, WWE's industrial structure, as well as its larger work culture, places the burden of success or failure squarely on the individual; it is the responsibility of the performer to succeed not only within the larger neoliberal landscape of contemporary economics but also within WWE's specific corporate framework. When the company limits and controls how individuals are presented within their product, however, these nonunionized performers must find alternative ways to negotiate for creative freedom and economic success. These struggles largely play out indirectly through the performance of the characters, both in and out of the ring.

Characters as the Product: Semifictional Texts

WWE produces many texts, paratexts, and financial outlets in its contemporary period, including live shows, merchandise, home videos, television broadcasts, and more. The central feature that unites all these diverse media artifacts, however, is the professional wrestling *character*. Every live event, television broadcast, and piece of merchandise is centered on the appeal of the individual wrestlers' personae. While the narrative is driven by the serialized storylines that extend from week to week, WWE makes most of its money by selling the characters that are involved in those storylines. In their 2011 annual report, WWE describes their business as follows: "We develop unique and creative content centered around our talent and present it at our live and televised events. At the heart of our success are the athletic and entertainment skills and appeal of our WWE Superstars and our consistently innovative and multi-faceted storylines across our brands. Anchored by these brands, we are able to leverage our content and talent across virtually all media outlets."[14]

In short, the company's business model places talent—and therefore characters—front and center, positioned clearly as the primary source for their increasingly varied media content. Significantly, this business model would seem to disqualify the company from relying on independent contracts, since the US Supreme Court considers "the extent to which the worker's services are an integral part to the employer's business" a key factor in deciding whether a contract violates the Fair Labor Standards Act (FLSA).[15]

While little has been written about the creation of wrestling characters, the process can be usefully compared to the ways celebrities or stars are manufactured for cultural consumption. One of the defining features of professional wrestling is kayfabe: the tension between "the real" and "the work." In more cynical summations of professional wrestling, fakeness becomes the defining factor, separating it from other forms of (legitimate) sport. In this view, wrestlers are mere actors, whose performances are intended to dupe unsuspecting and naive audiences in a manner akin to the carnival shows of old. WWE's definition of itself as a "sports entertainment" business, however, allows for some official acknowledgment of the spectacle's fictional status. This self-awareness with regard to the work of wrestling is similar to the way celebrity is produced and marketed.

Gamson's concept of the semifictional text is particularly useful in unpacking professional wrestling's complex interplay between reality and fiction vis-à-vis performers and their characters. He describes the "active production of semi-fictional information" involving the formation of a "semi-real public personality. It is her, and it is not her."[16] For Gamson, semifictionality is a strategic maneuver for publicists and others invested in the creation and maintenance of celebrity commodities. The work of a celebrity publicist, for example, is primarily geared toward controlling the celebrity's image by controlling information flows or at least the context in which information is presented. A semifiction is created when real events are integrated into a celebrity's persona, at which point they become part of, and indistinguishable from, a carefully managed fiction that belies any clear-cut reality. In this way, the celebrity image is both reality based and narrativized into a form of fiction. This is why, as my case studies will later show, professional wrestlers often remain in character at all times, becoming semifictional in ways that encourage fans and audiences to play a game of consumption wherein authenticity is constantly in question. This "postmodern audience position," as Gamson calls it, "embraces the second story as its primary truth."[17] Engaging with a wrestler's persona—WWE's true product—thus offers both the primary pleasure of the fictional narrative and a secondary story about the processes involved in producing the fiction.

Professional wrestling characters are frequently semifictional, insofar as the performer is intrinsically tied to the character, not just in appearance but sometimes also in name. While there are instances of masked wrestling characters that can be performed by multiple people over time, the vast majority of characters are only performable by a single individual because of the indelible connection between the character and the performer.[18] Indeed, many wrestling characters are based on the real-world personalities and histories of the people portraying them. For example, when Dwayne "The Rock" Johnson returned to wrestling after starting a Hollywood movie career, his character shifted to become a take on the self-obsessed Hollywood celebrity trope. While Johnson himself was likely not as deplorable as The Rock, his semifictional character evolved to reflect well-known events from the performer's life. Such synergy allows for more believable scenarios as well as a deeper level of fan engagement, whereby viewers are encouraged to integrate metatextual knowledge into their understanding of the WWE storyworld.[19]

Like the creation of any cultural text, the production of semifictional professional wrestling characters is fraught with negotiations between various interested parties, resulting in "constant battles for control."[20] Various media outlets and cultural gatekeepers, including the actual celebrity/performer of the semifictional text, are involved in these struggles for creative control and power: "Although the workers in the various celebrity-producing industries are in many ways tightly allied, the relationships among those actively producing celebrity representations also pull in a variety of directions."[21] For professional wrestling, however, it is most often the performers that represent themselves, rather than a team of handlers;

in this particular industry, it falls to individual performers to voice any challenges or complaints directly to the company—in this case, WWE—regarding the creative direction of their character. As we'll see in the following section, such challenges can be both complex and contentious.

CM PUNK VS. WWE

Phil Brooks is the real name of former WWE wrestler CM Punk. Both Brooks and Punk are "straight edge," a lifestyle that involves abstinence from drugs, cigarettes, and alcohol. Speaking to his creative process, Brooks notes that "I had to create this persona. It never occurred to me I was a hell of a character myself."[22] At the suggestion of his then girlfriend, Brooks decided to incorporate this trait in order to play a heel to local crowds, figuring that beer-loving audiences would hate someone who refused to drink. Brooks's pride in the character is reflected in interviews, where he claims that "CM Punk was always my vision and predominantly 100% me."[23] In such statements, Brooks reclaims his creative authority over his semifictional character. This type of creative labor—the creation of marketable personae—is, of course, done in concert with WWE; Brooks's comments reinforce a sense of ownership over that creative labor that becomes contentious only when he leaves the company.

What is interesting about Brooks's statement is the word *predominantly*. It is within the space opened up by this qualification that the difference between Brooks and Punk becomes fuzzy and the semifictional reigns. When Punk performs on WWE programming, it is clear that he is part of its fictional world, which has its own rules and presentational style that distinguish it from the real world. However, when Brooks performs as Punk in *other* arenas—such as giving media interviews, fighting in UFC, or writing for Marvel Comics—the distinction becomes less clear. In fact, Brooks has continued to use the name CM Punk long after his tenure with WWE has ended, most likely because of the cultural capital and notoriety associated with it. The Punk character simply has better brand recognition than Brooks, so the latter has an economic imperative to continue to use it. Significantly, most WWE performers would be unable to follow in Brooks's footsteps in this way after leaving the company: WWE itself holds the copyrights to most character names, precluding their use outside the company. As a counterexample to Punk, Cody Rhodes (real name Cody Runnels) has been forced to perform on the independent circuit under his given name (or simply "Cody") since leaving WWE.

Taking control of one's cultural labor is not unique to wrestlers, and so professional wrestlers in WWE (and on the independent circuit, for that matter) can be usefully understood as what Michael Scott has called "cultural entrepreneurs."[24] With the rise of Web 2.0 and individualized networking, the professional responsibility of artists has extended beyond creative tasks to include industrial responsibilities like publicizing themselves, booking appearances, and interacting with fans. While Scott focuses on independent and emerging musical artists, Jeremy Morris explores how established celebrities and artists must now maintain and cultivate their online presence themselves, a kind of labor that overlaps with work traditionally delegated to publicists and public relations managers. Social media outlets like Twitter and Facebook allow for more publicity and direct fan interaction, both outside and within the industrial framework, and they are increasingly central to the work of identity formation and creation.[25] As Morris puts it, "these connections allow for artists and other famous people to *perform* celebrity in a way that seems more authentic and intimate than in other media."[26] As Alice Marwick and danah boyd point out, these interactions can create a stronger bond between performer and fan, creating a new outlet for informing and presenting identity.[27] This being the case, the opportunities for the advancement of storylines and character development offered by social media outlets like Twitter and YouTube are entirely new to the professional wrestling industry, changing not only the way performers engage with audiences but also how they strive for creative and industrial control.

Cultural entrepreneurship can also be fraught with potentially negative consequences for WWE performers. On November 20, 2012, Brooks used his verified Twitter account to promote a series of public appearances outside of WWE. The four tweets are presented below:

> "Yes, I will be on @AMCTalkingDead on Sunday. Shocking how WWE didn't promote it or get AMC the proper materials in time to announce it."[28]

> "I will also be the Grand Marshall in the Chicago turkey day parade. Also not announced or promoted by 'my' company. Shocking."[29]

> "This is what happens when you go over everyone's head to hustle and acquire your own outside appearances. #DIY"[30]

> "#disrespect"[31]

Brooks is accomplishing several creative and entrepreneurial tasks with these tweets: he is promoting upcoming personal appearances outside of WWE, thereby contributing to his personal celebrity; he is playing within the semifictional space, creating ambiguity about where his character ends and the real man begins; and he is explicitly challenging his employers and their refusal to support his work as an independent contractor.

In order to fully understand the import of these tweets, one must read them in relation to WWE programming. At the time of these tweets, Punk was a heel character whose primary motivation was his sense of being disrespected by both the fans and the company. In semifictional terms, the key to this Twitter rant is the final tweet of "#disrespect." Everything in 57 the first three tweets is true, from the perspective of both the character and the performer behind the character: Brooks made and booked those appearances on his own, and WWE failed to promote them on the preceding weeks' broadcasts (though the appearances were mentioned after the fact, both on WWE's website and on television programming). In the months prior to this, Punk often used the word *disrespect* and variations thereof in television promos and video packages. Thus, "#disrespect" can be understood as an example of what Mikhail Bahktin calls *hybridization*, a form of linguistic multivalence that he defines as "a mixture of two social languages within the limits of a single utterance."[32] Brooks's tweet simultaneously signals two different social contexts or, in the case of professional wrestling, two different realities. Brooks is speaking to the actual disrespect he feels as a laborer working for WWE, noting his lack of support from the company; at the same time, Punk is articulating his feelings within the fictional storyworld of WWE. In this case, Punk's semifictional status combines with Brooks's cultural entrepreneurship to specifically address the challenges and complexities of being a laborer within the wrestling industry.

These tweets serve a variety of purposes. First, they provide a way for Brooks to promote his public appearances, which would raise his stock independent of his role in the company (though he also refers to his status as a WWE Superstar on both shows). Though he is the one making money and gaining publicity through these appearances, WWE also receives free promotion as a result of their association with him. Simultaneously, the tweets also perform and build the Punk character *within* the WWE storyworld, albeit from outside WWE's creative jurisdiction. These non-WWE-sanctioned appearances are quite distinct from promos performed on WWE television, which are often scripted, at least in part, by WWE writers in conjunction with the performers. By contrast, Brooks operates his own Twitter account—under the watchful eye of WWE, it can be assumed—as a tool for building not just cultural and financial capital but also "character capital" by extending his WWE performance to the online space. Ultimately, Twitter becomes a site for Brooks to further invest in the creation of his character, as well as in his own status as a laborer within the wrestling industry.

The Work of Wrestling

In many ways, labor identity was at the heart of Brooks's decision to walk away from WWE in January 2014. The lack of clarity about precisely why and under what circumstances he left WWE was due to an effective radio silence from both WWE and Brooks himself over his decision. WWE simply and abruptly stopped acknowledging the character.[33] Brooks's first post-WWE public appearance billed him as "Phil Brooks 'AKA CM Punk,'" though no other mention was made of his wrestling career and background; this appearance was followed by one at the July 2014 Alternative Press Music Awards, where he acknowledged his departure from WWE, vaguely citing health and personal issues.[34] In November 2014, nearly ten months after abruptly walking out on the company, Brooks appeared on his friend and independent wrestler Colt Cabana's popular podcast, *The Art of Wrestling*, where he spent nearly two hours recounting the events leading up to and following his final days in WWE in detail. While there is plenty within this "publicly-disclosed deep text" that is worthy of analysis, I will focus here on those claims that relate directly to the profession and the labor status of professional wrestlers.[35]

Perhaps the most startling of Brooks's disclosures, and those that gained media attention from the likes of *Deadspin*, the *Washington Post*, and *Yahoo! Sports*, were accusations of malfeasance on behalf of WWE's medical staff.[36] While Brooks had previously cited a variety of vague reasons for his departure from the company, he now claimed that "the big thing that led to my decision was my health."[37] He recounts how a growth on his back went untreated; while WWE staff claimed it was nothing to worry about, Brooks sought out a second opinion from an external doctor, who determined that the growth was the product of a dangerous staph infection. Brooks also criticized WWE's concussion-prevention system and the company's publicization thereof, claiming that "WWE doesn't do anything to protect wrestlers, they do things to protect themselves . . . they don't let everybody know that they're doing all these fantastic things for concussions for the boys. They do it so it looks good on them in the public."[38]

Brooks follows this assertion up with his first reference to unionization, claiming that "the [National Football League] is getting fucked in the ass because there is a union for the football players and the union is saying 'you need to pay these guys this much for medical for past injuries, whatever.' And the NFL is doing it."[39] Brooks's citation of the NFL is intriguing, as the league has been beset with controversies over concussions and player compensation in recent years; however, the credit Punk ascribes to the NFL is perhaps misplaced. As David Shoemaker writes in an editorial for *Grantland*, "The NFLPA didn't clamor for concussion protocols; the public did, and the NFL rushed them into effect to stem the tide of public outrage. What's more, the NFL is paying a settlement because of a class-action lawsuit filed by former players."[40] Brooks's focus on unionization nevertheless makes sense: WWE performers listed as independent contractors would stand to benefit immensely from the protections and negotiating power offered by collective action.

Brooks had previously taken legal action against WWE, stemming from when he was terminated by the company for breach of contract. WWE responded by effectively keeping Brooks's royalties for all CM Punk merchandise sold, even though these sales are often a primary source of income for professional wrestlers, even at the WWE level. Since the case was settled out of court, Brooks is unable to talk publicly about the terms of the settlement, but he does boast to Cabana that "I don't think I'll get in trouble for saying I got everything I wanted and then some." According to Brooks, WWE's willingness to settle relates back to their classification of performers as independent contractors: "For ten years of my life I was legally listed as an independent contractor, and they were terrified that I was going to go to court and ruin the way they do fucking business."[41]

Brooks is hardly the only former performer to take WWE to court, as new lawsuits continue to emerge in response to WWE's labor practices as well as possible liabilities for concussion-related injuries. In January 2015, plaintiffs Vito LoGrasso (a.k.a. "Big Vito") and Evan Singleton (a.k.a. "Adam Mercer") filed a class-action lawsuit against WWE that was directly modeled after the successful concussion lawsuits that led to massive payouts by the NFL to former players for mental and physical injuries. The major difference between these lawsuits is that it is much more difficult for professional wrestlers to prove that WWE specifically is legally at fault for their injuries. Wrestlers' independent contractor status, combined with the likelihood that they have worked for other promotions over the course of their careers, seems to absolve WWE of legal culpability for their performers' long-term well-being.

Ultimately, labor disputes within WWE and the professional wrestling industry more broadly are bound to be settled with lawyers rather than unions. In fact, Brooks's case has continued with Dr. Christopher Amann, the WWE doctor singled out by Brooks on *The Art of Wrestling* podcast, who filed a defamation lawsuit against both Brooks and Cabana seeking nearly $4 million in damages; on February 20, 2015, three months after the initial claims, WWE publicly backed their physician by releasing on their website a statement and video in which they shared the results of their own "internal investigation," which they claim prove Brooks's allegations to be false.[42] A jury ruled in Brooks and Cabana's favor in June 2018.[43]

CONCLUSION

In the end, the inequitable nature of labor in professional wrestling and the overall culture within the industry both suggest that unionization may be impossible in WWE, despite its potential benefits. Future conflict will likely center not just on the company's insistence on independent contractor status for its performers but more specifically on their unique and particularly restrictive definition of that concept. This is precisely why lawsuits have been and will continue to be the primary weapon wielded by aggrieved workers, though the cost and inconvenience of the court system make this approach less than ideal. The unique history of professional wrestling's evolution from circuses and carnivals to modern television screens and beyond, paired with the near-monopolistic control exerted over the industry by the contemporary WWE, has created a unique working environment in which worker autonomy and creative control are in constant negotiation, as new technologies and trends in market capitalism become tools for performers and promoters alike to exert and contest these powers. Online and social media have become the latest outlet for WWE performers to establish and exert their creative and professional capital through a dual-purpose cultural entrepreneurship, through which wrestlers are able to create personal publicity and professional worth through semifictional acts of performance.

There are many problems with the current employee-employer relationship in professional wrestling, and they go beyond WWE. Independent promoters have also been known to swindle performers, promising larger paydays than what is ultimately delivered, making unreasonable (and often dangerous) demands for match performances, all within a high-risk and relatively unregulated work environment. As in any other sport, injuries are common in WWE, but as independent contractors, performers are required to provide their own health care. WWE has trainers and staff who provide treatments backstage at WWE shows, but if wrestlers require long-term care, they must pay out of pocket or purchase an independent insurance plan. This practice trickles down to smaller professional wrestling promotions as well: if the largest company in the industry doesn't hire performers as full-time employees, the rest of the industry finds it easier to follow suit. For years, there have been calls for unionization and collective action, echoing those made by David Hesmondhalgh and Sarah Baker for trade unions as a means of increasing social justice in the cultural industries writ large.[44] But as they note, worker self-exploitation is often the root cause: with an industry as built on passion and tradition as professional wrestling, that is certainly the case here.[45] In 2017, former WWE CEO Linda McMahon was confirmed as the head of the Small Business Administration under President Donald Trump, an implicit endorsement of WWE's way of doing business from the American government. Criticism of her appointment largely cited WWE's use of independent contractors, which law professor Robert Solomon bluntly described as "taking advantage of laborers."[46]

The struggles that WWE performers endure are certainly unique; in the transmedia era, the profession demands constant character portrayal across a variety of media, peak physical conditioning, and flexible living that allows for a relentless travel and performance schedule. The semifictional nature of professional wrestling characters leads to a higher degree of cultural entrepreneurship, as well as an increase in the exploitation of workers' emotional and creative labor. As Eero Laine recounts in the preceding chapter, contemporary professional wrestling draws upon a new set of narrative tools and creative strategies to build and maintain its semifictional world across a variety of media; we must also pay attention, however, to the ways in which these new forms of creative expression lead to new forms of worker struggle.

NOTES

1. Punk, *Art of Wrestling.*
2. See, for instance, Chow, Laine, and Warden, *Performance and Professional Wrestling.*
3. Mazer, *Professional Wrestling.*
4. Havens, Lotz, and Tinic, "Critical Media Industry Studies," 243.
5. Ibid., 246.
6. Gamson, *Claims to Fame,* 62.
7. Turner, Bonner, and Marshall, *Fame Games,* 160.
8. Caldwell, *Production Culture.*
9. Shoemaker, "CM Punk's Parting Shot."
10. Middleton, "WWE Changes Contracts."
11. Butryn, "Global Smackdown," 285.
12. Shoemaker, *Squared Circle,* 40.
13. Butryn, "Global Smackdown," 283.
14. World Wrestling Entertainment, Inc., *Annual Report.*
15. United States Department of Labor, "Independent Contractors."
16. Gamson, *Claims to Fame,* 76–77.
17. Ibid., 155.
18. Sharing characters is much more common in the Mexican lucha libre tradition, where the use of masks makes personae more easily transferable between different performers.
19. See Eero Laine's chapter in this volume for a closer look at similar interactions between our reality and WWE's storyworld.
20. Gamson, *Claims to Fame,* 85.
21. Ibid., 80.

22. *CM Punk: Best in the World.*

23. Ibid.

24. Scott, "Cultural Entrepreneurs," 237.

25. The promise of direct interaction between fans and celebrities is emphasized in the use of Twitter's "verification badge"—a blue check mark that appears on accounts to affirm they are actually under the control of the people in question. Of course, the badges are no guarantee that the celebrities themselves, rather than those under their employ, are writing and posting each individual tweet.

26. Morris, "Artists as Entrepreneurs," 277 (emphasis added).

27. Marwick and boyd, "To See and Be Seen."

28. CM Punk, November 20, 2012 (1:39 p.m.), tweet, "Yes, I will be on @AMCTalkingDead on Sunday. Shocking how WWE didn't promote it or get AMC the proper materials in time to announce it," https://twitter.com/CMPunk/status/270959369175306241.

29. CM Punk, November 20, 2012 (1:47 p.m.), tweet, "I will also be the Grand Marshall in the Chicago turkey day parade. Also not announced or promoted by 'my' company. Shocking," https://twitter.com/CMPunk/status/270961592475209729.

30. CM Punk, November 20, 2012 (1:48 p.m.), tweet, "This is what happens when you go over everyone's head to hustle and acquire your own outside appearances. #DIY," https://twitter.com /CMPunk/status/270961956633059328.

31. CM Punk, November 20, 2012 (1:50 p.m.), tweet, "#disrespect," https://twitter.com /CMPunk/status/270962233234817024.

32. Bahktin, "Discourse in the Novel," 358.

33. There have since been winking nods to Punk's absence. For example, when WWE performs in Brooks's hometown of Chicago, crowds will frequently erupt into "CM Punk" chants, prompting figures such as Stephanie McMahon and Paul Heyman to refer to "that guy" in negative terms.

34. *Talking Dead*, "The Grove," episode 43, directed by Russell Norman, AMC, March 16, 2014.

35. Caldwell, *Production Culture*, 27.

36. Nadkarni, "CM Punk Rips Apart the WWE," Payne, "CM Punk Slams," and Vanderburg, "CM Punk Rips WWE."

37. Punk, *Art of Wrestling.*

38. Ibid.

39. Ibid.

40. Shoemaker, "CM Punk's Parting Shot."

41. Punk, *Art of Wrestling.*

42. WWE refers to him as CM Punk throughout the article, despite the lawsuit being filed against Phil Brooks—an odd quirk of kayfabe and the semifictionality of WWE characters. See Mrosko, "WWE Fires Back at CM Punk."

43. Konuwa, "CM Punk vs WWE."

44. Hesmondhalgh and Baker, *Creative Labour*, 222.

45. Smith, "Passion Work," 157.

46. Waldron, "Donald Trump's Small Business Pick."

Bibliography

Bahktin, Mikhail. "Discourse in the Novel." In *The Dialogic Imagination*, edited by Michael Holquist, 259–422. Translation by Caryl Emerson and Michael Holquist. Austin, TX: University of Texas Press, 1981.

Butryn, Ted. "Global Smackdown: Vince McMahon, World Wrestling Entertainment and Neoliberalism." In *Sport and Neoliberalism*, edited by David L. Andrews and Michael L. Silk, 280–93. Philadelphia: Temple University Press, 2012.

Caldwell, John T. *Production Culture: Industrial Reflexivity and Critical Practice in Film and Television*. Durham, NC: Duke University Press, 2008.

Chow, Broderick, Eero Laine, and Claire Warden, eds., *Performance and Professional Wrestling*. London: Routledge, 2016.

CM Punk: Best in the World. WWE Studios, 2012. Film.

Gamson, Joshua. *Claims to Fame: Celebrity in Contemporary America*. Los Angeles: University of California Press, 1994.

Havens, Timothy, Amanda D. Lotz, and Serra Tinic. "Critical Media Industry Studies: A Research Approach." *Communication, Culture & Critique* 2 (2009): 234–53.

Hesmondhalgh, David, and Sarah Baker. *Creative Labour: Media Work in Three Cultural Industries*. London: Routledge, 2011.

Konuwa, Alfred. "CM Punk vs WWE: News and Notes from Trial after Jury Rules in Favor of CM Punk." *Forbes*. June 6, 2018. https://www.forbes.com/sites/alfredkonuwa/2018/06/06/cm-punk-vs-wwe-news-and-notes-from-trial-after-jury-rules-in-favor-of-cm-punk/.

Marwick, Alice, and danah boyd. "To See and Be Seen: Celebrity Practice on Twitter." *Convergence: The International Journal of Research into New Media Technologies* 17, no. 2 (2011): 139–58.

Mazer, Sharon. *Professional Wrestling: Sport and Spectacle*. Jackson: University Press of Mississippi, 1998.

Middleton, Marc. "WWE Changes Contracts after High Profile Departures, WWE Reportedly Signs Top Indie Star." *Wrestling Inc*. December 31, 2014. http://www.wrestlinginc.com/wi/news/2014/1231/588121/wwe-changes-contracts-after-high-profile-departures/.

Morris, Jeremy. "Artists as Entrepreneurs, Fans as Workers." *Popular Music and Society* 37, no. 3 (2014): 273–90.

Mrosko, Geno. "WWE Fires Back at CM Punk, Supports Dr. Amann after 'Investigation' into Medical Mistreatment Claims." *Cageside Seats*. February 20, 2015. https://www.cagesideseats.com/wwe/2015/2/20/8080127/wwe-fires-back-cm-punk-dr-amann-investigation-medical-mistreatment.

Nadkarni, Rohan. "CM Punk Rips Apart the WWE in Revealing Interview about His Departure." *Deadspin*. November 27, 2014. http://deadspin.com/cm-punk-rips-apart-the-wwe-in-revealing-interview-about-1664130050.

Payne, Marissa. "CM Punk Slams WWE's Health and Wellness Policy, Says He Was Fired on His Wedding Day." *Washington Post*. November 28, 2014. https://www.washingtonpost.com/news/early-lead/wp/2014/11/28/cm-punk-slams-wwes-health-and-wellness-policy-says-he-was-fired-on-his-wedding-day/.

Punk, CM. Interview by Colt Cabana. *The Art of Wrestling*. Podcast audio. Accessed June 28, 2017. http://www.stitcherpremium.com/colt.

Scott, Michael. "Cultural Entrepreneurs, Cultural Entrepreneurship: Music Producers Mobilising and Converting Bourdieu's Alternative Capitals." *Poetics* 40, no. 3 (2012): 237–55.

Shoemaker, David. "CM Punk's Parting Shot." *Grantland*. December 3, 2014. http://grantland.com/the-triangle/cm-punk-podcast-colt-cabana-why-he-quit-wwe-vince-mcmahon-concussions-health-concerns-wrestlers-union/.

———. *The Squared Circle: Life, Death, and Professional Wrestling*. New York: Gotham Books, 2013.

Smith, R. Tyson. "Passion Work: The Joint Production of Emotional Labor in Professional Wrestling," *Social Psychology Quarterly* 71, no. 2 (2008): 157–76.

Turner, Graeme, Frances Bonner, and P. David Marshall. *Fame Games: The Production of Celebrity in Australia*. Cambridge: Cambridge University Press, 2000.

United States Department of Labor. "Independent Contractors." United States Department of Labor. https://webapps.dol.gov/elaws/whd/flsa/docs/contractors.asp.

Vanderburg, Marcus. "CM Punk Rips WWE, Doctors in Interview about His Departure from Company." *Yahoo.* November 27, 2014. http://sports.yahoo.com/blogs/the-turnstile/cm-punk-rips-wwe--medical-doctors-in-explosive-interview-225851818.html.

Waldron, Travis. "Donald Trump's Small Business Pick Has a History of Crushing Smaller Competitors." *Huffington Post.* December 15, 2016. http://www.huffingtonpost.com/entry/linda-mcmahon-business-history_us_5852efdbe4b012849c0609ca.

World Wrestling Entertainment, Inc. *Annual Report.* Stamford, CT: WWE, 2011.

ANDREW ZOLIDES is Assistant Professor of Digital Media at Xavier University.

chapter three

MAPPING THE WWE UNIVERSE: TERRITORY, MEDIA, CAPITALISM

Dru Jeffries and Andrew Kannegiesser

While it is far from the only professional wrestling brand in the contemporary marketplace, Vince McMahon's World Wrestling Entertainment is certainly the most financially successful and culturally ubiquitous. WWE boasts historical longevity, global name recognition, and a significant presence in the media landscape; and as a family-owned and -operated business as well as a multinational conglomerate, its success across multiple spheres of media is arguably unprecedented. Thanks to McMahon's business acumen, WWE effectively transformed a small territorial wrestling promotion into "a perfect company for early twenty-first-century global capitalism and the neoliberal agenda."[1] As Ted Butryn has demonstrated in his essay "Global Smackdown: Vince McMahon, World Wrestling Entertainment, and Neoliberalism," the company's explosive growth can be credited specifically to McMahon's ruthless adherence to market-driven organization and neoliberal values, qualities that have largely taken a backseat to the often contentious and contradictory ideological content of the televised product in scholarly examinations of professional wrestling. It is precisely that ideological content—including its engagement with sexually charged, nationally charged, and class-charged discourse—that constitutes the *entertainment* half of the *sports entertainment* hybrid that WWE packages so effectively.[2] But arguably more salient is the rationale behind the coinage of the term itself: this designation, which is the preferred nomenclature used by the company to describe its product, was invented by Linda McMahon in 1989 to dodge a 10 percent tax on sporting event tickets sold in the state of New Jersey.[3] Effectively, the invention of sports entertainment was initially little more than a successful attempt to avoid government regulation and taxation, to pursue capital largely unchecked; it thereby not only represents WWE's generic affiliation but also functions as a concise embodiment of the company's neoliberal ethos. As Butryn demonstrates, this particular agenda is also demonstrated in the company's conspicuous

support of the US military, their staunch resistance to worker unionization, and McMahon's stance on steroid use and public health.[4]

In this essay, however, we will focus specifically on the concept of *territory*, which—as we'll see below—not only is crucial to the development

of the American wrestling industry and the emergence of WWE but is also
revealing in terms of the company's contemporary business strategy. The
concept of territory, particularly in the humanities, is largely associated
with Gilles Deleuze, who theorizes how cultural and ideological spaces
are delimited and appropriated through discourse for particular ends.
While professional wrestling opens itself to this sort of reading, we wish
to begin at a more fundamental level, viewing territory first in terms of
discrete and material space. This finite grounding of the narrative spectacle can be elided all too easily when examining the more abstract qualities of narrativity, representation, and ideology; yet it is only by unpacking
WWE's treatment of territory that its unique hybridization of sports and
entertainment, and its commitment to neoliberal business practices, can
be best understood.

In analyzing the particulars of WWE's treatment of territory and
space, however, we cannot overlook the importance of the *sports* in *sports
entertainment*, and the operative logic that it represents. As noted, much
professional wrestling scholarship is chiefly concerned with the *entertainment* aspect of this hybrid genre, and yet the performance of wrestling
begins with the constructed approximation of organized sport. The regulation and rule-bound state of "legitimate" sporting leagues is assumed,
only to be challenged and destabilized through the performance of professional wrestling. As sports geographer John Bale argues, "the traditional
sports stadium's regulation-sized fields and strict demarcations between
the playing area and spectatorial areas make it the very model of a 'controlled and controllable space'"; this becomes an ironic designation when
applied to professional wrestling, given its historical ties with carnival and,
as John Fiske and others have noted, Mikhail Bakhtin's necessarily trans-
gressive concept of the carnivalesque.[5] As Fiske writes: "Sport's celebration of the body beautiful becomes, by contrast, a depoliticized ideological
celebration of physical labor in capitalism. The sporting male body is, consequently, an active hegemonic agent. The sporting values of fairness and
equality for all its players, of respect for the loser and proper celebration of
the winner, are the moral equivalent of the body beautiful and represent
the dominant ideology by which democratic capitalism values itself. But
if sport is clean, if capitalism is clean, then wrestling is triumphantly, defi-
antly dirty."[6]

Fiske's binary between "clean" capitalism and "dirty" wrestling, however, no longer holds in WWE. Indeed, democratic capitalism is something of a paradox in a society governed by the principles of neoliberalism, wherein WWE thrives as a "neoliberal poster child."[7] Under neoliberalism, the rhetoric of social liberalism and the drive for progressive advancement is contrasted, if not outright negated, by its conceptual linkage to market capitalism and its "winner take all" logic. By aligning the market with the state, neoliberalism creates the perception that what is beneficial to the market is invariably beneficial to the nation, while masking that the benefits of capitalism are not evenly distributed across the population. This internal tension is reflected in professional wrestling, which adopts the formal presentation of collective sport within a scripted narrative system. In WWE, storylines work to convince the audience that on any given night, any competitor can conquer any opponent and thereby overcome the hierarchical organization of the company itself. In both instances, lip service is paid to fair play and merit-based advancement, but both systems ensure systemic imbalances and entrenched positions of privilege. The shared values of sport and democratic capitalism that Fiske notes—fairness and equality—thus contrast sharply with those shared by professional wrestling and neoliberalism, both of which emphasize individual achievement and the creation of self-disciplining subjects while also minimizing the social safety net and dampening any impulse toward collectivism.

McMahon first publicly admitted that wrestling matches were scripted in order to avoid paying the aforementioned state tax on ticket sales for sporting events, a regulatory dodge that fits neatly within neoliberal ideology and its insistence on self-governance. Behind the curtain, the company's subsequent embrace of *sports entertainment* equally represents its category-defying product as well as its commitment to profits and resistance to government constraints on business; in the ring, meanwhile, the narratives of professional wrestling triumphantly expose the lack of fairness and equality under neoliberalism, whether in the form of conspicuously corrupt authority figures, heel characters who disregard honor in pursuit of victory, or the arbitrary and inconsistent enforcement of rules: "the fix" is on spectacular display as much as the feats of athleticism. This tacit admission is mediated through narrative content, which seeks to celebrate traditional values of integrity, determination, respectful competition, and physical prowess. This celebration occurs even as WWE's actions as a company proceed in the opposite direction, denying its workers union representation or comprehensive health coverage, blackballing performers for various reasons, and maintaining a locker room environment predicated upon masculine aggression, bully-ing, and sycophancy.[8] Within the diegesis, antagonistic authority figures may receive their comeuppance at the hands of performers who beat the odds while refusing to compromise their integrity; offscreen, however, this comeuppance rarely occurs, as the centralization of power in profes-sional wrestling cannot be overturned with a mere three count. Televisual content may position the WWE Universe as ultimately egalitarian, just, and rational, which serves as an ironic counterpoint to the corporate logic of the company itself. Accepting this schism—or denying it outright by embracing kayfabe and disregarding its underlying realities—becomes the cost of entry into the WWE Universe.

In exploring issues relating to territory and space, this essay also par-ticipates in what has been referred to as the *spatial turn* in the humanities and social sciences. Through the work of geographers like David Harvey, space and geography have been increasingly recognized as central to vari-ous aspects of cultural production.[9] The connection between geography and sport in particular has long been crucial to our understanding of the ways in which sport shapes global culture (through national pastimes, [inter]national competitions, the formation of local fan communities, etc.) and our world more generally (through the construction of sporting ven-ues, ranging from modest local parks to the grandest stadiums). But since WWE is by its own admission not a sport but rather sports entertainment, it makes sense that the company's deployment of space would unfold in a manner distinct from "legitimate" sport. WWE uses the familiar mark-ers of sport—an organized athletic contest within a regulated setting, supervised by an identifiable referee—but, as Fiske notes, its product can be more accurately described as "a parody of sport: it exaggerates certain elements of sport so that it can question both them and the values that they normally bear."[10]

One of the key functions of sport is to express local pride, which is accomplished through the "sport-place bond." As Bale writes, "sport is a potent source of topophilia—situations where sentiment is coupled with place and characterized by an intense identification between people and place," with the stadium functioning not unlike a present-day Greek agora.[11] Like major sports teams, WWE travels across North America (and sometimes beyond), holding events in different stadiums from day to day; the key distinction between WWE and other sports is that each WWE event constitutes a *narrative* event rather than an individual sporting con-test. It is not simply the company or the show (be it *Monday Night Raw* or *SmackDown Live*) that travels but the storyworld(s) that these shows collectively constitute. It is significant, then, that WWE subsumes both its nomadic narrative universe and its fandom within a single all-consuming spatial metaphor: the WWE Universe. Following the logic of this metaphor to its logical conclusion, the WWE Universe assumes the role of *place* in the traditional sport-place bond, replacing whatever geographic locality happens to be hosting WWE on a particular night with an imaginary locality associated with the company's brand.

Despite the company's near monopoly over professional wrestling in North America, such nomenclature reveals the extent to which WWE remains acutely concerned with notions of territory and space in the contemporary era. Expanding from this observation, we argue that WWE's relationship to issues like globalization, mass media, and capitalism can be most productively understood as an inversion of the wrestling industry's territory system, wherein the concept of territory no longer is tied to discrete geographic spaces but rather is based on fluid linkages between spaces in the world, in media, and in the marketplace. These concrete and imaginary spaces act as nodal points within an ever-expanding WWE Universe, as individualized territorial identities are repurposed into homogeneous sites of neoliberal consumption. As we'll see, however, these attempts at branded reterritorialization are not entirely successful in their attempts to erase the local, resulting in a dynamic relationship of exchange between the discrete and empirical site of performance and the more abstract and increasingly diversified WWE brand.

Television, Media Culture, and the Legacy of the Territory System

Understanding our concern with the dynamics of space and place requires some historical understanding of professional wrestling as a sport and business. First, however, it's necessary to briefly summarize our working understanding of space, which we take from David Harvey. For Harvey, space ought to be defined in three distinct ways, each of which should be considered in dialectical tension with the others in order to produce a properly nuanced understanding:

> If we regard space as absolute it becomes a 'thing in itself' with an existence independent of matter. It then possesses a structure which we can use to pigeon-hole or individuate phenomena. The view of relative space proposes that it be understood as a relationship between objects which exists only because objects exist and relate to each other. There is another sense in which space can be viewed as relative and I choose to call this relational space— space regarded in the manner of Leibniz, as being contained in objects in the sense that an object can be said to exist only insofar as it contains and represents within itself relationships to other objects.[12]

To summarize Harvey's position, we have (1) the absolute Euclidian space of empirical measurement; (2) the concept of space as relative to people, locations, and points in time; and (3) a linked notion of space as a quality produced in space-time via relational processes of production.[13] In this third aspect, space is not an inert preexisting vacuum in which action occurs but is instead a property that becomes constructed and defined through material and affective processes, which include the social. In short, events produce space, and space, in turn, produces events. This third aspect is akin to place, the sociocultural identity that emerges from events in discrete locations. This tripartite definition encourages us to think about space simultaneously as an empirical limit factor *and* as a dynamic construction emerging over time, through various events and social relations. By this logic, an affectively loaded space such as New York City's Ground Zero is simultaneously "an absolute space at the same time as it is relative and relational in space-time"; while it exists in empirical and material space, its *meaning* can only be grasped by thinking "in relational terms."[14] Where a positivist or empirical understanding of space can tell us, for our purposes, the audience capacity and dimensions of a given stadium, it does little to explain the social or cultural value the space offers to its patrons or the significance of the events unfolding within it. More critically, in this formulation, space is both a product of economic, social, and cultural factors as well as a constructive force in production itself.

The production and instrumentalization of space are of particular import, given professional wrestling's history as a mobile and nomadic form of performance. Professional wrestling first emerged on the carnival circuit in the early part of the twentieth century, where stereotypical strongmen, often with a background in amateur or Greco-Roman wrestling, would tour North America and Europe, offering locals the chance to pay a fee and attempt to pin the champion.[15] The popularity of these exhibitions increased to the point where promoters could sustain crowds in larger performance spaces, like small arenas and exhibition halls. As promoters and performers were driven to seek progressively larger crowds to maximize their profit potential, space and place strongly exerted themselves as limit factors: the size of local performance spaces enforced a maximum number of customers, while regionally specific tastes and values informed the style of the performance itself. At that point, professional wrestling was a firmly regional business; despite the marketing of individual wrestlers as "world champions," these performers could only perform within strictly demarcated geographical areas, known as territories, or else would face the economic and personal wrath of other promoters.[16] In the late 1940s, however, the National Wrestling Alliance (NWA) was formed as a means of overseeing the business, mediating conflicts between promoters and performers, and legitimating a single "true" world champion; the NWA World Champion would then travel across the country, defending his title against a variety of opponents by wrestling within various territorial promotions, while its constituent members were bound by the organization's charter to adopt a standardized set of business and contract practices.[17] In short, this territory system was primarily based on a strictly empirical treatment and delimitation of geographical space; however, the sport-place bond also produced relative relationships within a given region (e.g., between fans and wrestlers) and between discrete regions (e.g., when a wrestler defends a championship in a foreign territory). But the empirical measurement of space certainly dominated the industry at that point in its development.

The introduction of television to professional wrestling thus marked a number of profound shifts in how the industry operated, both immediately and over time. While national touring and broadcasting would become the singular business model that the majority of viable promotions adhered to, promoters initially lacked access to a national broadcast infrastructure. Consequently, when wrestling events were televised, their reach was necessarily limited by the broadcasting power of the local over-the-air station, which effectively demarcated the boundaries of each promotion's territory. At first, then, television failed to open up new and distant markets but rather only provided greater visibility and access within prescribed geographical regions. The shift from local live performance to television broadcast, however, resulted in tangible changes to viewers' consumption practices. As Henry Jenkins, Sam Ford, and Joshua Green write in *Spreadable Media*, wrestling fandom was radically transformed by a practice known as tape sharing, whereby fans would record local televised wrestling events and exchange them with fans in other territories: "Prior to the VCR, fans treated pro wrestling show results quite like legitimate sports. With tapes, fans could start evaluating wrestling as performance art, comparing the ability (or 'workrate') of performers rather than their character's win-loss records."[18] Tape sharing allowed professional wrestling to spread beyond the sanctioned circuits of production and distribution while also granting individual viewers the ability to compare different brands and national styles of wrestling, and to replay and rewatch footage, thereby facilitating a greater understanding and appreciation of the skill and athleticism required to create such performances. It not only created a new kind of fan engagement with the industry and its narratives but also effectively allowed fans to transcend the empirical geographical boundaries between discrete territories: two crucial steps on the path leading to the WWE Universe that exists today.

While the potential for expansion lay incipient within these technological changes, entrenched operating conventions and long-standing promoter agreements prevented any one promotion from unilaterally making the leap to the national stage. This business model would remain largely unchallenged until 1979, when Vince McMahon Jr. assumed control of the World Wide Wrestling Federation (formerly the Capitol Wrestling Corporation) from his father. Almost immediately, McMahon rebranded the company as the WWF (World Wrestling Federation) and sought to reposition it as a national company, able to tour across the entire United States and secure television rights in every major market, a move that would single-handedly undo the regional containment of the territory system. His base of operations in New York provided him with access to major television content providers, and his finances allowed him to offer regional stars far more lucrative (and exclusive) contracts, which smaller promoters could not compete with.[19]

McMahon also simultaneously emphasized the theatricality and spectacle inherent to professional wrestling. In order to take wrestling from the regional to the national, McMahon needed to demonstrate the wider appeal of wrestling beyond the confines of the local: to this end, seemingly larger-than-life stars like Hulk Hogan and Andre the Giant, an increased emphasis on pageantry and high production values, and cross promotion with other mainstream media outlets gave each televised WWF card the appearance of a high-profile media event. This business strategy turned many of his performers into household names while differentiating the style of WWF wrestling in a saturated marketplace. McMahon's gambit paid off, and by the first *WrestleMania* in 1985, held at Madison Square Garden and broadcast nationwide via closed-circuit television, the WWF had become the most prominent wrestling organization in America.

At that point, the territory system began to dissolve as more and more of its constituent federations went under. McMahon lacked monopolistic control of the industry, but his actions convinced fellow promoters that the only viable strategy for competition lay in national touring and broadcasting, a strategy that necessarily required regular television programming. As Fiona McQuarrie puts it, "By the late 1980s the NWA's power was almost completely broken and the WWF was the major power in professional wrestling," a cultural and economic coup that would have hardly been possible without a televisual infrastructure.[20] Fittingly, Jim

Crockett Promotions would be purchased by media mogul Ted Turner and rebranded as World Championship Wrestling (WCW), a move that set the stage for the WWF's main competition throughout the 1990s. Turner's national television "superstation" TBS provided WCW with a preestablished programming base and reach into the national market, and in an ironic twist, WCW's access to Turner's finances even allowed them to poach major stars like Hulk Hogan and Bret "the Hitman" Hart away from the WWF. By the mid-1990s, WCW's flagship program *Nitro* was consistently beating the WWF's *Monday Night Raw* in the ratings—in an era that WWE has since endlessly mythologized as the "Monday Night Wars"— which by extension translated into beating the WWF in terms of brand visibility and penetration into mass culture.

Although power within the professional wrestling business had previously been associated with control over discrete territories, geographical space was now shared among all the major players; in this newly mediated environment, power shifted to the cultural and financial capital associated with media dominance, as measured by television ratings, merchandise and ticket sales, and cultural visibility. To consolidate this power, Turner and McMahon would feature appearances by celebrities—actors, musicians, and "real" athletes—in their programming, a move that sought to legitimate professional wrestling as a form of popular entertainment. The first ten editions of the WWF's annual *WrestleMania*—the self-proclaimed "grandest stage of them all"—featured appearances by musicians Willie Nelson, Liberace, Cyndi Lauper, and Run-DMC; actors Mr. T, Jonathan Taylor Thomas, and Leslie Nielsen; television hosts Morton Downey Jr., Bob Uecker, and Ray Combs; and public figures including Donald Trump and Marla Maples, among others. In this way, WWF programming was presented as an organic component of the broader landscape of media entertainment, and over the following three decades, professional wrestlers also began to spread outward into the broader cultural matrix. Hulk Hogan frequently appeared on *The Tonight Show with Jay Leno*, teasing a presidential run, and starred in several feature films, including the WWF's first production, *No Holds Barred* (1989).[21] Diamond Dallas Page and Raven's feud extended to a joint appearance on MTV's *Total Request Live*, where they staged a brawl to hype their match at an upcoming WCW pay-per-view. In the late 1990s, "attitude era" Superstars "Stone Cold" Steve Austin and Dwayne "The Rock" Johnson crafted catchphrases that entered the popular vernacular, and both men appeared on mainstream programs such as *Saturday Night Live* and *Good Morning America*, acting both in and out of character. WCW briefly sponsored NASCAR racer Mark Martin, leading to Martin appearing in vignettes on WCW programming while his race car was adorned prominently with the WCW logo. Such appearances and brand extensions indicate a profound shift in the industry: if the goal of wrestling promotions prior to 1985 was to occupy clearly defined and delineated physical spaces, the goal of promotions following the WWF's national expansion was to occupy increasingly heterogeneous and fluctuating cultural spaces, legitimizing each promotion as an entertainment spectacle on par with the best that Hollywood films and other mainstream media had to offer. The central role played by geographical space now takes a backseat to a more relative concept of space, as companies compete to create meaningful connections between their core product and audience members through a wide variety of mediated forms.

The WWF ultimately won the Monday-night ratings war and was able to purchase WCW outright in 2001.[22] But rather than solidify its branding and programming efforts around its primary demographic of adult males, the WWF has continued to evolve and diversify as it sought to capitalize on new demographics in a changing cultural and media landscape.[23] The first indicator of this evolution occurred in 2002 when the WWF was legally ordered to change its name after a protracted lawsuit from the World Wildlife Fund. Tellingly, McMahon rebranded his company as World Wrestling Entertainment. This change in nomenclature strongly signaled WWE's transformation from a wrestling company into a provider of diversified media content while further diminishing the linkage between professional wrestling and competitive sport. In the years that followed, this desire has manifested in the creation of diverse media ventures, such as WWE Studios, which produces feature films in-house as vehicles for its performers (e.g., *The Marine* and its sequels, which have been vehicles for WWE Superstars such as John Cena, Ted DiBiase Jr., and Mike "the Miz" Mizanin) and also provides funding for externally developed films with no relation to professional wrestling (e.g., *The Call*). Along these same lines, WWE has recently produced new lines of narrative content aimed at children and adults alike, including a line of comic books (*WWE Superstars*), the *Slam City* morning cartoon, *Scooby Doo!* animated films featuring WWE performers in key roles, and the adult-oriented animated series *Camp WWE*.[24] These instances are particularly interesting when taken collectively, as each of these standalone narrative storyworlds reimagines the WWE Universe as a discrete geographical territory: *Slam City* takes place in the titular city, which is populated entirely by WWE Superstars who must take on new careers outside the wrestling ring; the first arc of the *WWE Superstars* comic book series takes place in Titan City, a film noir–style city populated by WWE characters, while a later arc involves WWE terraforming Mars for the purposes of wrestling; *Scooby Doo! WrestleMania Mystery* (2014) reimagines the WWE Universe as WWE City, another geographically demarcated space defined by branding and seemingly populated entirely by wrestlers and wrestling fans; finally, *Camp WWE* reimagines the WWE Universe as a children's summer camp, where Superstars and WWE executives alike find themselves reimagined alternately as young campers and teenage counselors.

These are not merely attempts to diversify the company's programming but also implicit acts of corporate self-mythologizing. Collectively, these texts make it abundantly clear that the company continues to understand itself in terms of space and territorialization. In *Show Sold Separately*, Jonathan Gray writes that "we are all part-time residents of the highly populated cities of Time Warner, DirecTV, AMC, Sky, Comcast, ABC, Odeon, and so forth."[25] The territorial metaphor that Gray employs is particularly appropriate to WWE, both in practical terms and as the aforementioned texts above demonstrate; however, the launch of the WWE Network in January 2014 also places WWE on nearly equal footing with brands like AMC, Sky, and ABC. Through the Network's combination of 24-7 programming and an extensive on-demand streaming library (which includes the archives of many of WWE's fallen competitors, including WCW), it's now possible to be a full-time resident of the WWE Universe. In this regard, the Universe has extended itself in both time and space, condensing half a century of content and history into a manageable platform for on-demand consumption.

THE SUN NEVER SETS ON THE WWE UNIVERSE:
PLACELESSNESS AND BRANDED SPACE

To this point, we have been concerned with WWE's engagement with space on a macro level, as it provides insight into their navigation and transformation of the wrestling industry over time. However, WWE's engagement with physical spaces on a micro level—that is, the local stadiums in which its live performances are staged and, often, filmed for live televisual broadcast—is also indicative of a desire to territorialize space in the name of capitalist consumption. What E. Relph refers to as the "placelessness" that has long defined the sports arena is mobilized to great effect by WWE, and indeed it forms the operational logic of the brand's aesthetics.[26] As Bale puts it, contemporary stadiums "are ambiguous places, defying neat and tidy land use categorizations. Consider the Skydome in Toronto—is it indoor or outdoor?—a sports stadium or a hotel or both?—a night club or a sports facility?—used for sports events or a television studio?—a studio where people watch live sport on the giant TV screen in the stadium itself?"[27] These kinds of arenas, often bearing the name of a global conglomerate—Bale's example of the SkyDome has since been rebranded as the Rogers Centre—now aspire "'to a condition of absolute placelessness' with no 'regional inflection.'"[28] And just as a McDonald's restaurant in the United States will be uncannily similar to one in Japan, WWE imposes a set aesthetic upon each venue they visit for an event. The Titantron screen, the entrance ramp, the stadium seating, the squared circle itself: all are remarkably consistent from one arena to the next, from one city or country to the next, and from one televisual broadcast to the next, such that any home viewer would be hard-pressed to identify the geographical location of an event from the homogenous WWE space alone. Whereas sports fans tend to identify with a particular (often local) team and its players, WWE fans become sublimated into identification with WWE's global brand: this is the unspoken price of the fan's "citizenship" in the WWE Universe.[29] Viewers and attendees may take pride in the vicarious successes of their favorite wrestlers, but since the performers' characters, catchphrases, images, and gestures are generally owned and trademarked wholly by WWE, every cheer and jeer speaks to fans' emotional and financial investment not only in particular characters but in the product and the company as a whole.[30] The irony of placelessness is that it enables WWE to be everywhere, rather than nowhere; not limited by geographical borders, the WWE Universe both territorializes physical space and occupies mediated cultural space. Nevertheless, placelessness is not without its losses: as Bale argues, "having erased external references, the sport no longer connects to anything else," becoming "hostile to the bounds imposed by locale and history."[31] Indeed, for most sports this *would* constitute a loss; for WWE, however, it represents the ultimate triumph: to sever all ties to other companies, to produce and deliver its increasingly diverse array of content entirely independently, for the empire of the WWE Universe to conquer all.[32]

However, professional wrestling also poses some interesting complications to Bale's conceptualization. As a business model predicated upon touring from city to city, WWE lacks the geographic tether that other forms of sport possess, which in turn influences how sport and space become linked through performance. Top-level sports teams typically hold their games in purpose-built areas, a fact we are reminded of every time a sports franchise collaborates with municipal and state entities to finance a new stadium, often using public funds to do so.[33] By contrast, while WWE has been symbolically and historically associated with particular venues, like Madison Square Garden in New York, it lacks a fixed point that acts analogously to a team's home field; it also lacks markers of specific geographic branding akin to local sports teams. As a result, WWE and professional wrestling as an industry bear a different relationship to locality: while individual performers may drop local references in order to elicit either a pop or heat from a given region's homegrown audience—a tendency best embodied in The Rock's promo-opening catchphrase, "Finally, The Rock has come back to [insert city here]," and ironically echoed in Hulk Hogan's infamous gaffe at *WrestleMania XXX*, where he mistakenly identified the Superdome in New Orleans, Louisiana, as the Silverdome in Pontiac, Michigan—such attention to locality is most often at odds with the creation and maintenance of the fictional WWE Universe. At these events, the symbolic association with a given team or sport and place is replaced with an association with the WWE brand: when audiences file into a given stadium that has been given the WWE makeover, they literally enter into the WWE Universe, a fictional storyworld that occupies real geographical space, coterminous with that of the stadium, not unlike the parallel universes postulated by string theory. The aesthetic consistency with which this storyworld migrates from stadium to stadium and city to city is precisely what enables narrative continuity from show to show, from week to week. In this regard, the placelessness of sport and other multinational enterprises becomes necessary from a storytelling and world building standpoint.

At this point, it is crucial to return to Harvey in order to unpack the layers of meaning operating within the contemporary WWE's treatment of space. Most obviously, we can speak of the empirical space of the stadium, including its dimensions and the placement of various elements within that absolute space (including the ring, ramp, Titantron, announce table, barriers, floor space, spectator seats, etc.). At the same time, the events taking place within this space can only be experienced relatively by individuals according to their placement around the stadium: a spectator standing directly in front of the barrier at ringside will have a very different experience than a spectator seated in the nosebleeds. Crucially, this also applies to the television viewer, who enters the space in a figurative sense through the mediation of the broadcast. Such viewers possess a greater mastery over the space, having multiple cameras and points of view at their disposal, as well as access to the explicit narration provided by the ring announcers via voiceover. This viewer's mediated and disembodied gaze, however, is also controlled more fully by WWE, whose cameras will move or cut away from any aspects that aren't meant to be seen. For instance, during the September 10, 2012, episode of *Raw*, announcer Jerry

Lawler suffered a heart attack at the announce table and had to be carried away on a stretcher by medical personnel. Attendees at the live event were understandably distracted from the concurrent in-ring action, while television viewers continued to watch the match in total ignorance of Lawler's condition. Later, this dynamic was reversed, as television viewers were given regular updates on Lawler's health by the remaining announcers while the live audience continued to watch the show without knowing what precisely had befallen Lawler. We see, then, the powerful effect that mediation has on viewers' relative experiences of time and space.

Arguably, however, the heretofore-unexplored relational component of space is most crucial, especially in the company's contemporary phase. The current product is known among fans as the "reality era," so-called for the tenuousness of the line that separates fiction from reality in the WWE Universe and for the difficulty of maintaining kayfabe in the age of social media and the unprecedented level of direct interaction between fans and performers that it enables. This kind of extratextual knowledge— including wrestlers' real names, their histories in the industry outside of WWE, details about their personal lives, and so on—has always separated marks from smarts, those viewers who immerse themselves fully in the fiction just as they would any other and those who deliberately and conspicuously resist the narrative pull of the WWE Universe, respectively; in the reality era, however, smarts have become increasingly visible and vocal, to the extent that the company now actively courts and encourages this kind of oppositional viewing practice.[34] How is this relevant to space? As Harvey describes it, "Individuals in the audience bring to the absolute space and time of the [event] all sorts of ideas and experiences culled from the space-time of their life trajectories and all of that is co-present in the room."[35] In short, relational space concerns "where peoples' heads are at" in relation to events occurring in empirical and relational space-time: are they fully inside the fictional WWE Universe, or are they actively attempting to disrupt its attempt at territorialization?[36] Just as likely, viewers may keep one foot firmly planted in each domain, popping for certain narrative events while always remaining aware of their presence within a fictional storyworld. The salient point here is that audience members navigate the line between these overlapping worlds in myriad ways according to their own preferences and experiences.[37]

CONCLUSION

Notions of space, place, and territory have always been central to the industry of professional wrestling, and even in the absence of viable competition, they remain central to our understanding of WWE in the present, both as a globally distributed media object and as a company seeking to brand real and imagined spaces under its imprint. As WWE's reach becomes increasingly global through emergent digital technologies and platforms, it's all the more important to reiterate the centrality of space and materialism within these efforts. Just as the physical reality of the human body underpins the diegesis of WWE, we must remind ourselves that this fictional storyworld rests upon a decidedly real material base, which is itself subject to various economic, technological, social, cultural, and political influences. The previous century saw wrestling transform from a carnival novelty into a worldwide media phenomenon, and it is now our task in the present to grapple with the cultural, ideological, and geographical consequences of this transformation.

Notes

1. Butryn, "Global Smackdown," 290.

2. For example, Vaughn May sees professional wrestling as proposing a moralistic and conservative model of social politics through content (see "Cultural Political and Professional Wrestling"); Henry Jenkins typifies televised professional wrestling as masculine melodrama (see "Never Trust a Snake"); Phillip Serrato focuses on how the construction of performer masculinity is structured through the lenses of race and nation at the level of image (see "Not Quite Heroes"); Douglas Battema and Philip Sewell discuss how the spectacular masculine body constitutes the primary commodity of professional wrestling (see "Trading in Masculinity"); and Sina Rahmani argues that the character of the Iron Sheik allows for American viewers to mediate their anxieties over postrevolution Iran through a restorative narrative of conquest (see "Wrestling with the Revolution"). These approaches are unified through their focus on televisual content and narrative and formal transmission, collectively situating the televised product as the primary legible "text" of professional wrestling.

3. McQuarrie, "Breaking Kayfabe," 247–48.

4. Butryn, "Global Smackdown," 287, 285, and 281. See also Eero Laine's and Andrew Zolides's chapters within this volume for more detailed discussions of WWE's relationships with the US military and unionization, respectively.

5. Bale, "Cartographic Fetishism," 81.

6. Fiske, *Understanding Popular Culture*, 79.

7. Butryn, "Global Smackdown," 290.

8. While the nature of the wrestling business makes it difficult to verify information of this nature, stories of locker room hierarchies and backstage politicking within WWE are legion. See, for instance, Thorne, "10 Wrestling Careers."

9. Warf and Arias, "Introduction," 1.

10. Fiske, *Understanding Popular Culture*, 70. In contrast to Fiske, Roland Barthes sees professional wrestling as an exaggerated performance linked strongly to historical and cultural mythology. In this regard, professional wrestling seeks to *reaffirm* traditional values by demonstrating their endurance over time. See Barthes, "World of Wrestling."

11. Bale, "Cartographic Fetishism," 77.

12. Harvey, "Space as a Keyword," 271.

13. Ibid., 271–73.

14. Ibid., 275–76.

15. Shoemaker, *Squared Circle*, 9–10.

16. Ibid., 35.

17. Wrestling historian Tim Hornbaker is one of the few contemporary scholars to have acquired primary documents from this period, using minutes, correspondence, and transcripts to illustrate precisely how promoter concerns manifested at the level of binding policy. See Hornbaker, *National Wrestling Alliance*, 1–29; Shoemaker, *Squared Circle*, 37.

18. Jenkins, Ford, and Green, *Spreadable Media*, 108.

19. Shoemaker, *Squared Circle*, 45.

20. McQuarrie, "Breaking Kayfabe," 234.

21. *No Holds Barred* is a particularly interesting film given WWE's tendency to self-mythologize through tangentially related fictions. In the film, Hulk Hogan plays a wrestler firmly devoted to his promotion (a fictional version of the WWF) who is courted by an evil television executive who wants to create a rival professional wrestling program. WCW had emerged as a legitimate competitor to the WWF on the national televisual stage in 1988, and the film very clearly reads as McMahon's perspective on the rivalry between the two companies.

22. The causes of WCW's bankruptcy were numerous and are still debated among fans. Frequently cited reasons include their inability to create new stars, frequent reuse of storylines and angles, illogical booking that favored sensationalism over verisimilitude, and a bloated roster with high-priced contracts. Many in the industry single out Time Warner's merger with America Online, approved in January 2001, as a particularly destructive moment for the company. The merger placed WCW under committee control and oversight, and many board members had little interest in professional wrestling, leading to a scaling down of production expenses and ultimately the cancellation of all WCW programming on Turner-owned stations. In some respects, this enormous corporate merger is indicative of neoliberal logic, though it provided McMahon and Turner with dramatically different results. For further reading, see Reynolds and Alvarez, *Death of WCW*.

23. WWE's Q1 2016 conference call to investors announced new metrics for assessing brand visibility, primarily oriented toward social media mentions and website traffic. Television ratings, once used as the primary measure of a professional wrestling promotion's success, have now become a secondary concern. Whether this will result in long-term changes to WWE's business strategy and product development remains to be seen. See World Wrestling Entertainment, "WWE Reports Strong First-Quarter 2016 Results."

24. It's worth noting that this strategy is not new; it dates back to the Saturday-morning cartoon *Hulk Hogan's Rock 'n' Wrestling*, which aired on CBS for two seasons beginning in 1985. The company has also boasted some high-profile failures in its attempts at diversification, including the World Bodybuilding Federation in the 1980s and the Xtreme Football League (XFL) in 2001. In the present, the WWE Network allows the company to bypass the traditional model, allowing them to produce new ventures at a lower cost while depending less on ratings and advertising for financial solvency.

25. Gray, *Show Sold Separately*, 1.

26. On placelessness and contemporary sport, see Bale, "Cartographic Fetishism," 79–80.

27. Bale, "Cartographic Fetishism," 80.

28. Frampton, quoted in Bale, "Cartographic Fetishism," 79.

29. As an example, it is not uncommon for fans to reward particularly violent or hardcore sequences with chants of "E-C-W! E-C-W!"—a reference to Philadelphia-based promotion Extreme Championship Wrestling, which operated from 1993 to 2001 and which is credited with popularizing the "hardcore" style in North America. By contrast, few baseball spectators would reward a particularly dazzling double play with chants of "M-L-B! M-L-B!" While professional sporting leagues are globally visible brands, they exhibit far less concern with centralized branding, in turn forming a different relationship between the audience, the performer, and the brand that envelops and connects them.

30. Of course, WWE fans are notoriously subversive in their reading practices and their engagement with the product, often behaving in ways that are unexpected or even outright

hostile to the product's ostensibly intended reading. For more on such practices, see the next section of this volume.

31. Bale, "Cartographic Fetishism," 82.

32. This is not to say that geographic space is always rendered anonymous; in 2018 alone, WWE's heavily promoted Network special events in Saudi Arabia and Melbourne, Australia—the *Greatest Royal Rumble* and *Super Show-Down*, respectively—demonstrate that geography still has some significance within the product. Yet these spaces only retain their identity so that WWE can celebrate their expansion into new areas; the moment that new spaces are visited, they are rendered homogeneous as yet another point within the branded Universe.

33. On the economic impact of sports stadiums on local economies, see Bale, *Sports Geography*, 108–28.

34. See Christian Norman's chapter in this volume.

35. Harvey, "Space as a Keyword," 276.

36. Ibid., 277.

37. See Sam Ford's chapter in this volume for a more in-depth analysis of how fans negotiate their various roles.

BIBLIOGRAPHY

Bale, John. "Cartographic Fetishism to Geographical Humanism: Some Central Features of a Geography of Sports." *Innovation: The European Journal of Social Science Research* 5, no. 4 (November 1992): 71–88.

———. *Sports Geography.* 2nd ed. New York: Routledge, 2003.

Barthes, Roland. "The World of Wrestling." In *Steel Chair to the Head: The Pleasure and Pain of Professional Wrestling*, edited by Nicholas Sammond, 23–32. Durham, NC: Duke University Press, 2005.

Battema, Douglas, and Phillip Sewell. "Trading in Masculinity: Muscles, Money and Market Discourse in the WWF." In *Steel Chair to the Head: The Pleasure and Pain of Professional Wrestling*, edited by Nicholas Sammond, 260–94. Durham, NC: Duke University Press, 2005.

Butryn, Ted. "Global Smackdown: Vince McMahon, World Wrestling Entertainment, and Neoliberalism." In *Sport and Neoliberalism*, edited by David L. Andrews and Michael L. Silk, 280–93. Philadelphia: Temple University Press, 2012.

Fiske, John. *Understanding Popular Culture.* 2nd ed. London: Routledge, 2010.

Gray, Jonathan. *Show Sold Separately: Promos, Spoilers and Other Media Texts.* New York: New York University Press, 2010.

Harvey, David. "Space as a Keyword." In *David Harvey: A Critical Reader*, edited by Noel Castree and Derek Gregory, 270–93. Oxford: Blackwell, 2006.

Hornbaker, Tim. *National Wrestling Alliance: The Untold Story of the Monopoly That Strangled Pro Wrestling.* Toronto: ECW, 2007.

Jenkins, Henry. "'Never Trust a Snake': WWF Wrestling as Masculine Melodrama." In *Steel Chair to the Head: The Pleasure and Pain of Professional Wrestling*, edited by Nicholas Sammond, 33–66. Durham, NC: Duke University Press, 2005.

Jenkins, Henry, Sam Ford, and Joshua Green. *Spreadable Media: Creating Value and Meaning in a Networked Culture.* New York: New York University Press, 2013.

May, Vaughn. "Cultural Politics and Professional Wrestling." *Studies in Popular Culture* 21, no. 3 (1999): 79–94.

McQuarrie, Fiona. "Breaking Kayfabe: 'The History of a History' of World Wrestling Entertainment." *Management and Organizational History* 1, no. 3 (2006): 227–50.

Rahmani, Sina. "Wrestling with the Revolution: The Iron Sheik and the American Cultural Response to the 1979 Iranian Revolution." *Iranian Studies* 40, no. 1 (2007): 87–108.

Relph, E. *Place and Placelessness*. London: Pion Books, 1976.

Reynolds, R. D., and Bryan Alvarez. *The Death of WCW*. 10th anniversary edition. Toronto: ECW, 2014.

Serrato, Phillip. "Not Quite Heroes: Race, Masculinity, and Latino Professional Wrestlers." In *Steel Chair to the Head: The Pleasure and Pain of Professional Wrestling*, edited by Nicholas Sammond, 232–59. Durham, NC: Duke University Press, 2005.

Shoemaker, David. *The Squared Circle: Life, Death, and Professional Wrestling*. New York: Gotham Books, 2013.

Thorne, Sam. "10 Wrestling Careers Damaged by WWE Backstage Politics." *WhatCulture*. October 18, 2014. https://whatculture.com/wwe/10-wrestling-careers-damaged-by-wwe -backstage-politics.

Warf, Barney, and Santa Arias. "Introduction: The Reinsertion of Space in the Humanities and Social Sciences." In *The Spatial Turn: Interdisciplinary Perspectives*, edited by Barney Warf and Santa Arias, 1–10. New York: Routledge, 2009.

World Wrestling Entertainment. "WWE Reports Strong First-Quarter 2016 Results." May 10, 2016. http://corporate.wwe.com/investors/news/press-releases/2016/05-10-2016 -133323161.

DRU JEFFRIES teaches in the Cultural Studies Department at Wilfrid Laurier University. He is author of *Comic Book Film Style: Cinema at 24 Panels Per Second*.

ANDREW KANNEGIESSER is an independent scholar living in London, Ontario.

chapter four

NARRATIVE SMARTS: NEGOTIATIONS OF CREATIVE AUTHORITY IN WRESTLING'S REALITY ERA

Christian Norman

"Times changed. Just telling a story and people accepting that storyline for what it is, as a storyline, is gone."[1] Paul "Triple H" Levesque, current executive vice president of talent, live events, and creative for WWE, made this statement on the February 2, 2015, episode of *The Steve Austin Show—Unleashed!* podcast when asked about the difficulties of running a professional wrestling company in an age when fans have become smarter about the product. At its heart, professional wrestling is a genre of narrative entertainment: the matches are all placed within a broader narrative context that gives fans a reason to care about who wins and who loses, and while it mimics the emotional highs and lows of legitimate (i.e., unscripted) sporting events, it also heightens those moments and ensures their frequency.[2] Historically, the professional wrestling industry has abided by a strict adherence to *kayfabe*, whereby performers were expected to maintain the fictional illusion at all times, both inside and outside the squared circle. Over the past two decades, however, wrestling promotions like WWE have allowed the kayfabe storyworld and external reality to coexist more and more. As Triple H's comments reveal, this shift is largely due to the fans, whose increased knowledgeability about the inner workings of the industry have made a "pure kayfabe" approach to storytelling more and more untenable. Professional wrestling journalist David Shoemaker has described the results of this new dynamic as the "reality era" of WWE, a designation that has been adopted by fans, scholars, and even performers on WWE television.[3] More than just a passing trend, the reality era represents a paradigm shift not only in what kinds of narratives can be told in professional wrestling but also in how those stories are told and to whom they are addressed. The reality era also exemplifies what media scholars have recognized as a general trend toward increased audience participation in the media industries.[4] While studies have largely focused on understanding fan behaviors in this changing media context, it's equally important to recognize how the producers of media texts have adapted to accommodate new kinds of audience participation as the lines between production and consumption become increasingly blurred.[5]

WWE serves as an ideal case study for understanding how the producers of media texts change their rhetorical strategies to adapt to different power dynamics between authors (in this case, WWE's creative team) and audiences (WWE fans). In this chapter, I will focus on how WWE's narrative approach has evolved over time, specifically in terms of the relationship posited by the author of the text toward its viewing audience. As wrestling fans have become more knowledgeable and participatory, WWE has gradually shifted from addressing the audience as "marks" (who believe wrestling is unscripted or real) to "smarts" (who "know the inside of the business and the secrets behind the ruses—what is real and what is staged both in terms of story lines and moves").[6] As my analysis will show, the trajectory from the former to the latter has resulted in three distinct eras of professional wrestling storytelling, each with a distinct mode of address: first, the kayfabe era, which stretches from the early days of wrestling in the 1900s to the mid-1990s, is characterized in WWE by addressing the audience as marks who believe the action is real; second, the entertainment era, which spans the mid-to-late-1990s through the early 2010s, saw WWE shift to an implied audience of smart fans while nevertheless continuing to address viewers as marks; finally, the reality era, which began around 2012 and continues today, reflects an effort by WWE to acknowledge and work with a participatory fan culture by addressing the narrative audience as smarts.[7]

My primary case study focuses on the contemporary period and what is arguably its most representative storyline: that is, Daniel Bryan's journey from a fan-favorite midcarder to the main event of *WrestleMania XXX*. This story serves as an ideal text because it exemplifies the reality era's unique style of narrative audience address. Further, this storyline realizes the potential of the audience to embrace what Aristotle characterized as the role of the "judge who renders a decision."[8] By making the creation of wrestling narratives part of the storylines themselves, WWE put its own creative choices and narrative direction on trial for the approval of the audience. WWE thereby effectively positioned the audience as an ersatz quality control department, a more powerful subject position than that typically occupied by spectators and an invitation to exercise agency in the production process. In this story, the actual audience of fans exerted unprecedented influence over the creative decision-making process. In short, the fans exercised creative authority in helping to put Bryan in the top spot of the show despite WWE as producers not initially wanting to go that route in the narrative.

Scholars in media studies have long investigated the processes through which audiences come to understand themselves and their place in society relative to particular texts. As media theories of audience developed, scholarship moved from thinking of fans as passive consumers to viewing them as more participatory and knowledgeable subjects capable of exercising creative authority over the production of meaning in media texts.[9] More recently, critics have looked at the tension that arises between consumers and producers of media content, as well as the power dynamic between them as fans become more participatory, pointing out the ways in which producers attempt to either co-opt or fight against participatory consumption behaviors.[10] Bryan's rise to the main event at *WrestleMania XXX* shows the potential of fans to influence the creative direction of media narrative content, as well as the potential for the commodification and co-option of fan investment by media producers.

For this study, my methodology is based on a rhetorical approach to narratology. Starting with the work of Wayne Booth, narratology has treated fictional narratives as rhetorical texts. Specifically, I will look to the ways the wrestling narrative addresses the audience as marks or smarts by examining how the narrative address shifts across the three eras of wrestling. Ultimately, by paying special attention to the modes of audience address in the narrative, this study demonstrates the usefulness of a narrative rhetorical approach to understanding how producers of mass media texts negotiate changing power dynamics between media professionals and increasingly participatory fan cultures. To do so, I must first elaborate on the terms *author* and *audience* as developed in rhetorical narratology.

GRAPPLING WITH NARRATIVE THEORY

Within the field of narratology, the author is never simply the person who wrote the text; rather, the author is determined by who tells the narrative. This figure can be understood as three distinct (though potentially overlapping) entities: the *actual author*, the *implied author*, and the *narrator*. The actual author is the physical person who writes the story. Seymour Chatman points out that a narrative may have many actual authors.[11] When this conception of authorship is applied to WWE, the actual authors are the writers who script the dialogue (often in collaboration with the performers), the bookers who craft the overarching story, and WWE management (especially Vince McMahon), all of whom exert direct control over the creative direction of the text. The actual author, however, doesn't manifest in the text itself; Booth coined the term *implied author* precisely to distinguish between the flesh-and-blood person(s) writing the text and the image thereof that is produced by that text.[12] Rather, the implied author is "the version of himself or herself whom the actual author constructs and who communicates through the myriad choices—conscious, intuitive, or even unconscious—that he or she makes in composing and revising a narrative."[13] Booth argued that the same actual author may "imply different versions" of himself/herself into different narrative texts.[14] Thus, the implied author is a textual effect that is "reconstructed by the reader from the narrative" and, as Chatman points out, is necessarily singular.[15] The implied author of WWE narratives, therefore, is a singular abstract notion of the various actual authors that is encoded into the text through the various creative choices made (and not made) in presenting the text to an audience. In short, the implied author is the vision of WWE that the storylines being told present to the world, which may or may not reflect the reality of the physical person(s) actually writing the stories. For example, during the period in which WWE maintained that wrestling was a genuine competitive sport, they essentially attempted to deny the existence of actual authors but, in so doing, nevertheless presented an image of the company (an implied author) to those who understood that wrestling was scripted. By switching its focus to "sports entertainment," WWE altered its production of wrestling, presenting a vastly different implied author through their creative choices.

Finally, the narrator differs from the real or implied authors in that the narrator is a part of the storyworld of the narrative.[16] The narrator, the teller of the story within the narrative text, can take many forms, including a character within the story (homodiegetic) or an omniscient narrator who seems to "see from above" the events going on in the story (heterodiegetic).[17] In the text of wrestling, the narrators are the wrestlers (homodiegetic) and commentators (heterodiegetic) who perform and describe the story for audiences in the arena and at home. Thus, in wrestling there is one implied author but many narrators (performers on the screen). Further, the personae that performers embody onscreen are often indistinguishable from those of the persons performing the characters: where, for instance, does Hulk Hogan end and Terry Bollea begin? Nevertheless, the basic distinction is that the narrator is speaking from within the storyworld, while the implied and actual authors are not.

The concept of audience within narrative theory can be broken up into a similar tripartite arrangement of the actual audience, authorial audience, and narrative audience.[18] The actual audience, much like the actual author, refs to the flesh-and-blood readers of the narrative text, consisting of many individual readers, who are all different and complex. The authorial audience, on the other hand, is who the author has in mind as the reader when crafting the narrative.[19] In wrestling, the actual audience refers to the flesh-and-blood fans in the stadium or watching at home, while the authorial audience is who WWE has in mind as they craft the stories. The text of professional wrestling reveals certain assumptions about the authorial audience of the narrative that may or may not be true about the actual audience reading the text but that nevertheless provide insight into the power dynamics underlying the mode of narrative address, as well as the content of the story itself.

Finally, the narrative audience refers to the audience of the narrator: that is, the persons to whom the narrator directs the address. The narrative audience is different from the previous two audiences in that the narrative audience "treats the narrator as 'real.'"[20] The narrative audience is one "that exists in the narrator's world, that regards the characters and events as real rather than invented, and that accepts the basic facts of the storyworld regardless of whether they conform to those of the actual world."[21] In wrestling, the narrative audience consists of the live crowd and the television viewership whom the performers in the ring are addressing in their promos and before whom they are wrestling. The narrative audience differs from the authorial audience in that the former is part of the narrator's diegetic world while the latter is extradiegetic. James Phelan and Peter J. Rabinowitz argue that "readers typically join (or try to join) the authorial audience, the hypothetical group for whom the author writes" and "*pretends* to join the narrative audience, the audience that receives the narrator's text."[22] Thus, the narrative audience recognizes the narrative as an invitation to invest in the world of the narrator, usually by making an emotional connection with the elements and characters present only in the narrator's fictional world. In this respect, the narrative audience is a reflexive participant in the production of textual meaning.

For the purposes of this study, the distinction between these three types of audiences is crucial to understanding how producers of wrestling texts address their audience. While the following section of this volume features several analyses of professional wrestling's actual audience—that is, the "real" flesh-and-blood fans of professional wrestling—I will focus instead upon the authorial and narrative audiences as implied or produced by WWE's narratives. In so doing, this study shows that a rhetorical theory of narrative reveals and interrogates the dialectic of power between author and audience, which is necessary for a robust account of media responses to fan cultures past and present.

The kayfabe era was defined by narratives that addressed the audience as marks. The term *kayfabe* refers to a culture within professional wrestling that maintains the illusion that wrestling is real. While authors like Shoemaker argue that most fans, even in the early days of wrestling, understood implicitly that wrestling was fixed, they nonetheless participated as if they took the action at face value.[23] In any case, WWE addressed its fans during the kayfabe era *as though* they were true marks. This mode of address called upon the audience, as Roland Barthes observed, to "abandon itself to the primary virtue of the spectacle, which is to abolish all motives and all consequences: what matters is not what it thinks but what it sees."[24]

The entertainment era shifted the address of WWE's implied audience to a smart audience. A combination of technological and cultural changes around this time gave fans greater access to previously unavailable insider secrets and terminology, erasing the boundaries between insider and outsider and thereby making it more difficult to maintain the illusion of kayfabe. Faced with this changing fan culture, WWE openly admitted the scripted nature of its product. Even though wrestling fans had long been aware of the genre's fictional status, this was an unprecedented gesture: never before had a wrestling text so openly admitted that it was being created for an audience that was in on the con. However, while the implied audience shifted to one comprised of smarts, the actual audience was nevertheless still *addressed* as marks by the performers. For example, while McMahon formally inaugurated this era with a direct address to the audience from outside the storyworld, speaking openly about "telling stories" that did not "insult the fans' intelligence," within the WWE storyworld itself wrestlers like The Rock continued to address the fans in the crowd and those watching on television as though they believed that the action was real—in short, as marks.[25]

The reality era is distinguished by a full switch to addressing the audience as smarts, both by WWE Creative and in the performances themselves. Not only are the stories written with the understanding that the audience knows the matches are fixed, but in many cases they are self-reflexive to the point that "smart" knowledge about the production of wrestling industry texts is a necessary precondition to understanding the narratives. For example, contemporary WWE storylines include the production and creative processes as part of the diegetic rationale behind the storylines. Wrestlers like the Miz cut promos about how entertaining their matches are as evidence for success rather than sticking with the kayfabe logic that success is based on besting one's opponent in competition. Fans' approval or disapproval of certain wrestlers being pushed has become part of the diegetic world of the narrative. Further, WWE has given fans a far greater participatory role, incorporating fans' perception of where certain wrestlers should be positioned into the narrative. In effect, WWE now addresses fans both as consumers and as participants in the production of wrestling texts. Importantly, this is achieved by addressing the narrative audience—that is, the audience addressed in real time during the performance—as smarts rather than marks.

The shift from the entertainment era to the reality era further broke down the barriers between production and consumption by foregrounding the production process as part of the narrative. Whereas the prior shift left producers in the position of experts, the reality era positioned the fan perspective as the basis for what should happen in wrestling narratives. Thus, smart fans are now positioned to wield greater influence over the product than they did in previous eras. Moving forward, this newly empowered fan position required WWE to re-center the consumption process in the wrestling narrative to appropriate fan desire for their own financial benefit. While CM Punk's "pipe bomb" promo is often credited as the starting point for the reality era, I would argue that Daniel Bryan's rise to the main event of *WrestleMania XXX* in 2014 better epitomizes the change in audience address that defines the era.[26]

What's Best for Business: The Daniel Bryan Story

On April 6, 2014, in New Orleans, an unlikely champion found himself standing triumphant in front of more than seventy-five thousand fans chanting "Yes! Yes! Yes!" at WWE's biggest event of the year, *WrestleMania XXX*.[27] This figure, Daniel Bryan, largely owed his rise to the efforts of his fan base. Through a series of interventions, these fans compelled WWE to alter its planned narrative, in which Bryan would occupy a middling position, in order to make him the company's top star. In this section, I examine the role of narrative address in the events leading up to this moment, arguing that WWE's earlier efforts to constrain fan participation by addressing the narrative audience as smarts backfired; this strategy instead *invited* an unprecedented level of fan participation.

Bryan's storyline perfectly exemplifies the mode of address unique to WWE's reality era. As in the entertainment era, the implied author addressed the authorial audience as smart fans wise to the scripted nature of wrestling. The lead-up to *SummerSlam*, the company's second-largest event each year, featured the initiation of the onscreen storyline centering on WWE management questioning Bryan's credibility as a top Superstar in the company—based not upon his competitive success but rather on his marketability *as a character*. Within the storyworld, McMahon voiced his lack of faith in Bryan as a top star, a view Bryan claims the WWE chairman held offstage as well.[28] At *SummerSlam*, Bryan defeated John Cena for the WWE Championship, but his title reign was short-lived, as Triple H—performing, like McMahon, a fictionalized version of the WWE corporate executive role he holds offscreen—attacked Bryan during his celebration. This action enabled perennial main event star Randy Orton to defeat a weakened Bryan for the championship mere minutes after he had won the belt. While Bryan did not walk out of the event as champion, the decision to have him beat the top star in the company elevated him to the main event level, albeit only briefly. Bryan himself relates in his autobiography that even during that time he felt that the company had little faith in his ability to be a true top star.[29]

The fallout of the *SummerSlam* main event led to a self-reflexive storyline that epitomizes the reality era of WWE programming. Over the next few months, Bryan and Orton feuded over the WWE heavyweight title. During this feud, Orton was backed onscreen by Triple H and Stephanie McMahon (Vince McMahon's daughter and Triple H's wife, both in and out of storyline), who dubbed themselves "the Authority." The storyline revolved around the Authority trying to hold Bryan down while elevating Orton as "the face of the WWE." On the *Raw* following *SummerSlam*, Stephanie McMahon confronted an angry Bryan, defending her husband's actions. She explained that Triple H cost him the title because Bryan did not fit the mold of a WWE Superstar who could be the public face of the company. McMahon infamously assessed Bryan as a "solid B+ player" during this promo.[30] These remarks resonated with fans precisely because they correctly perceived that Vince McMahon and the rest of WWE Creative truly felt that way about Bryan. Of course, remarks like these were used in the storyline to fuel fan support for Bryan as a top babyface character against the heel characters of Orton and the Authority.

During this time, WWE introduced a phrase that would be repeated by the Authority throughout this storyline. Stephanie McMahon explained to Bryan and the viewing audience that the Authority was simply doing "what's best for business" by promoting Orton as the face of the company. This phrase focused the story on the outside-the-ring aspects of the wrestling industry, those elements of the company that were deliberately left off camera throughout the kayfabe era. McMahon cast herself and her husband as characters representing WWE Creative (i.e., the actual authors of the wrestling text); they became the onscreen manifestation of the real authorial choices that determined which wrestlers were pushed and which wrestlers got buried. McMahon also made comments about the fans not knowing how to run a successful business, precisely because they cheered "B+" wrestlers like Bryan. These comments cast the fans not only as viewers but also as *characters* in the storyline. The Authority attempted to get heat by claiming that fan opinion should not factor into their creative decisions. Of course, WWE was still pushing Bryan's character as the top face star at the time, so the idea that the Authority was holding him back reeked of dramatic irony. If anything, the jabs at Bryan's ability to be a main event Superstar only further solidified his popularity with the fans, if only to spite the heel Authority figures.

The storyline of the Authority *appearing* to hold Bryan back makes sense dramatically if WWE planned to pay off fans' collective frustration by having Bryan ultimately vanquish the dastardly heel authority figures and prove he truly belonged among the elite in the business. However, by all indications, WWE had no such long-term plans. By October, Bryan had fallen back down into a midcard feud and out of WWE Championship contention. Notably, Bryan's run as the main event babyface character ended as soon as perennial top star John Cena returned from rehabbing an elbow injury. Once Cena returned, WWE began a main event feud involving Randy Orton and John Cena while Bryan resumed his role as a solid competitor on the undercard. The storyline of the WWE Creative powers that be not having faith in Bryan to be more than a "solid hand in the ring" played out in the actual booking decisions made by the company. However, while WWE seemed poised to put the main event push of Daniel Bryan behind them, the fans still yearned for a triumphant ending for Bryan's feud with the Authority.

The "Yes! Movement" Takes Control

Moving into 2014, many fans hoped that WWE would use the Royal Rumble match to elevate Bryan back into the main event picture for a title shot at *WrestleMania*. Vince McMahon and the rest of WWE Creative, however, had other plans. Namely, former main event Superstar Batista, who had left the company in 2010, returned on January 20, 2014, vowing to win the Rumble match. In his time off from WWE, Batista had embarked on an acting career, and WWE could not resist the potential for mainstream crossover appeal. Thus, WWE attempted to push Batista as the top face character who would defeat the villainous Orton and the Authority at *WrestleMania*. Fans voiced their disapproval in unprecedented fashion at the *Royal Rumble* pay-per-view. As the match wore on and Bryan had still not entered, fans began to chant his name in anticipation of each new entrant. Batista entered the match as the twenty-eighth wrestler and, at first, received a mildly positive reaction from the audience. During the countdown to the final entrant's appearance, the crowd was chanting "Yes!" in anticipation that Bryan would be the final wrestler. Instead, Rey Mysterio appeared as the thirtieth and final competitor, entering to a chorus of boos from the live crowd in Philadelphia. The hyperbolically negative reaction to Mysterio, a popular babyface, owed simply to the fact that he was not Daniel Bryan.

Once the crowd realized that WWE had excluded Bryan from the Royal Rumble match, they loudly voiced their displeasure at the creative decision. The crowd booed whenever Batista was on offense and repeatedly chanted Bryan's name in protest. When Batista eventually emerged victorious, he was met with the loudest boos of the night and more chants for Bryan. The fans outright rejected the proposed conquering babyface character. Batista himself appeared visibly shaken by the crowd reaction. After the show ended, Batista visually mocked Bryan's poses and extended his middle finger at the crowd. Following the event, wrestling-related websites focused on how the crowd hijacked the event by rejecting WWE's handpicked top star. Even the BBC covered the crowd's overwhelmingly negative reaction in an extremely rare instance of the news organization covering anything wrestling related.[31] WWE initially attempted to stick with Batista as the top face character, but fans continued to voice their displeasure with this creative direction. After two months of overwhelmingly negative fan reaction, WWE showed signs of changing their plans for the main event at *WrestleMania*.[32]

As fans more readily exercised agency in expressing their displeasure, WWE eventually cast the audience members who were hijacking their shows as more active characters within the narrative itself, self-reflexively addressing the narrative audience as smart fans. The March 10, 2014, episode of *Raw* featured a segment known as the "Occupy *Raw* Movement." Drawing from contemporaneous news coverage of the Occupy Wall Street protests, WWE staged a fan protest aimed at getting Bryan added to the *WrestleMania* main event. Bryan entered the ring and stated, "Tonight we're gonna make it so you have to listen to us because tonight the Yes! Movement is in full effect. And tonight we are going to occupy *Raw*!" At that point several extras emerged, all dressed in Daniel Bryan T-shirts, filling the ring and the area around it. As the Yes! Movement entered the ring, Bryan yelled, "We are not going to take it anymore. We are one! We stand together! We are united! And we are not going to leave this ring until the Authority give us what we want." The visual of fans crowding the ring, in shirts that were designed to make Daniel Bryan's image reminiscent of iconic Marxist revolutionary Che Guevara, reflected in fictional form the very real dissent expressed by fans regarding WWE's recent booking decisions. Eventually, Triple H acquiesced to the occupiers, and they left the ring chanting "Yes! Yes! Yes!" The "Occupy *Raw*" segment self-reflexively narrativized the dynamic between producer and consumer leading into *WrestleMania*, indicating the extent to which fans had become empowered and the ways in which WWE would incorporate that power into their ongoing storytelling.

At *WrestleMania*, Bryan and Triple H wrestled in the opening match. Bryan defeated Triple H, as expected, in a match that lasted over twenty-five minutes, thereby earning him a position in the main event later in the evening. After the match, however, Triple H attacked Bryan with a steel chair, furthering the idea that the Authority would screw Bryan out of the championship yet again. But Bryan showed up for the main event match against Batista and Orton, albeit with his shoulder taped up. During the match, Triple H again emerged to attack Bryan, who this time was put on a stretcher and carted up the ramp as the match continued without him. However, Bryan got off the stretcher and reentered the match. Ultimately, Bryan would pin Batista to win the WWE World Heavyweight Championship. The biggest professional wrestling event of the year went off the air with Daniel Bryan celebrating before a sea of fans chanting "Yes!" repeatedly.

By embracing participatory behaviors beyond simple or passive consumption, the narrative audience exerted unprecedented influence over the production of the media text. The fans exerted enough pressure on the actual authors of WWE Creative that they successfully initiated a change in the show's ongoing narrative. WWE used narrative audience address to maintain sole control over its narrative from the kayfabe era, through the entertainment era, and into the reality era. However, by addressing the narrative audience as smart fans and characters within the diegetic storyworld capable of judgment and armed with meaningful agency, WWE opened the door to the fans participating in the coproduction of wrestling narratives.

One can argue that fans have always had a degree of agency regarding WWE's creative choices: they could simply choose to spend their money elsewhere. In the case of the Daniel Bryan storyline, however, fans exerted pressure by acting out. In a sense, the angle was a good draw because fans were coming to shows to see how the narrative would progress from week to week, spending money to do so. However, the fans who were purchasing tickets were also the ones hijacking the shows. Wrestling journalist Dave Meltzer argued that WWE changed the Orton-Batista main event because they feared that the reaction from fans at the show would make the product and the company look bad, not because they feared that the event would draw less money.[33] Thus, the fans found an *active* method of influencing the creative production process even as they engaged in consumption practices that redounded to the benefit of WWE.

While fans exerted more influence over the creative direction of the narrative storylines in WWE during this period than in any previous era, WWE did not necessarily lose its power in the process. Michel Foucault argues that power should not be seen as a thing one wields over another but rather as "a more-or-less organized, hierarchical, coordinated cluster of relations."[34] Indeed, while acquiescing to fans' desires in the lead-up to *WrestleMania*, WWE nonetheless benefited from the positive reception to the show and the mainstream exposure the Bryan storyline gave them. The disruptive behavior of the fans therefore exposes the limits of WWE's ability to control fans and the narrative direction of its product in the face of such participatory behaviors. At the same time, the case study also exposes the limits of such movements to work contra the interests of the dominant discourse. In staging the "Occupy *Raw*" segment, WWE used the "Yes!" chant as a floating signifier, which Ernesto Laclau defines as signifiers that are suspended and reused by alternative fronts.[35] In this case, WWE used the "Yes!" chant, along with the visual of supporters pointing their fingers to the sky in unison, within their own narrative to increase sales. The Che-style T-shirts worn by every member involved in the "Occupy *Raw*" crowd associated merchandise with the pseudopopulist movement, thereby circumscribing the power the fans wielded to the broader financial interests of WWE.

The epilogue to the Daniel Bryan story, however, calls into question the true power of the consumers to meaningfully change the creative direction of WWE over the long term. Yes, the fans were able to sway WWE into changing their *WrestleMania* plans; just one month later, however, Bryan announced that he needed major surgery on his neck and would be out of action for a significant amount of time.[36] He never returned to the main event picture, and on February 8, 2016, he reluctantly announced his retirement because of lingering health issues stemming from the multiple concussions he suffered throughout his career.[37] He continued to work for the company after his retirement, including a two-year stint as the baby-face general manager of *SmackDown Live* (a particularly ironic role, given his character's history in the aforementioned storyline) and an ongoing role in one of WWE's reality television series, *Total Bellas* (2016–).[38] In early 2018, Bryan was medically cleared to wrestle again in WWE, and he returned to in-ring competition at *WrestleMania 34*.[39] Despite widespread fan enthusiasm for his long-speculated return to WWE, Bryan has nevertheless not become the next face of the company as fans desired. WWE assuaged fan protests by temporarily giving fans what they wanted in terms of narrative direction, but only temporarily and in small doses. This case study further illustrates the unlikelihood and difficulty of fans to effect meaningful change. WWE, as producers, allowed the Yes! Movement to gain leverage in support of Daniel Bryan, but without a key figure around which to rally, the movement ultimately lost steam, as casual and hardcore fans alike had less reason to unite against a common foe.

The idea that fans can hijack shows to force their choices onto the creative direction of WWE has implications for the narrative process beyond who is the champion at a given time. WWE is not alone in having to navigate the pressures of fan expectations when creating its narratives. Fan pressure has influenced other producers of popular narrative content to alter their creative plans. For example, George Lucas claimed that he significantly changed his creative direction in the *Star Wars* prequels because of negative fan reactions to *Star Wars: Episode I—The Phantom Menace* (1999).[40] Because of its status as a live event and television broadcast, however, WWE is unique insofar as fan pressure can coincide with the narration of the story in real time, which is quite distinct from how fans express their frustrations with a movie. Like other popular culture industries, WWE now struggles with how much and how often to acquiesce to fan desires in its narrative choices.[41] In the wake of Bryan's departure from the company, WWE seems to find itself on the losing end of its ongoing battle with its own audience over the creative direction of the narrative, with ratings for both *Raw* and *SmackDown* at all-time lows.[42] The fate of WWE's battle with fans may have implications for other kinds of media producers as well: giving too much or too little heed to fan desires can prove equally dangerous when crafting narrative content.

CONCLUSION

The narrative address in the reality era paved the way for an extended struggle over creative authority. The Yes! Movement exerted unprecedented influence over the creative direction of a professional wrestling narrative. In part, this creative authority to influence change resulted from the narrative's construction of narrator characters, representing the actual authors of WWE Creative, as antagonists to the protagonist-narrator characters, representing the Yes! Movement. But the power to influence change also led to an entrenched battle between producer and consumer over the direction of the content, which ultimately left both sides unhappy. WWE continues to find itself battling fan hijacking when trying to push certain stars—most notably and noticeably, Roman Reigns—in accordance with its planned narrative. Fans, in turn, have stopped watching in massive numbers as the producers attempt to regain control of the narrative. The future of wrestling narrative remains uncertain, as WWE is now showing some signs of pulling back from its reality era style of narrative address. On the one hand, the company may adopt narrative strategies exhibited by Triple H in WWE's developmental brand, NXT. On the other, rival wrestling promotions like New Japan Pro Wrestling and Lucha Underground have had success by crafting narratives that again address the narrative audience as marks rather than smarts.[43] Regardless of WWE's future narrative strategies, by foregrounding the production process as a central component of their narratives in the reality era, WWE opened a door for audience participation to influence the creative process, and they will not likely be able to close it.

Notes

1. Levesque, *Steve Austin Show.*
2. Jenkins, "'Never Trust a Snake,'" 51–53.
3. Shoemaker, "Pro Wrestling for Auteurs."
4. Jenkins, *Fans, Bloggers, and Gamers,* 2.
5. For example, see Jenkins, Ford, and Green, *Spreadable Media,* 5.
6. Laine, "Professional Wrestling," 226.
7. Other writers have attempted to divide wrestling history into distinct eras. For example, Shoemaker divides his book *The Squared Circle* into various eras distinguished largely by changes in the thematic content of wrestling or the technological means of production. Rather than dividing wrestling history through thematic means, I propose to use audience address to mark the divides between eras; despite thematic differences in content, most of Shoemaker's eras address the audience in overwhelmingly similar manners.
8. Aristotle, *Rhetoric,* book 1, part 3.
9. See Adorno and Horkheimer, *Dialectic of Enlightenment;* "Culture Industry Reconsidered" in Adorno, *The Culture Industry;* and Jenkins, *Textual Poachers,* 3.
10. Graham, "New Kind of Pandering," 131.
11. Chatman, *Story and Discourse,* 149.
12. Booth, *Rhetoric of Fiction,* 70.
13. Phelan and Rabinowitz, *Narrative Theory,* 30.
14. Booth, *Rhetoric of Fiction,* 71.
15. Chatman, *Story and Discourse,* 149.
16. James Phelan and Peter J. Rabinowitz give a quick way to conceive of these differences by reference to a familiar narrative text. In *The Adventures of Huckleberry Finn,* the actual author is the flesh-and-blood person Samuel Clemens, the implied author is the image of Mark Twain that Clemens wishes to embed in the text of the book, and the narrator is the character Huck Finn. See Phelan and Rabinowitz, *Narrative Theory,* 30.

17. Genette, *Narrative Discourse*, 244–45.

18. Rabinowitz, "Truth in Fiction," 126–28.

19. Booth initially conceived of the implied audience as a counterpart to the implied author but later agreed with Rabinowitz's tripartite audience distinction in the afterword to the second edition of *Rhetoric of Fiction*. Therefore, I use the term *authorial audience* as coined by Rabinowitz. For a more thorough discussion of the differences between the terms, see Shen, "Implied Author," 151–56.

20. Phelan and Rabinowitz, *Narrative Theory*, 140.

21. Ibid, 6.

22. Ibid.

23. Shoemaker, *Squared Circle*, 77.

24. Barthes, *Mythologies*, 15.

25. WWE, "Mr. McMahon."

26. CM Punk gave his "pipe bomb" promo on the June 27, 2011, episode of *Raw*. In this "worked shoot," which was scripted but also contained elements of usually nondiegetic talking points, Punk broke wrestling norms by directly referring to the production and creative processes in the wrestling business. During the speech, CM Punk engaged in a self-reflexive critique of the stories being told in WWE. He criticized why certain wrestlers were pushed over others despite being better wrestlers (using a criterion of production). See Jansen, "Yes! No! . . . Maybe?," 637–38, and Dru Jeffries's introduction to this volume.

27. The "Yes!" chants initially started while Bryan portrayed a heel character who would put on an exaggerated show of pointing both index fingers in the air while chanting "Yes!" whenever he was doing well in matches, a gesture intended to provoke the fans into booing him. However, once fans began to rally behind Bryan around 2012, they began chanting along, and eventually the chants spread to various sporting events outside WWE in a rare instance of mainstream notoriety for the company.

28. Bryan and Tello, *Yes!*, 260.

29. Ibid, 264.

30. Dave Meltzer, *Wrestling Observer Newsletter*, August 26, 2013.

31. Butterly, "Royal Rumble."

32. Dave Meltzer, *Wrestling Observer Newsletter*, February 3, 2014. WWE had to change some plans for the big event anyway due to CM Punk abruptly walking out on the company following the *Royal Rumble*. But by most accounts, even with Punk leaving, the main event was supposed to stay the same and Bryan was not in line for a push to the main event. For more on Punk's departure from WWE, see Andrew Zolides's essay in this volume.

33. Dave Meltzer, *Wrestling Observer Newsletter*, April 14, 2014.

34. Foucault, *Knowledge/Power*, 119.

35. Laclau, *On Populist Reason*, 131.

36. WWE stripped Bryan of the championship because he could not defend it. Wrestling insiders later reported that Bryan was originally scheduled to lose the title to Brock Lesnar at that year's *SummerSlam* event in August. Upon his return in early 2015, Bryan found himself back on the midcard.

37. For more on Bryan's career and retirement, see Sean Desilets's chapter in this volume.

38. For a detailed discussion of *Total Divas*, the precursor to *Total Bellas*, see Anna F. Peppard's chapter in this volume.

39. Ironically, Bryan entered *WrestleMania 35* holding the WWE Championship, this time as a heel. In an extended callback to the build to *WrestleMania XXX*, Bryan's babyface challenger Kofi Kingston was denigrated by Vince McMahon (and Bryan himself) as a "B+ player" throughout the angle.

40. Dodge, "They Didn't Use Any of My Ideas."

41. Logically, WWE cannot always put over the fan-favorite wrestlers. If Bryan always won because he was the audience favorite, the dramatic product would suffer. Part of the enjoyment

of wrestling comes in hoping the face character can overcome the odds and win the prize after a long and difficult journey. Therefore, the protagonists must suffer setbacks in wrestling.

42. Dave Meltzer, *Wrestling Observer Newsletter*, May 23, 2016.

43. New Japan Pro Wrestling (NPJW) has expanded its market globally in recent years with English language broadcasts. The NJPW narrative style foregrounds the competitive nature of professional wrestling as a sport, largely addressing the audience as marks. Similarly, upstart lucha libre promotion Lucha Underground has seen success in the United States by implementing a narrative style similar to that of a telenovela, embracing the inherently campy nature of professional wrestling storylines. Lucha Underground also addresses the fans in attendance as marks, or in their own terms, *believers*.

Bibliography

Adorno, Theodor. *The Culture Industry: Selected Essays on Mass Culture*, edited by J. M. Bernstein. London: Routledge, 1991.

Adorno, Theodor, and Max Horkheimer. *Dialectic of Enlightenment*. Translated by Edmund Jephcott. Berkeley: University of California Press, 2002.

Aristotle. *Rhetoric*. Translated by W. Rhys Roberts. Accessed July 20, 2016. http://classics.mit .edu/Aristotle/rhetoric.2.ii.html.

Barthes, Roland. *Mythologies*. Translated by Annette Lavers. New York: Macmillan, 1972.

Booth, Wayne. *The Rhetoric of Fiction*. Chicago: University of Chicago Press, 1961.

Bryan, Daniel, and Craig Tello. *Yes! My Improbable Journey to the Main Event of WrestleMania*. New York: St. Martin's Press, 2015.

Butterly, Amelia. "Royal Rumble: Daniel Bryan Blames WWE for Exclusion." *BBC Newsbeat*. January 27, 2014. http://www.bbc.co.uk/newsbeat/article/25911039/royal-rumble-daniel -bryan-blames-wwe-for-exclusion.

Chatman, Seymour. *Story and Discourse: Narrative Structure in Fiction and Film*. Ithaca, NY: Cornell University Press, 1978.

Dodge, Shyam. "'They Didn't Use Any of My Ideas': George Lucas Says New Star Wars Film Is Not How He Envisioned It." *Daily Mail*, January 21, 2015. http://www.dailymail.co.uk /tvshowbiz/article-2920541/George-Lucas-says-new-Star-Wars-film-not-envisioned-it .html.

Foucault, Michel. *Knowledge/Power: Selected Interviews and Other Essays*. Edited by Colin Gordon. New York: Pantheon Books, 1980.

Genette, Gérard. *Narrative Discourse: An Essay in Method,* translated by Jane E. Lewin. Ithaca, NY: Cornell University Press, 1980.

Graham, Annissa M. "A New Kind of Pandering: *Supernatural* and the World of Fanfiction." In *Fan CULTure: Essays on Participatory Fandom in the 21st Century*, edited by Kristin M. Barton and Jonathan Malcolm Lampley, 131–45. Jefferson, NC: McFarland & Company, 2014.

Jansen, Brian. "'Yes! No! . . . Maybe?': Reading the Real in Professional Wrestling's Unreality." *Journal of Popular Culture* 51, no. 3 (2018): 635–56.

Jenkins, Henry. *Fans, Bloggers, and Gamers: Exploring Participatory Culture*. New York: New York University Press, 2006.

———. "'Never Trust a Snake': WWF Wrestling as Masculine Melodrama." In *Out of Bounds: Sports, Media and the Politics of Identity*, edited by Aaron Baker and Todd Edward Boyd, 48–80. Bloomington, IN: Indiana University Press, 1997.

———. *Textual Poachers: Television Fans and Participatory Culture*. New York: Routledge, 1992.

Jenkins, Henry, Sam Ford, and Joshua Green. *Spreadable Media: Creating Value and Meaning in a Networked Culture*. New York: New York University Press, 2013.

Laclau, Ernesto. *On Populist Reason*. New York: Verso, 2005.

Laine, Eero. "Professional Wrestling: Creating America's Fight Culture." In *American History through American Sports: From Colonial Lacrosse to Extreme Sports, Volume 2,* edited by Danielle Sarver Coombs and Bob Batchelor, 219–36. Santa Barbara, CA: Praeger, 2013.

Levesque, Paul. Interview by Steve Austin. *The Steve Austin Show—Unleashed.* Podcast audio. February 5, 2015. http://podcastone.com/pg/jsp/program/episode.jsp?programID=436 &pid=482164.

Phelan, James, and Peter J. Rabinowitz. *Narrative Theory: Core Concepts & Critical Debates,* edited by David Herman, James Phelan, Peter J. Rabinowitz, Brian Richardson, and Robyn Warhol. Columbus, OH: Ohio State University Press, 2012.

Rabinowitz, Peter J. "Truth in Fiction: A Reexamination of Audiences." *Critical Inquiry* 4 (1977): 121–41.

Shen, Dan. "Implied Author, Authorial Audience, and Context: Form and History in Neo-Aristotelian Rhetorical Theory." *Narrative* 21 (2013): 140–58.

Shoemaker, David. "Pro Wrestling for Auteurs." *Grantland.* May 23, 2012. http://grantland.com /features/how-documentary-films-explain-wwe-reality-era-preview-weekend-limit-pay -per-view/.

———. *The Squared Circle: Life, Death, and Professional Wrestling.* New York: Gotham Books, 2013.

WWE. "Mr. McMahon Ushers in the Attitude Era." YouTube video, 2:17. Posted January 6, 2014. Accessed August 16, 2018. https://www.youtube.com/watch?v=PjBeCwz2fXg&t=30s.

CHRISTIAN NORMAN is Assistant Professor of Communication at Middle Georgia State University.

PART II

MARKS AND SMARTS: WWE'S UNRULY FANDOMS

chapter five

SPORT VS. SPECTACLE: FAN DISCONTENT
AND THE RISE OF SPORTS ENTERTAINMENT

Shane Toepfer

WWE's rebranding of professional wrestling as sports entertainment is a contentious topic among fans and critics of professional wrestling. As wrestling historians Greg Oliver and Steven Johnson summarize, "In 1984 the world of wrestling changed forever when WWF owner Vince McMahon seized the industry, recast it as sports entertainment and marched it to the forefront of popular culture."[1] This chapter focuses on the consequences of this terminological recasting and the discontent that it has engendered within wrestling fandom. As we shall see, this represents more than a mere shift in appellation; indeed, many wrestling fans interpret *sports entertainment* as a direct affront to the very structure of their beloved genre. The following analysis examines the distinction between professional wrestling and sports entertainment as evidenced by the discourse of wrestling fans, many of whom lament the changes McMahon has wrought upon the professional wrestling landscape. This is one aspect of a wider sense of discontent among wrestling fandom that is revealed by the responses to a questionnaire I distributed over the weekend of *WrestleMania XXX* in New Orleans, Louisiana, in 2014. In particular, the results of this questionnaire highlight the contentious nature of WWE's use of *sports entertainment*, which fans view as symptomatic of wider changes that have lessened the quality of WWE's product. I will conclude the chapter by gesturing toward some of the ways in which WWE has attempted to adapt to these criticisms, seemingly as an attempt to maintain their global dominance over the professional wrestling marketplace.

First, however, it is worth briefly noting that the professional wrestling landscape has never been fully homogenous, as the prevalence of different national styles (e.g., Mexican lucha libre, Japanese "strong style") demonstrates. Prior to WWE's national expansion, regional promotions offered many varieties of professional wrestling across the United States, each tailored to the tastes of its local audience. Despite the variety inherent to professional wrestling, the genre was unified by a common understanding that professional wrestling events ought to resemble and reproduce the aesthetics and pleasures offered by legitimate sport. Contemporary wrestling journalist Bryan Alvarez defines the genre thus: "At its core, it's two people fighting over something important. . . . It should be a worked sport."[2] For Alvarez and a large segment of like-minded fans, the structural core of professional wrestling is a worked sport wherein athletes simulate competitive combat under the diegetic premise that the action and events are authentic, even though the audience is fully aware of the genre's scripted (or "worked") nature. It is precisely this structural core that is destabilized in WWE's presentation of sports entertainment, which many fans feel abandons the worked sport foundation at the heart of professional wrestling in favor of spectacle and other less regulated narrative pleasures.

The conflict between these two distinct visions of what professional wrestling can or should be has enormous stakes, for both wrestling fans and WWE itself. As the industry leader, WWE has the power to unilaterally define the genre of professional wrestling in American popular culture; it's particularly notable, then, that their preferred mode of presentation is quite distinct from the way professional wrestling has appeared throughout its history. Compared to professional wrestling, sports entertainment is more easily monetized and consumed by mass audiences, whereas fans would not flock to arenas or subscribe to the WWE Network if professional wrestling were presented as two athletes simply competing to see who is the best. On the one hand, wrestling fans who prefer their wrestling to mirror the conventions of sport may be unsatisfied or frustrated by WWE's product; as a result of WWE's near monopoly over the professional wrestling industry in North America, such potential consumers might even become alienated from wrestling altogether. This discontent has led to a gradual withering of WWE's audience over time; as top wrestling journalist Dave Meltzer tweeted on November 23, 2015, "With the exception of the mid-90s, wrestling now least popular in my lifetime."[3] On the other hand, WWE apparently feels that adhering to Alvarez's vision of wrestling would severely limit the company's ability to appeal to general audiences, as a professional wrestling product that adheres to a sports-like presentation would always be seen as inferior to legitimate sport because of its scripted nature. Communication scholars such as Allen Guttmann contend that sport must be a "playful, physical contest," suggesting that the result of said contest cannot be known beforehand.[4] It is for this reason that Roland Barthes, in his famous essay about professional wrestling in French society in the 1950s, specifically insisted that wrestling is *not* a sport.[5] By WWE's logic, it's better to emphasize those aspects of professional wrestling that *distinguish* it from sport—the pageantry, the spectacle, the characters, the melodrama—and to downplay those qualities that beg a comparison that will always favor legitimate sporting contests.

WWE also attempts to leverage its hegemonic power to influence, if not control, the ways audiences understand and consume its products. In many ways, the 2014 launch of the WWE Network serves as the culmination of a project that began in the 1980s, when McMahon began to eradicate regional wrestling territories and position his company as the top brand of professional wrestling in the world.[6] On the WWE Network, wrestling fans can access the digitized tape archives of a variety of promotions that span the industry's diverse history—but all of it is filtered through the lens of WWE. The only tape libraries available are those that WWE has purchased, and many of those libraries are incomplete. For example, selected episodes of World Class Championship Wrestling (WCCW) can be viewed on the Network, but viewers are not able to experience the complete WCCW narrative is it unfolded week by week in the 1980s. Only the shows that WWE deems significant enough to its *own* corporate history, such as World Championship Wrestling's (WCW) long-running *Monday Nitro*, are presented in full, thereby creating a hierarchy of importance in wrestling history that is determined by, and to the benefit of, WWE.

Further, the content that WWE has emphasized since the Network's launch (via televised promotion and advertisements on the platform itself) indicates that WWE thinks of itself as much more than a mere professional wrestling promotion. Rather, it is a self-contained media production and distribution empire that specializes in a variety of media content, some of which is only tangentially related to its core product. WWE aggressively advertises its original programming, which features WWE talent in genres such as sketch comedy (e.g., *The Edge and Christian Show That Totally Reeks of Awesomeness*), adult-humor animation (e.g., *Camp WWE*), and reality television (e.g., *Holy Foley!*). This diversified media portfolio illuminates WWE's complex, and perhaps even hostile, relationship to professional wrestling as a genre, as the company devotes significant expense and effort to producing and advertising these types of programs in lieu of digitizing the archives of professional wrestling content to be mined from the company's vast tape library. This leaves many fans of professional wrestling— as it has been traditionally defined by wrestling promotions outside of WWE and as it continues to be presented by many of WWE's remaining competitors—clamoring in vain for more sports-like content while WWE instead seeks to expand the category of sports entertainment across an increasing variety of formats and genres.

WWE's evolution from professional wrestling promotion to media empire has understandably led to considerable consternation within professional wrestling fan communities. Fans perceive that WWE is embarrassed to be synonymous with professional wrestling, resulting in concerted attempts to subvert and redefine the genre and its connotations through the hybrid signifier of sports entertainment. Many wrestling fans feel alienated by WWE's contemporary product for precisely this reason; abandoned by the industry's primary content provider, they yearn for content that more closely resembles professional wrestling prior to WWE's dominance of the industry. This discontent is on display in the results of a questionnaire that I distributed online across several wrestling sites and forums as well as in person at *WrestleMania XXX* in New Orleans in 2014. The questionnaire asked wrestling fans about their preferences and tastes regarding professional wrestling; significantly, an overwhelming majority of the 316 respondents expressed negative attitudes toward WWE and its emphasis on sports entertainment, as well as toward the company's perceived embarrassment about professional wrestling as such. Specifically, the results of the questionnaire demonstrate that the most vocal members of the wrestling audience—"smart" fans who participate in online forums and research the history and backstage maneuverings of the industry—want WWE to embrace the worked sport model that defined professional wrestling throughout most of its history. These fans advocate making those conventions the foundation of WWE's business and media content, instead of continuing their current trajectory of deemphasizing professional wrestling contests in favor of sports entertainment. Accordingly, this chapter suggests that WWE's pursuit of general audiences risks alienating their most devoted viewers, who may begin seeking their professional wrestling content exclusively from less mainstream promotions. Before analyzing the results of the questionnaire in detail, however, I will first add some nuance to the distinction between professional wrestling and sports entertainment.

Professional Wrestling vs. Sports Entertainment

In an article for his website *Voices of Wrestling*, Brandon Howard asserts that "WWE is *not* pro wrestling. . . . If you're a wrestling fan who follows other wrestling companies today or if you're a longtime fan of the tradition of wrestling in the US or any other country, it often seems WWE has disowned itself from that tradition."[7] Such a statement speaks to the wide gulf separating the competing definitions of professional wrestling as either worked sport or sports entertainment. In order to fully understand how these two conceptions of professional wrestling are fundamentally oppositional, however, it is necessary to unpack each designation in greater detail. While both use the term *sport*, WWE's description of professional wrestling as sports entertainment subordinates the characteristics of sport to those of entertainment; in short, elements of sport survive the transition to contemporary WWE insofar as they serve the master of "entertainment" and no further. Worked sport, by contrast, indicates an allegiance to the conventions of sport as a governing principle, albeit with those conventions controlled in a way that is meant to regulate pleasures and ensure specific narrative outcomes. McMahon himself confirmed the implications of WWE's transition to sports entertainment in a 2000 interview with the *Boston Globe*, stating that their approach "treats professional wrestling as an action/adventure soap opera. . . . The WWF presents a hybrid of almost all forms of entertainment and sports combined in one show."[8] As has been discussed elsewhere in this volume, this linguistic dodge not only allowed McMahon to avoid paying licensing fees to state athletic commissions but also exempted his performers from any state-mandated drug testing, which was key to the company's national expansion in the 1980s, when herculean physiques distinguished McMahon's performers from those in competing promotions. The WWE chairman has also suggested that sports entertainment and professional wrestling are mutually exclusive categories, unequivocally stating that "We are not a wrestling company, we're an entertainment company."[9] A glance at the company's corporate website confirms this self-conscious attempt to distance WWE from professional wrestling. Most tellingly, the "Company Overview" section features no mention of the word *wrestling*; instead, WWE describes itself as "an integrated media organization and recognized leader in global entertainment. The company consists of a portfolio of businesses that create and deliver original content 52 weeks a year to a global audience."[10] In short, WWE describes itself as an entertainment company that delivers original content but doesn't indicate that wrestling—as a narrative genre, a style of performance, or a worked sport—is structurally crucial to that content.

In practical terms, WWE's alignment with sports entertainment rather than worked sport emphasizes aspects of the product that most obviously diverge from the conventions of sport. Todd Martin, a professional wrestling critic for *Pro Wrestling Torch*, states that "sports entertainment to me is about the tone of the product."[11] Martin contends that *sports entertainment* connotes frivolity, comedy, and melodrama within the loose confines of performers seeking to entertain fans in both televised and untelevised events. Eschewing the logic of sport, whereby scheduled competitions would determine the athletes' relative positions in the overall rankings, WWE is instead governed by whatever narrative logic the writers need to tell a particular story: the ultimate task of WWE and the Superstars in their employ is to entertain the fans with witty banter, elaborate entrances, and melodramatic scenarios. While wrestling matches do occur, the outcome in terms of wins and losses is less important than narrative progression, character development, and audience investment.[12] While matches on WWE's televised broadcasts are routinely interrupted by commercial breaks, it is much rarer for advertisements to take precedence over a long promo segment or Superstar entrance.

In addition, the commentary panel often seems more interested in discussing recent narrative developments and social media hashtags than calling the play-by-play of the match itself. R. Tyson Smith describes WWE's presentation as follows: "Intricate plots are generated with aggressive monologues, tense interviews, locker room mishaps, hokey humiliations, replays of recent conflicts, and colorful commentary by two ringside announcers. In a two-hour program, little more than 20 minutes consists of actual in-ring combat."[13] This may be slightly hyperbolic: for instance, the four-hour *WrestleMania XXX* featured 119 minutes and 55 seconds of in-ring wrestling, excluding entrance videos and interviews. Approximately half of this show was devoted to actual wrestling, which is significantly more than Smith's estimate of one-sixth. However, it is worth noting that *WrestleMania XXX* received accolades from wrestling fans for its emphasis on in-ring action, marking that event as an outlier compared to WWE's typical programming.[14] In contrast to a sporting event, where the game itself is the primary focus, WWE matches are often presented as superfluous within WWE's diegesis, something that is subordinate to other attractions rather than the primary draw for audiences. And even when the matches are featured prominently, the results of the staged competition are less consequential than the entertainment value of the performance. The founder of *Pro Wrestling Torch*, Wade Keller, echoes this sentiment in his review of WWE's July 2016 pay-per-view event *Battleground*, stating on his podcast that WWE's attitude seems to be as follows: "We hope we entertain you . . . instead of setting up the narrative that we are a governing body bringing these people together to fight for something that matters."[15] This stands in stark contrast to what many fans like most about professional wrestling: the athleticism and physical storytelling contained within the matches themselves.

In contrast to sports entertainment, the presentation of professional wrestling as worked sport emphasizes what goes on inside the ring between two (or more) wrestlers competing to see who is the superior athlete. For example, New Japan Pro Wrestling (NJPW) is often heralded for its realistic, sports-like presentation. In discussing the history of NJPW and professional wrestling in Japan, historian Chris Charlton states that "Japanese cards for the most part are presented and sold as legitimate sporting events, even if the audience is at least vaguely wise to the way things work. To whit [sic], victories and losses carry a heavy significance, and in-ring, a star taking punishment and fighting back is deeply appreciated."[16] Further, the main narrative in most of the matches in NJPW revolves around the trajectory of a wrestler's career as he attempts to win coveted championships and tournaments within the promotion, which is a significant departure from WWE and its more melodramatic storylines that are often the catalyst for the conflict in the ring.

The Wrestling Audience Observer

In order to accurately gauge how professional wrestling fans feel about WWE's original media content, I developed and distributed a questionnaire to wrestling fans during the weekend of *WrestleMania XXX* (April 4–7, 2014) in New Orleans, Louisiana. In addition to functioning as the culmination of WWE's storytelling each year, *WrestleMania* has become an annual destination for wrestling fans from across the world, with numerous smaller promotions capitalizing on WWE's global popularity by holding their own events in the host city on the same weekend. The thirtieth edition of *WrestleMania* was a particularly interesting historical moment for wrestling fans, as it featured the coronation of Daniel Bryan as the top star in the company. Bryan, who had previously wrestled outside of WWE under his real name of Bryan Danielson, was well known in wrestling fan communities for his excellent technical wrestling skills in independent promotions, including Ring of Honor (ROH) and Pro Wrestling Guerilla (PWG).[17] In my discussions with fans over that weekend, many expressed how happy they were to see someone so deserving succeed on "the grandest stage of them all." It was a rare moment in which WWE simultaneously satisfied the desires of two sets of fan communities: those niche fans who follow a variety of independent promotions in addition to WWE as well as the mainstream audiences that watch WWE exclusively and perhaps only casually. This historical anomaly therefore provided an ideal opportunity to gauge the tastes of a diverse set of wrestling fans.

The questionnaire featured open-ended questions designed to determine what type of wrestling the respondents preferred. Of course, WWE was prominently featured in the questionnaire since it is the dominant promotion in the industry. I distributed physical cards that featured the web address of the survey to fans outside the New Orleans Superdome at *WrestleMania XXX*, as well as at other wrestling shows that weekend.[18]

My intent was to be as inclusive of different wrestling fandoms as possible, as not everyone who identifies as a professional wrestling fan enjoys the same promotion or type of content. In addition, I sought to reach as many people as possible over the weekend; the smaller shows facilitated more direct interaction with individual fans than the Superdome's overwhelming capacity (over sixty thousand people) allowed.

In addition to distributing these cards in person, I also posted links to the questionnaire in three different online professional wrestling forums: the Freakin' Awesome Fan Network (http://officialfan.proboards.com/), ProWrestling.com, and WrestleCrap.com. I also posted a link to the survey in Bryan Alvarez's "Daily Update" at F4Wonline.com, a heavily trafficked destination for wrestling fans looking for news about the latest backstage occurrences in professional wrestling. Overall, the survey garnered 316 responses.[19] This overwhelming response from wrestling fans provided an enormous amount of data to parse and revealed tremendous insight about these fans' likes and dislikes regarding contemporary professional wrestling. The range of respondents was quite diverse, with 49.5 percent indicating that they contributed to online forums about professional wrestling, 48.1 percent indicating that they watch mixed martial arts (MMA) in addition to professional wrestling, and 52.4 percent professing to watch Japanese professional wrestling in addition to North American (though most of these respondents also indicated that their knowledge of Japanese wrestling was minimal). In addition, 66.1 percent indicated that they actively follow promotions other than WWE, with the remaining 33.9 percent watching WWE exclusively. The questionnaire offered open-ended questions, prompting fans to elaborate on their own preferences regarding professional wrestling. Although responses were diverse, several key themes clearly emerged. This section analyzes responses to the following questions:

- "What do you like/not like about the WWE product?"
- "What constitutes WWE style?"
- "What changes would you make to the WWE product?"
- "What do you like about promotions outside of WWE (Japan and smaller promotions like Ring of Honor)?"
- "What do you think about WWE terminology such as 'sports entertainment'?"

Overwhelmingly, the responses to these five questions paint a coherent picture of the antagonistic dynamic between contemporary WWE and its fans. The respondents indicate that, like McMahon, fans too understand professional wrestling and sports entertainment as diametrically opposed, mutually exclusive categories of content; but while WWE seems intent on pursuing the latter at the expense of the former, fans are more invested in the opposite, which is their chief complaint with the current product.

The first question posed to respondents regarding WWE was what they liked or did not like about the company's contemporary product, referring mainly to their television broadcasts and pay-per-view or special events (i.e., excluding WWE-branded reality shows, the WWE YouTube channel, films produced by WWE Studios, Superstars' social media accounts, etc.). The emphasis on sports entertainment was immediately evident, with response after response using this terminology. Some representative responses include: "Too much Sports Entertainment, Not Enough Wrestling"; "I am not a fan of 'Sports Entertainment'"; and "The product is too much sports entertainment based and has gotten away from pro wrestling being an athletic contest." Some respondents apparently felt that *sports* was sufficiently deemphasized by WWE's current programming that they dropped the word entirely, designating the product simply as *entertainment*. For example, one respondent stated that "What I don't like about it is that it is much more entertainment based . . . way less wrestling and way more drama. Not a fan of the amount of soap opera." Another wrote, "I find the entertainment aspect to be unfulfilling." In these instances, respondents are expressing dismay over the product's attempts to entertain audiences through contrived drama and spectacle, instead of allowing those qualities to emerge organically from a more sports-like presentation. Several respondents specifically bemoaned WWE's deemphasizing of sport in this section as well, a sentiment exemplified by comments such as "I wish it was presented as more of a legitimate sport." Overall, a large majority of respondents were more critical than supportive of WWE's sports entertainment presentation; nevertheless, several respondents praised these same elements, expressing admiration for the "soap opera" storylines and "big league feel" of the product, as well as the "top notch production values" and "big time stars" seen on WWE broadcasts.

Although many of the responses focused on sports entertainment in general terms, many respondents also singled out the tone of WWE programming for critique. One recurring theme was the lack of authenticity within WWE, with one respondent stating that it often "feels overproduced, artificial, and manufactured." In addition, many respondents focused on the product's frivolity, mentioning that they did not like the "lame comedy," "stupid skits and storylines," and the "immature humor." As Martin notes, the sense of frivolity is a defining characteristic of sports entertainment, as opposed to the competitive stakes inherent to a more sports-like presentation. One respondent summarized the overall tone of WWE by stating that they "No like [sic] the devalued emphasis on the basic premise of pro wrestling—the titles mean nothing, feuds are blown off for no reason, hot shot booking for ratings instead of slow building storylines." The underlying assertion here is that professional wrestling should have, at its core, some semblance of sport instead of constant representations of melodrama.

The second question asked respondents to define the "WWE style," which was intended to evoke sports entertainment without priming the type of responses provided. Many respondents focused on the matches themselves when offering their responses, indicating that WWE style was about "playing to the camera" and "being able to always know where the hard camera is located" during the performance of televised wrestling matches. This attention to detail demonstrates that fans are able to identify the salient stylistic features of wrestling's televisual production. Many respondents also pointed to WWE's mass appeal, stating that WWE represented a type of wrestling that is "slower paced and aimed at the masses," or "made for tv, meant to appeal to a wide audience." Such responses implicitly critique WWE by suggesting that, by aiming for a broad audience, they risk losing the interest of more ardent consumers of the genre. This question also prompted many respondents to raise the related issue of homogeneity, suggesting that WWE's attempt at mass appeal leads to everything looking and feeling similar. For example, one respondent stated that WWE style means that "most matches essentially look the same. . . . For the most part they follow the same formula." Terms such as *patterned matches, corporate wrestling*, and *sanitized* were mentioned repeatedly, indicating a frustration within fandom at the lack of variety within the promotion and, in particular, in the matches themselves. One respondent went so far as to describe WWE style as "paint by numbers wrestling" where performers "only do the moves that they tell you you can do." This same respondent went on to say that WWE style "never gives the appearance of a struggle or an athletic contest," once again connoting the disparity between WWE's content and worked sport. The respondents shared a widespread belief that WWE emphasizes spectacle at the expense of impressive athletic performances; as one respondent put it, WWE style "means working light, entertainment and showmanship FIRST. Wrestling itself is last."

My third question asked what changes respondents would make to the WWE product if they were in a position of authority. In contrast to the first two questions, which were open ended and allowed respondents room to praise or disparage WWE according to their individual tastes, this was an unambiguous invitation to critique the WWE product. However, numerous respondents stated that they would change nothing about WWE, a clear rejection of the question's premise. An overwhelming majority of responses, however, echoed the themes identified above, deriding the frivolous nature of the current product and the company's preference for sports entertainment rather than worked sport. One respondent claimed they would institute "less artificiality, no more scripting of promos, and more attention to wins and losses. Less outlandish storylines, make the focus on titles and winning matches." This change represents a wholesale rejection of WWE's vision of sports entertainment, clearly pointing toward worked sport as a preferred alternative. This sentiment was echoed repeatedly, with answers such as "I would change it into a pro wrestling company, by making things more real and not phony"; "put more emphasis on wins and losses"; "more wrestling oriented"; and "make it more competition oriented. The idea of people fighting their way to the top while gathering support from the fans." The consistency of these responses demonstrates the sweeping changes that many fans feel ought to be made to the WWE product and their approach to professional wrestling as sports entertainment. One respondent articulated this explicitly: "I would change it into a pro wrestling company, and not sports entertainment."

The fourth question invited respondents to make comparisons between WWE and other wrestling promotions, asking what they liked about wrestling beyond WWE. This question produced the most pointed critique of WWE's sports entertainment approach, with respondent after respondent emphasizing the ways in which other promotions took the diegetic premise that professional wrestling is a legitimate sport more seriously. When referring to Japanese wrestling in particular, many respondents expressed admiration for the high quality of the matches: "My favorite aspect of wrestling is the matches, specifically the athleticism and craftsmanship that goes into a great match. In Japan, that is put at the highest priority and actual ability is valued more than anything." This comment suggests that, at its best, a professional wrestling promotion ought to resemble a meritocracy, where actual skill determines who moves up and down the cards, instead of looks, charisma, nepotism, or simple favoritism. Many others echoed the sentiment that Japan places greater value on wrestling as a legitimate (although still worked) sport: "Japan takes professional wrestling very seriously and the content they produce is of the highest caliber." Other respondents agreed, preferring "the adherence to a more traditional 'wrestling is real' narrative" or "the emphasis of pro wrestling as a sporting contest" compared to WWE's product. In short, Japan's presentation of professional wrestling as a worked sport is widely praised and even held up as a model from which WWE could learn. Fans made similar claims in relation to smaller North American wrestling promotions like ROH and PWG as well, with many respondents applauding these companies for their "more realistic matches" with "less focus on nonsense." One fan stated that the North American independent wrestling scene "is more true to traditional pro wrestling rather than polished sports entertainment," referring to the homogenization and sanitized nature of the WWE product. Others stated that they liked the "more serious approach" of these smaller promotions, on the grounds that "the presentation is more akin to Japanese wrestling, which I prefer over WWE style." Ultimately, the overwhelming consensus from those who answered this question was that they wanted the focus to be "primarily on the in-ring product." In light of this preference, the fact that a standard WWE program devotes somewhere from one-sixth to one-half of its broadcast time to actual wrestling is particularly damning.

The final question focused on respondents' thoughts about WWE's use of terminology, including terms like *Superstar* for wrestler, *WWE Universe* for fandom, and *sports entertainment* for wrestling. The goal of this question was to efface the distinction between sports entertainment and professional wrestling, explicitly couching the terms as synonyms in order to more accurately assess fans' thoughts on WWE's specific vocabulary. It was this question, however, that yielded the widest range of responses, with an overwhelming majority of respondents expressing little opposition to these terms. While most respondents indicated that they disliked the terms, they also accepted them as part of WWE's diegesis and brand. Common responses to this question included "I'm fine with them. Don't use them personally but they don't offend me"; "Stupid, but I understand why and am numb to it now"; and "It's jargon, I know it annoys some people but I've kind of just gotten used to it and it doesn't bother me." Such responses speak to the extent of WWE's hegemonic power over the professional wrestling industry, having literally set the terms of the discourse. Response after response expressed distaste for WWE's corporate language, but most also thought that it was "no big deal." In fact, while many fans resigned themselves to the omnipresence of these terms in WWE programming, others went so far as to praise the company for its successful branding strategy. In this vein, respondents offered the following: "It's a business, all businesses have buzzwords that they want people to remember and associate with them to keep them caring and to differentiate themselves"; "It's the branding that all companies try to use these days." One respondent claimed that WWE's unique branding makes them "seem much bigger than any other wrestling promotion in the world," further demonstrating how successful the company has been in dictating its vision to wrestling fans, while others claimed that WWE's ability to enforce the use of these terms is emblematic of the company's position at the forefront of the professional wrestling industry. Nevertheless, such acceptances were often tinged with a sense of resignation: "It doesn't bother me at all, they have the right to call it whatever they want"; "I'm a realist. I don't like it, but it's their game now. They can make the rules as they see fit."

The hegemony of WWE's vision of professional wrestling as sports entertainment, however, was not accepted entirely without resistance; in contrast to the tone of the above-mentioned respondents, others were clearly furious about the company's terminology in general and the term *sports entertainment* in particular. Many fans argued that *sports entertainment* reveals McMahon's own sense of shame over being a professional wrestling promoter. One respondent wrote that *sports entertainment*, *Superstars*, and *WWE Universe* are "stupid terms for Vince to feel like he isn't doing wrestling . . . and it is a slap in the face." Another suggested that "it seems like they are embarrassed that it's wrestling they're selling." While these responses demonstrate some attempt to understand McMahon's motivation for using these terms, other respondents were less empathetic. One fan exclaimed that the terms "make me want to burn my fucking tv," while another wrote, "Fucking kill me now. These are my thoughts. It's insulting and obnoxious." A particularly memorable, if plainly hyperbolic, response asserted that "justifiable homicide is the term that comes to mind." Such responses indicate the consternation many wrestling fans feel regarding WWE's status as the global leader of the professional wrestling industry. Placed in a historical context where McMahon and WWE were not always in this exalted position, one fan stated that "it's stupid and insulting to anyone who grew up watching the product before the Hulk Hogan era," referring to the beginning of the national expansion period of the WWF in the 1980s—and, significantly, prior to the coinage of *sports entertainment*. In short, these responses illustrate the tension between WWE and many wrestling fans, who feel that the spectacle of sports entertainment has completely overshadowed the worked sport aspect of professional wrestling.

CONCLUSION

This chapter demonstrates that WWE's insistence on presenting professional wrestling as sports entertainment is at the root of many wrestling fans' frustration with the company and their current product. While such fans covet and privilege those qualities of professional wrestling that align it with legitimate sport, it's also important to recognize that a wholesale abandonment of sports entertainment in favor of a "pure sports" approach would likely alienate just as many fans of WWE, if not more. In the years since this data was collected, WWE has simultaneously entrenched its reliance on sports entertainment in its main programming while also offering some olive branches to these disenfranchised fans in Network-exclusive programs and competitions. As the industry leader, WWE exerts hegemonic control over the entire wrestling industry, and increasingly so: their most recent wave of new Superstars includes top performers who had already established themselves in promotions like NJPW and ROH before landing in WWE, simultaneously legitimizing the worked-sport approach favored in such promotions while also cementing their own position at the top of the industry ladder. For example, current NXT standouts at the time of this writing include Adam Cole, who made his name in ROH and PWG prior to signing with WWE, and Ricochet, an international star who is best known for his work in NJPW, PWG, and Dragon Gate. While these performers enjoy considerable subcultural capital among wrestling fans who follow promotions outside of WWE, they were also seen as only having reached the pinnacle of the industry upon signing with WWE. Perhaps no WWE Superstar better represents this transition from a career in sport (worked or legitimate) to sports entertainment than Ronda Rousey, who made her debut at the *Royal Rumble* in January 2018. Rousey has legitimate sports credibility from her years in Ultimate Fighting Championship (UFC), and WWE hopes that her celebrity and cultural capital in the world of legitimate sports will translate to the realm of sports entertainment.

Recent years have also seen WWE make concessions to precisely those fans who espouse a strong distaste for sports entertainment. Programs such as the *Cruiserweight Classic, 205 Live,* and *NXT,* all of which air exclusively on the WWE Network, have incorporated more of the desires of fans who want professional wrestling to be a worked sport, emphasizing workrate (i.e., the quality of matches) over storytelling and spectacle. When describing the differences between the *Cruiserweight Classic* and WWE's weekly televised programming, Garrett Martin of *Paste Magazine* writes that "it's all in the presentation. Whereas *Raw*'s non-match moments usually veer between inane and insulting, and titles are openly treated like glorified props, the Cruiserweight Classic is being portrayed as a legitimate sport. . . . Opponents were respectful, there was basically no cheating, and it was all presented as a legitimate athletic contest."[20] The differences between WWE's normal programming and the *Cruiserweight Classic* take to heart many of the criticisms levied against sports entertainment in this chapter. As a result, many wrestling fans lauded the *Cruiserweight Classic* for adhering to the worked sport elements of professional wrestling that had characterized the genre prior to WWE's rise in the 1980s. Speaking on behalf of these fans, Chris Mueller at *Bleacher Report* wrote, "I can honestly say that I was looking forward to this event more than any pay-per-view since I knew Daniel Bryan was going to win the WWE World Heavyweight Championship at WrestleMania 30. . . . It's shows like this that make us remember why we are fans of the most ridiculously over-the-top form of entertainment in the world."[21] John Canton of TJRWrestling.net repeated this sentiment: "I'm just glad that this tournament existed, that they were given the chance to have pure wrestling matches like this and tell stories in the ring the way that they did."[22] Featuring a roster of wrestlers who made their names in promotions outside of WWE, programs such as the *Cruiserweight Classic* give fans a reason to be optimistic about the future of WWE, insofar as it represents the company's willingness to widen the range of wrestling content designed to appeal to different kinds of fans. However, these programs remain under the auspices of WWE and therefore feature the same problematic terminology and polished aesthetic associated with WWE's more mainstream efforts. It therefore remains an open question whether WWE's efforts to expand their programming to appeal to fans who prefer worked sport will be worthwhile or if such fans will continue to be seen by WWE as a vocal but ultimately unimportant minority of their audience.

NOTES

1. Oliver and Johnson, *Pro Wrestling Hall of Fame*, 11.
2. Alvarez, "WOL 12/24."
3. Dave Meltzer (@davemeltzerWON), November 23, 2015 (6:29 p.m.), tweet, "With the exception of mid-90s, wrestling now least popular in my lifetime," https://twitter.com/davemeltzerWON/status/668934426013757440.
4. Guttmann, *From Ritual to Record*, 11.
5. Barthes, "World of Wrestling," 23.
6. For more on the dissolution of the territory system and its consequences in contemporary WWE, see Dru Jeffries and Andrew Kannegiesser's chapter in this volume, as well as Reynolds and Alvarez, *Death of WCW*.
7. Howard, "Language of WWE."
8. Katz and Jhally, "Manhood on the Mat."
9. Dave Meltzer, *Wrestling Observer Newsletter*, July 11, 2011.
10. World Wrestling Entertainment, "Company Overview."
11. Todd Martin expressed this position in private correspondence with the author on August 27, 2016.

12. For instance, a Superstar like Bray Wyatt continues to receive top title opportunities despite a miserable win/loss record because of his strong character work and enduring popularity with fans.

13. Smith, "Raw Export," 66.

14. For instance, the *Monday Night Raw* that preceded *WrestleMania XXX* featured only 50 minutes and 37 seconds of wrestling across its three-hour runtime.

15. Keller, "724: WWE Battleground."

16. Charlton, *Lion's Pride*, 13.

17. See Christian Norman's chapter in this volume for more on Daniel Bryan's narrative leading up to and following *WrestleMania XXX*.

18. In total, I solicited fans to take the questionnaire at five shows over the course of the weekend, including two Ring of Honor shows, a Kaiju Big Battel show, a Dragon Gate USA show, and *WrestleMania XXX*.

19. Coincidentally, this number connotes "Stone Cold" Steve Austin's famous catchphrase of the 1990s, "Austin 3:16 says 'I just kicked your ass.'"

20. Martin, "WWE's Cruiserweight Classic."

21. Mueller, "WWE Cruiserweight Classic 2016."

22. Canton, "John Report."

Bibliography

Alvarez, Bryan. "WOL 12/24: Christmas Eve Show with News and Revelry." *Wrestling Observer Live*. Podcast audio. December 22, 2015. http://www.f4wonline.com/wrestling-observer-live/wol-1224-christmas-eve-show-news-and-revelry-204366.

Barthes, Roland. "The World of Wrestling." In *Steel Chair to the Head: The Pleasure and Pain of Professional Wrestling*, edited by Nicholas Sammond, 23–32. Durham, NC: Duke University Press, 2005.

Canton, John. "The John Report: WWE Cruiserweight Classic 09/14/16 Review." September 14, 2016. http://tjrwrestling.net/the-john-report-wwe-cruiserweight-classic-090716-review-the-finale/.

Charlton, Chris. *Lion's Pride: The Turbulent History of New Japan Pro Wrestling*. Self-Published, 2015.

Guttmann, Allen. *From Ritual to Record: The Nature of Modern Sports*. New York: Columbia University Press, 1978.

Howard, Brandon. "The Language of WWE." *Voices of Wrestling*. July 15, 2015. http://www.voicesofwrestling.com/2015/07/15/the-language-of-wwe/.

Katz, Jackson, and Sut Jhally. "Manhood on the Mat: The Problem Is Not That Pro Wrestling Makes Boys Violent. The Real Lesson of the Wildly Popular Pseudo Sport Is More Insidious." *Boston Globe*, February 13, 2000.

Keller, Wade. "724: WWE Battleground PPV Roundtable." *Pro Wrestling Torch PPV Roundtable*. Podcast audio. July 24, 2016. http://vip.pwtorch.com/2016/07/24/vip-audio-724-wwe-battleground-ppv-roundtable-keller-bryant-mcneill-mitchell-shield-three-way-for-wwe-title-orton-on-highlight-reel-bayley-wrestle-first-main-roster-match-more-98-m/.

Martin, Garrett. "WWE's Cruiserweight Classic Is an Exciting Glimpse of a More Serious WWE." *Paste Magazine*. December 26, 2016. https://www.pastemagazine.com/articles/2016/07/wwes-cruiserweight-classic-it-feels-real-to-me-dam.html.

Mueller, Chris. "WWE Cruiserweight Classic 2016: Winners, Grades, Reaction for September 15." Bleacher Report. September 15, 2016. http://bleacherreport.com/articles/2663763-wwe-cruiserweight-classic-2016-winners-grades-reaction-for-september-15.

Oliver, Greg, and Steven Johnson. *The Pro Wrestling Hall of Fame: The Heels*. Toronto: ECW, 2007.

Reynolds, R. D., and Bryan Alvarez. *The Death of WCW*. Toronto: ECW, 2004.
Smith, R. Tyson. "A Raw Export." *Contexts* 8, no. 2 (2009): 65–67.
World Wrestling Entertainment. "Company Overview." http://corporate.wwe.com/who-we-are
/company-overview.

SHANE TOEPFER is Assistant Professor of Media Studies and Communication at the University of North Georgia.

chapter six

THE MARKS HAVE GONE OFF-SCRIPT: ROGUE ACTORS IN WWE'S STANDS

Sam Ford

Modern professional wrestling is unique as a storytelling form. It's part sleight of hand, a carnival con in which performers imagine they are "duping the marks" by staging a fight that can cause the audience to lose willing suspension of disbelief.[1] It's part street theater, a morality play in which immediately intelligible characters carry out the core human struggles we all face in exaggerated form. And it's part dramatization of the modern sports arena event, with hyperbolic representations of all the trappings of contemporary sports performance. In the televised era, it's also become part serialized storytelling in the vein of the US soap opera, boasting an ensemble cast carrying out storylines that are always "to be continued," continually delaying narrative closure in favor of new twists and turns and ensuring that any characters who hit upon a moment of triumph will soon find themselves in peril. And, finally, it's part participatory theater, with a casting call going out at each new show, in each new town, for thousands of performers to come to the arena and pay money not to be a spectator but to actively *play the part* of the sports spectator.

Thus, wrestling fans don't just experience the show "as pure theater," as Gerald Craven and Richard Moseley have written; they also overtly see themselves—quite rightly—as an essential part of the show.[2] Wrestling's performance art has traditionally been built on how to work the crowd—how to draw heat from the marks, those true believers who can be emotionally manipulated by the convincing simulation of an athletic contest. However, this imperative means that, from the beginning, an audience filled with people who seem like true believers has been an essential element of any professional wrestling performance; without someone to con, the performance is just a rehearsal. As Broderick Chow, Claire Warden, and Eero Laine put it, "The entertainment form itself would not exist without the stadiums full of active participants."[3] That need in the wrestling performance to have an arena full of marks to work is ingrained both in the logic of professional wrestling performance and in the ways onstage performers have talked about their craft.

Today's fans have unprecedented access to information about the professional wrestling business through the memoirs of wrestling performers and creative talent, the work of digital columnists and journalists who report on the creative decisions backstage, and the ways in which professional wrestling storylines themselves have increasingly featured fictionalized versions of "the backstage" over the past two decades. Dedicated fans have incorporated much of the carny parlance of wrestling and of the vernacular theory of wrestling performers that underpins it, in how they understand and talk among themselves about these performative dynamics.[4] Yet even as the fandom moves toward a desire to be addressed as "smarts" and to have their increased knowledge playfully recognized in the narrative itself, there's still the overt knowledge that the core wrestling narrative relies, to a significant degree, on their successful performance as dupes not in on the con—that the suspension of disbelief necessary for wrestling to maintain its dramatic appeal necessitates their own performance as marks.

The positioning of wrestling audiences as marks was, from the beginning, a foundational narrative construct on which the performance relied, but one that often led promoters and wrestlers alike to confuse the fandom as performed in the arena with the actual people who populate the stands.[5] However, the modern professional wrestling scene is one where wrestling promotions' overt acknowledgment of the scripted nature of their programming and fans' understanding of it is no longer new. In that environment, the art of kayfabe—the carny term for doing everything possible to preserve the fiction—becomes not only the responsibility of the performers on stage but also, crucially, the responsibility of the performers in the stands: the fans themselves.

This essay specifically explores the performative environment of the live arena wrestling show that is simultaneously being televised to an at-home audience, with an emphasis on the performing fans in the arena. In many respects, the fans in the stands are more important as performers than as spectators, since the at-home audience is much larger and, in most cases, more profitable. In the contemporary wrestling industry, fans feel more empowered than ever before to shape, tweak, resist, or even protest the narrative direction of the creative team of companies like World Wrestling Entertainment (WWE), which has—for most of the past thirty years—been the dominant international producer of professional wrestling's unique form of "sports entertainment." However, the fandom also understands and openly discusses the responsibility they hold in their performative role at the arena to make the performance work; without individual fans playing their role, the show falls apart. First, I'll examine in further detail the unique dynamics of the performative wrestling audience at a live event. Then, I'll explore how that performance shifts as fans move from an environment where they are the intended end audience for the performance to the televised wrestling show, where they are more explicitly called on to be an active part of the performance ultimately staged for the viewer at home. Finally, I'll reflect on the tensions within wrestling fandom when it comes to, on the one hand, exerting more control over the narrative through their performance while, on the other, fulfilling the primary duty of playing marks in the stands.

Elsewhere in this collection, Christian Norman provides a compelling look at the narrative and rhetorical practice of WWE in light of fan resistance to the direction the creative team has taken stories. Complementing Norman's essential work—and the illustrative case study he provides in the rise of character Daniel Bryan to the top of WWE's competitive ranks on the back of intense fan support and overtly against the wishes of WWE's head executives—I explore the in-arena fan-producer dynamic by concentrating on the fandom's own negotiations with how to handle this increased power and on the continued responsibility they have within the televised narrative. As Norman writes in his piece, wrestling provides an ideal case study for all those who study media texts and live performance to better understand the dynamic between producers and audiences; but it's also an extreme and unusual case study because fans play such an overt role not just in the reception of the fictional text but also in its very creation. Just as professional wrestling often holds a carnivalesque mirror to our culture, absurdly exaggerating the cultural tensions it explores, so too might we look at the wrestling arena as a hyperreal, larger-than-life setting in which we can explore dynamics that exist throughout other fandoms and fan-producer relationships.

Understanding the Nature of In-Arena Performance

Shane Toepfer has described the performative nature of professional wrestling fandom as a "playful audience," referring specifically to the ways in which fans enter the wrestling arena, ready and willing to play their role.[6] As Stephen Di Benedetto argues, these performative practices are significantly amplified in the live arena by the sense of community with fellow fans: "Participation and camaraderie is central to getting the most out of the experience."[7] These in-arena performative practices include coming in costume, adopting an alternative persona for the evening, participating in call-and-response with performers onstage, reacting to the narrative unfolding onstage, and possibly resisting the ways in which the in-ring performers and the creative team seem to intend for the fans to perform. It also potentially includes overtly seeking to engage in a playfully antagonistic relationship with other fans in the arena—for instance, arguing over which performer they want to see win a match, whether in one-on-one discussion or in arena-wide dueling chants (e.g., "Let's go Cena!"/"Cena sucks!").

Using in-arena and outside-the-arena interviews, I've previously researched fans' attitudes toward their own in-arena performances. In those conversations, I found that some fans explained their performances through a sense of obligation to the show, acknowledging the fact that those in the ring—and those writing the script—rely on their active performance to provide the heat necessary for the performance to truly work. Some fans also invoked their obligation to fellow fans (children in particular, but also adults) who they imagine may not yet be in on the con—a justification one person I interviewed likened to preserving the myth of Santa Claus for a child.[8] In her work, Sharon Mazer explores the conflicted feelings smart fans may have regarding these perceived marks—simultaneously establishing their superiority as smarts while also admiring marks' ability to effortlessly give themselves over to the performance as the believing fan.[9] Smart fans are on a constant quest to learn as much as possible about the creative process and what is likely to happen in WWE, and potentially even to use that knowledge to critique and oppose the company's creative decisions. But at the same time, they also seek moments where they are pleasantly surprised by a performance, narrative twist, or storyline such that they can "mark out," expressing the genuine emotion associated with fully immersing themselves in the role of the "believing sports fan."[10]

For the in-arena wrestling audience, I've identified five modes of engagement that fans slip into and out of: their baseline role as spectators (accomplished via merely attending and providing their attention for the duration of the show); their role as community members (whether a smaller-scale, more tightly knit regional community surrounding local independent wrestling promotions or a larger-scale global fan community like the WWE Universe); their role as critics, sharing observations with others in attendance about the quality of the athletic performance or the storyline; their role as vernacular theorists, reflecting on wrestling performance, the state of wrestling storytelling, and what makes a good show more broadly (which can happen between fans before and after a show or during breaks between matches); and their role as performers.[11] This expands on Cassandra Amesley's notion of "double-viewing" into what I've categorized elsewhere as "quintuple viewing."[12]

A trip into the wrestling arena often reveals fans cycling quite expertly through these modes. Consider, for instance, this moment captured by Toepfer, quoting a fan: "'I fucking love the Briscoes.' He then turned his head back towards the ring and started chanting, 'Fuck-You-Bris-Coes (Clap; Clap; Clap, Clap, Clap).'" As Toepfer writes:

> The chants were hostile in sound only, however, as this fan smiled throughout his jeering of the Briscoes, obviously enjoying the wrestlers' portrayal of heels as much as he was enjoying playing along by deriding their actions in the ring. This fan loved the performance of the Briscoes and confessed to admiring the wrestlers' abilities in the ring, but also knew that since they were villains the desired response from the crowd was for the wrestlers to be jeered. In this way, chants of "Fuck-You-Bris-Coes" become supportive demonstrations of appreciation by the fans, calling out that they are appreciative of the efforts of these performers pretending to be villains in the ring.[13]

The struggle within wrestling fandom, and even within individual fans, can perhaps be best demonstrated by how fans collectively and individually navigate or combine their various roles as spectators, community members, critics, theorists, and performers while attending live events. Fans are conflicted between desiring to influence the direction of the narrative through the power afforded by wrestling's unique placement of fans in the text and the responsibility they feel to play their part in the performance. If they don't perform or are too resistant to the narrative of the show en masse, they may well see the work of the writers and performers on the stage fall apart.[14]

Much of their power comes from combining modes of engagement. The spectator-performers, even if performing in a way that is contrary to the writers' intentions, still act within the confines of their role in the narrative. The critic-performers don't merely analyze the in-ring action internally or in quiet conversation but rather express that critique openly, effectively engaging as part of the show but from a perspective external to the fictional construct. However, as fans band together in the arena to subvert or resist storylines—whether from within the fiction or outside it— they engage in what Toepfer calls "macro rejections."[15] They may do so as community-spectator-performers, challenging where the writers and in-ring performers want to take the script by cheering the villain, booing the hero, or providing a bigger reaction to a midcard performer than to someone in the main event. Or they may act as community-critic-performers, critiquing performances and creative directions with chants like "You fucked up" when wrestlers botch a move or "Boring" when they don't like what is unfolding on the screen. Such macro rejections have a strong ability to influence the direction of the show in ways that individual acts of resistance would not. Or they may stay in a community-spectator role and collectively refuse to participate in the show with a significant performative reaction, which many in-ring performers might argue is the most damaging result of all—an arena with no heat. As Claire Warden writes, silence generated by "a crowd [who] is not fully invested in an angle" is a particularly tough scenario for in-ring performers to navigate.[16]

The more literate and knowledgeable wrestling fans become about the structure of wrestling performance and the business of the wrestling industry, the more they become cognizant of their abilities to influence the individual show itself and the ongoing creative direction of the story; this results in increased ambivalence regarding when, where, and how to exert that autonomy. When attending an untelevised live event (called a house show, in wrestling parlance, since the intended audience is limited to those in the house), aberrant fan behaviors may disrupt the night's card but are unlikely to substantially influence the ongoing direction of the storyworld. However, when fans attend a televised event, they are cognizant that their choices may have significant consequences not just for the viewer at home but also on the ongoing direction of the storyline, since each of those shows represents a canonical installment in WWE's primary serialized narrative.

The Wrestling Arena as Collective Performance for a Media Text

Again, as WWE and other wrestling organizations have become media companies that are built on live events but whose primary product is arguably the media text created from those shows, fans become more important as cast members than as audience members. In the words of Jon Ezell, "The live, physically present audience is now an element of production rather than its means."[17] Thus, we can see the televised live event as WWE's overt invitation for fans to directly become part of the company's immersive storyworld—a serialized narrative that unfolds in real time, in our real world.[18] No other fictional media franchise gives fans such a privileged position. As I've written elsewhere: "Even more vital to understanding wrestling is acknowledging that it is a 360-degree performance between on-stage talent and 'in-the-stands' talent. . . . (Note that WWE itself calls both its narrative world and its fandom the 'WWE Universe'—indicating that fans are, themselves, part of this fictional world. Perhaps, then, pro wrestling can best be understood as a continuous alternate reality game.)"[19]

However, as opposed to the company's employees and independent contractors involved in the production of their televised events, WWE has no direct control over these fans' live performances. As writers, producers, and performers prepare each new chapter in WWE's ongoing serialized plots, they collectively hypothesize how fans will act, they shape scripts and onstage execution to attempt to manipulate that reaction, and they respond and revise based on the fans' performance at each show. WWE chairman Vince McMahon has frequently likened each live arena they produce shows in to a vastly superior version of the traditional media industries' focus group.[20] The creative team's job—in addition to determining the ongoing direction for the serialized narrative unfolding week by week on shows like *Monday Night Raw, SmackDown Live, Main Event, NXT,* and *205 Live* and their important supercard events, which act as the culmination of several weeks' worth of televised storylines—is to constantly monitor the feedback they receive from fans in the arena and to tweak the creative direction based on what seems to be resonating, what falls flat, and what draws fan ire.

When wrestling troupes largely performed on a geographically regional circuit, writers only had to get to know the collective performance of a limited number of fans at the local arenas on their regular route. As WWE and other companies have focused more on television narratives meant for national and international distribution with more geographically broad touring routes to match, this process of predicting and accounting for potential fan response has become even more complicated. Consider, for instance, a 1997 WWE storyline in which Canadian character Bret "the Hitman" Hart was treated alternately as a villain by US fans and as a hero by Canadian fans, whereas his rival "Stone Cold" Steve Austin received the inverse reaction. This was perhaps one of the earliest and most overt examples of how WWE's writers learned to be more cognizant of fans' role in shaping the narrative, accounting for potentially drastic differences in fan response from one city to the next—effectively acknowledging the unique subculture of various cities' fans.

Today, you can still see this kind of local flavor being overtly performed at televised shows. WWE's creative team must think ahead to what might happen as they hold a show in the hometown of a villain or a lower-card performer and thus may see a reaction opposite to, or out of proportion with, what can usually be expected. Today's WWE writers must anticipate and deal with a variety of location-specific actions: for instance, performed fan anger on each televised show in Montreal over an incident that happened to character/performer Bret Hart there two decades ago (via chants of "You screwed Bret"); the tendency of Toronto-based fans to regularly cheer characters who are supposed to be villains while jeering the supposed heroes (prompting WWE commentators to label Toronto as WWE's version of Bizarro World); and the inevitable fan support of character CM Punk in his native Chicago, despite the fact that Punk's performer walked out of WWE in anger years prior. Additionally, they must brace for what happens when major events like WWE's annual *Wrestle-Mania*, and the live televised shows airing in the following days, draw their most ardent fans from around the world, creating an arena environment where a good portion of the attendees are not actually from the local town but rather represent their most knowledgeable and dedicated fans—fans who perhaps have the greatest potential to slip into the community-critic-performer mode.[21]

Likewise, many wrestling fans are well aware not only of the role they have to play in the text but also of the differences in various arena environments. WWE fans may conjecture what a Toronto audience will do during the next televised show in that city, or whether the next Chicago audience will persist in its chants for Punk, or what antics the "supercrowd" of *WrestleMania* and its subsequent shows may pull. In fact, WWE may even overtly draw on speculation of how the fans will perform at a particular arena in the script as a way of creating drama and as a means of mitigating fan performances that might interrupt or challenge their long-term storytelling plans. For instance, commentators sometimes build tension by speculating how fans will react to notoriously divisive characters like John Cena or Roman Reigns, or by foreshadowing a night of unpredictable or atypical audience responses to television viewers (e.g., at the beginning of a telecast like the *Raw* after *WrestleMania*).

WWE has long had to prepare for and contend with how fans' in-arena performances in one town may influence fans in the next, who saw the previous city's reaction on television, to give a similar reaction. This is often how a fan chant or a new gimmick or catchphrase's popularity builds.[22] But in a digital communication era when fans across cities frequently collaborate online to dissect storylines, discuss rumors of what is happening backstage, and collectively organize how they will respond to current plots, the relationship between WWE's creative teams and the fans has become increasingly complicated. Thus, while WWE writers and performers work as diligently as they can to predict how the fans who gather in a particular arena on a particular night for the production of a particular installment of an ongoing narrative will behave, as Ezell puts it, "The imaginary audience is not always the one that shows up."[23]

Fan Performance as Resistance and Collaboration

The most intense and dedicated wrestling fans are what David Shoemaker calls "meta-fans," those for whom "history and reality matter as much as the onscreen narrative."[24] As described by Nicholas Ware, meta-fans "are not just fans of the diegetic drama of professional wrestling but fans of the business itself, and follow the meta-narrative of business deals, backstage politics, and real-world relationships that inevitably influence the pro wrestling product as presented on television."[25] Lawrence B. McBride and S. Elizabeth Bird have written about such wrestling fans' "elaborate criticism of wrestling," ascribing to them a "sophisticated grasp of nuance" and a penchant for critiquing the politics inherent in promoters' decisions.[26] Mazer writes that "the fans who might be considered fanatic addicts . . . are the least passive purchasers."[27]

Online fandom practices—including weekly critiques of WWE shows and "fantasy booking" upcoming events—help refine those critiquing skills. These activities often overtly or subtly critique the politics behind WWE's choices about who the top stars should be and who should go over in matches. Fans react to such decisions with a great deal of nuance, noting not only who the writers choose to have win and lose matches but also how the narrative positions characters to have the opportunity to resonate with fans. Thus, fantasy booking often functions similarly to other forms of fan fiction, providing individual fans a venue for creative commentary on which stories WWE chooses to tell, how it chooses to tell its stories, and how it values the size, physique, gender, class, ethnicity, cultural identity, and various other attributes of a given character.[28]

Over the past twenty years in particular, as the culture and norms of the internet wrestling community have become widespread, fans have organized movements to protest creative decisions or influence which characters are pushed to the top of the card: for instance, by rallying to see the character Mick Foley treated as a top star and champion in the late 1990s; by persistently pushing, beginning in 2015 with the Twitter hashtag #GiveDivasAChance, to have women's wrestling treated as seriously as men's matches; and by hijacking and protesting for the rise of Daniel Bryan to the top of the card beginning in 2013.[29] In his examination of the fan protests surrounding Bryan, Eero Laine writes that online fans planning to attend live events "shared proposals for various protest actions to be performed in the stadium, from standing and turning their backs on The Authority [members of the McMahon family who run the WWE] to starting distracting and off-topic chants to agreed-upon responses when certain predictable things would take place during the show." In this online communication environment, fans brainstormed these actions with fellow event attendees, attendees at upcoming events in different towns, and many others who may have contributed to brainstorming the protests without planning to attend a show.[30]

Fan resistance is a familiar frame for fan studies scholars; however, it rarely takes place as dramatically and as overtly as it does in professional wrestling.[31] When we look at wrestling fan resistance, we can see an ongoing cycle in which WWE presents fans with the next installment of the narrative; the fans resist; and WWE attempts to ignore, adjust to, or else co-opt that resistance into the ongoing narrative. For wrestling fans, Mazer writes that even when moments of fan resistance don't drive change, "the act was more important, more felt and somehow more significant, than its failure."[32] Wrestling fandom is thus pitted in an eternal collar-and-elbow tie-up with wrestling promoters. Mazer writes:

> The true tension is between the cynicism that tells us it's all a game owned by the guy with the money at the expense of the rest of us and the optimism that keeps us in it, keeps us trying to find a way to be more smart than mark, and barring that, at least to acquire the self- and social-awareness to see how we are made into marks, and with that knowing to learn to act outside the box, to break free of the squared circle, of its ethos and of the dominant culture pro wrestling so richly represents.[33]

In this view, just as wrestling narratives are person vs. person, wrestling fandom is built around promoters vs. fans.

However, we must contrast this antagonism with the dynamic between the actors on the stage and the actors in the stands described throughout this chapter. As I've written elsewhere, "If the wrestling industry's hyperbole is built around pretending that fans are being deceived and fans are dedicated to performing being deceived, we can ultimately see both the wrestling industry and wrestling fandom engaged together in maintaining this 'con' on the rest of the world."[34] From this perspective, if the modern wrestling narrative is one where the narrative calls on fans to critique and even feud with promoters, we instead see wrestling fans engaged with promoters and performers in a collaborative performance of contention; any feud between the fandom and the promoters may be just as staged as the choreographed matches happening in the ring.[35] If the evolution of wrestling in the transmedia era is primarily the result of increased fan knowledge about the vernacular of the industry—of fans being brought deeper under the carnival tent and into the backstage of the arena—then we might understand performed fan resistance as, to some degree, a critical component of modern kayfabe.

The degree to which wrestling fans are engaging in passionate resistance or merely performing is hard to parse. Just as the debate between real and fake is central to the discussion of professional wrestling overall, it's hard to tell exactly where the line of reality is drawn when wrestling fans protest the powers that be while also paying for a seat and the opportunity to do so. After all, the types of fan activities described throughout this essay as indicative of dedicated wrestling fans blur the lines between affirmational and transformational fandom practices. As defined by obsession_inc, *affirmational fandom* refers to communities where the source author's vision of a text is accepted and upheld and where most of the practices of the fandom are sanctioned and encouraged, while *transformational fandom* is "all about laying hands upon the source and twisting it to the fans' own purposes."[36] Online, you can see both types of fan activities displayed simultaneously: for instance, the online fan base might use the WWE-sanctioned Twitter hashtags appearing on the upper-left side of their screen during a broadcast while also adding unsanctioned hashtags meant to question or mock the creative direction (such as the 2014 hashtag #Bluetista to mock a new pair of blue tights wrestler Batista began wearing, or the aforementioned #GiveDivasAChance). In the arena, many of the fan performances described in previous sections involve moving fluidly between affirmational and transformational modes of engagement. And even fans' strongest critiques of WWE practices have genre-imposed limitations that fans rarely break from. As I write elsewhere, critical fans "aren't going to call for tensions to be resolved through peer mediation rather than pro wrestling contests, most likely."[37] Thus, WWE fandom's fantasy booking is unlikely to lead to scenarios like the parody piece that *ClickHole* once published, titled "Wow: No One on 'WWE RAW' Was Mad Enough to Fight Each Other Last Night, so They Just Sent All the Fans Home."[38] Just as many wrestling veterans say the best in-ring performers are "playing themselves, with the volume turned up," perhaps fans are performing their resistance in a similar fashion—a truly felt critique, but performed in exaggerated fashion. It's therefore important that we understand fan resistance and collaboration with wrestling's producers as inevitably intertwined.

In some ways, the dynamic between WWE Creative/performers and WWE fans captures the dichotomy inherent to the narrative of WWE's "traveling road show" in general. On the one hand, these characters are all pitted against one another in the ring at each arena. On the other, they overtly acknowledge that they are a troupe who travel on the road together, share a locker room with one another, and ultimately are there to entertain fans with their athletic performances. WWE's writers, performers, and their fans are likewise all simultaneously adversaries in the game of shaping the narrative and partners in staging a collective con.[39]

CONCLUSION: NEGOTIATING THE BORDERS OF PERFORMED FAN RESISTANCE

While this essay has outlined how performed resistance from in-arena wrestling fans has become an integral part of modern wrestling performance, storytelling process, and kayfabe, it's worth concluding with a look at the ways in which wrestling fandom continues to negotiate the parameters of this evolving role. In the past, wrestling veterans worked hard backstage to police the borders of kayfabe and the rest of the unwritten rules of conduct among wrestlers; today, we can see the same policing of borders happening within the stands by a fan base trying to collectively perform as believing sports fans while also potentially engaging as critic-performers and community-critic-performers. Within the arena, communities of fans may challenge the behavior of individuals who they believe have gone outside the boundaries of the fandom's unique code of kayfabe.

Toepfer provides multiple instances of such policing, moments when fans critique their fellow performers in the stands for engaging in "expressions of unproductive resistance."[40] For example, he describes a situation at a Ring of Honor show where one fan, who had said he was going to "Fuck with ROH by cheering the heels and booing the faces," was eventually met with chants of "Shut the fuck up"—"a representation of hegemonic struggle where the audience at large seemed to decide that this fan's transgression was pushing the limits of acceptable behavior."[41] At the same show, fans who interrupted the performance of female wrestlers with lewd sexual remarks were met with the same chant, which silenced them. Toepfer writes, "In this instance the subculture was negotiating the limits of acceptability for its collective identity, and the battle between catcalling fans and subcultural community standards was on full display."[42]

But this self-policing of performative boundaries doesn't just take place in specific arenas or virtual communities; increasing fan attention is given to critiquing the performance of whole arenas of fan performers or questioning the performative practices of sections of the fandom overall. For example, fans may critique a particular night's crowd—or the consistent performance of a certain city—as being insufficiently enthusiastic, thereby compromising the quality of a particular show.[43] Regularly, reviewers writing about one of WWE's weekly shows or special supercards will evaluate whether the audience generated an appropriate level of fervor. These critics may lay blame upon the performers in the stands, rather than those in the ring, for failing to provide the appropriate fan reaction to essential points in the drama.[44]

The most intense of these fan debates focus on when it is appropriate for fans to engage in the community-critic-performer mode. There are moments, like the massive fan protests described earlier in this essay, when a wide range of WWE fans may feel a communal sense that pushing back is justified. There are particular cities or episodes (like the *Raw* and *SmackDown Live* immediately following each year's *WrestleMania*) where a heightened performance of protest from fans in attendance has become part of the expected fan culture. But these behaviors are debated heavily in online discussions of community practice.

Consider, for example, a situation at WWE's 2016 *SummerSlam* event in Brooklyn in which fans disrupted one of the main events, a match between Finn Bálor and Seth Rollins, to voice discontent about the chosen color of the new WWE Universal Championship belt, which was at stake for the first time. A common refrain from fans and critics in reaction to the event was that the fans in the arena had gone too far in trying to make their performance of protest the story at the expense of the narrative of the show and the performance of the wrestlers themselves. For instance, in his piece "Smart Crowds Are Often Complete Idiots," Jason Martin compares such fans to the stereotype of the wrestler who has become a "mark for himself," with fans losing all sense of the collective performance they are supposed to be engaged in in favor of blind self-promotion.[45] In fact, this was a case where even onstage performers chastised the Brooklyn fans for their performance. WWE legend Mick Foley wrote an impassioned Facebook post titled "When Smart Fans Turn Dumb," in which he claimed that fans were responsible for needlessly undermining a meritorious in-ring performance: "Instead of that element of magic necessary to turn that great match into a classic, what Finn and Seth got instead was the stench of self-congratulatory snarkiness from a very vocal minority."[46] Rollins himself took to Twitter to critique the fans' reaction, writing, "More important than a title's appearance is what it represents for the men fighting over it. You really let me down tonight, Brooklyn."[47]

A similar critique emerged around the 2018 *Extreme Rules* event in Pittsburgh. In light of many WWE fans' ongoing complaints that character Roman Reigns's matches were too often given pride of place as the main event, many smarts expressed delight online when they realized that Reigns's match against Bobby Lashley was not going to headline the event as the night's narrative played out. Instead, the aforementioned Rollins and Dolph Ziggler—both considered top performers by many of these ardent fans—went last in a thirty-minute Iron Man match that many online pieces predicted could be one of the best WWE in-ring performances of the year. When the Pittsburgh audience chose to chant a ten-second countdown for every minute of the countdown clock posted on the screen during the match, though, it significantly disrupted the narrative tension of the performance in the ring. Citing tweets from wrestling fans (and retired wrestler Bubba Ray Dudley) about the fan performance, Raza Kazi concludes, "What seems to irritate most of the fans online, however, is the fact that the majority of fans are always complaining that the same big names are featured in the main event matches time and time again. When the WWE listens and gives them what they want, they decide to take over the show themselves, rather than focusing on the excellent match two talented stars are putting on."[48]

As communities of wrestling fans debate the balance between collaboration and resistance—and where the line should be drawn between exercising the unique autonomy wrestling fans have in the live arena and fulfilling their duties as part of the media text being created for those viewing at home—we can see fans drawing on a sensed moral economy around these issues.[49] Much of this debate hinges on times fans feel WWE's creative team, through their storytelling choices, has violated the implicit contract between the company and its fan base, to draw on Alec Austin's work.[50] If WWE's media empire relies heavily on the fans' active performance at televised shows—which is not only unpaid labor but, in fact, labor fans are themselves paying sometimes significant costs per ticket to provide—it's perhaps not surprising that fans feel they have significant rights to and ownership over the story in exchange for that labor; creative decisions that defy fans' desires therefore violate a contract based on the value their performances provide to the company.[51] And yet, when writers, performers, and fellow fans feel that certain cities' live event attendees, or certain contingents within the fan base, have themselves engaged in behaviors that fail to fulfill their obligations to WWE and fellow fans watching at home—a perceived responsibility for in-arena fans to perform in a way that heightens the performance for at-home viewers and rewards strong performances and generally welcomed creative decisions—they may also feel that a contract has been broken: perhaps, in this case, the code of the carnival in maintaining kayfabe and preserving the suspension of disbelief.

The unique nature of wrestling fans' role within the primary media texts of the storyworld makes this particular fandom exceptional. That's precisely why all of us interested in the ways fans engage with media texts, the conflicts between producers and their audiences, and the ways in which affinity communities actively debate and enforce shared values might want to look toward this carnivalesque exaggeration. Here, in these performances where "the volume is turned up," we see some of the core debates of the modern media era, negotiated and contended in the stands of the arena of every televised wrestling event.

Notes

1. Coleridge, "Chapter XIV."
2. Craven and Moseley, "Actors on a Canvas Stage," 327.
3. Chow, Warden, and Laine, "Introduction," 2.
4. McLaughlin, *Street Smarts and Critical Theory*.
5. For more on this, see Christian Norman's discussion of WWE audiences in this volume.
6. Toepfer, "Playful Audience."
7. Di Benedetto, "Playful Engagements," 31.
8. Ford, "Pinning Down Fan Involvement," 27.
9. Mazer, *Professional Wrestling*.
10. While it is beyond the scope of this essay, further scholarship looking at where and how the pleasures and tensions described throughout this piece compare to the highly knowledgable and performative traditional sports fan in the dynamics of in-arena performance could prove especially useful.
11. Ford, "Pinning Down Fan Involvement."
12. Amesley, "How to Watch *Star Trek*"; Ford, "'I Was Stabbed 21 Times by Crazy Fans,'" 40.
13. Toepfer, "Playful Audience," 88.
14. Writing about this obligation, Toepfer offers, "These fans are acutely aware of their responsibility as members of the audience when they are there live. They are aware that for those watching on television and on the internet, their level of excitement is crucial for the overall spectacle of the event." He notes, for instance, a fan who acknowledges "the need to cheer" the efforts of the wrestlers in the ring because "they were working so hard." Ibid., 96.
15. Ibid., 139.
16. Warden, "Pops and Promos," 23.
17. Ezell, "Dissipation of 'Heat,'" 11.
18. We can also read fan opportunities to interact with characters on social media, in auto-graph signings, and in other settings in a similar fashion. For more on this dynamic, see Ford, "WWE's Storyworld."
19. Ford, "'I Was Stabbed 21 Times by Crazy Fans,'" 42.
20. Braun and McMahon, "Pinning Down McMahon."
21. For more on this, see Jenkins and Jenkins IV, "'Same Old Shit': Fan Resistance at Wrestle-mania 29 (Part One)"; and Jenkins and Jenkins IV, "'Same Old Shit': Fan Resistance at Wrestle-mania 29 (Part Two)."
22. As Jon Ezell writes, "*Raw* audiences generally behave like audiences on past episodes. . . . There is a continuity informed by prior televisual experience and dictated by the current ecology of performance." Ezell, "Dissipation of 'Heat'," 14.
23. Ibid., 15.
24. Shoemaker, "WWE SummerSlam."
25. Ware, "Wrestling's Not Real," 49.

26. McBride and Bird, "From Smart Fan to Backyard Wrestler," 175.

27. Mazer, "'Real' Wrestling/'Real' Life," 79.

28. For more on this balance, see Ford, "Fan Studies."

29. See Ford, "Mick Foley." For more on WWE's treatment of its female Superstars, see Anna F. Peppard's essay elsewhere in this collection.

30. Laine, "Stadium-Sized Theatre," 41.

31. For more on wrestling fandom and negotiations on representations of masculinity, see Ford, "'He's a Real Man's Man.'"

32. Mazer, "Epilogue," 201.

33. Ibid., 204.

34. Ford, "'I Was Stabbed 21 Times by Crazy Fans,'" 42.

35. For more on these competing frames, see the section "Resistance versus Participation" in Jenkins, Ford, and Green, *Spreadable Media*, 162–66.

36. obsession_inc, "Affirmational Fandom vs. Transformative Fandom."

37. Ford, "Fan Studies," 62. One contrast to fan practice that is so transformational that it moves WWE outside its genre completely is slash fiction that imagines tag-team partners or rivals as lovers. For more on this, see Salmon and Clerc, "'Ladies Love Wrestling, Too.'"

38. *ClickHole*, "Wow: No One on 'WWE RAW.'"

39. Again, for more on this collective con, see Ford, "'I Was Stabbed 21 Times by Crazy Fans'."

40. Toepfer, "Playful Audience," 141.

41. Ibid., 137–38.

42. Ibid., 143–44.

43. See, for instance, Ferguson, "*SmackDown* Proves the WWE Universe Really Does Matter."

44. See, for instance, Toepfer, "Playful Audience," 96.

45. Martin, "Smart Crowds Are Often Complete Idiots."

46. Foley, "When Smart Fans Turn Dumb."

47. Morrow, "WWE SummerSlam."

48. Kazi, "WWE Fans Critical of Pittsburgh Crowd."

49. The moral economy is originally a concept from historian E. P. Thompson, who used it in relation to late-eighteenth-century English peasants' reasons for feeling justified in engaging in food riots. Thompson, "The Moral Economy of the English Crowd." Henry Jenkins was the first to apply the concept to media fandom and debates around media fans' feeling of perceived rights in return for the economic benefits media companies derive from their engagement. See Jenkins, "*Star Trek* Rerun."

50. Austin, "Implicit Contract."

51. For an overview of academic work on these concepts of fan ownership of texts, and on fan labor, see Ford, "Social Media Ownership."

BIBLIOGRAPHY

Amesley, Cassandra. "How to Watch *Star Trek*." *Cultural Studies* 3, no. 3 (October 1989): 323–39.

Austin, Alec. "The Implicit Contract." Online essay for *Spreadable Media: Creating Value and Meaning in a Networked Culture*, edited by Henry Jenkins, Sam Ford, and Joshua Green. New York: New York University Press, 2013. Accessed January 19, 2017. http://spreadablemedia.org/essays/austin/.

Braun, Georgette, and Vince McMahon. "Pinning Down McMahon." *Rockford Register Star*. October 18, 2004. Accessed January 19, 2017. Archived at http://www.hack-man.com/Wrestling/Interviews/20041016-vince.html.

Chow, Broderick Claire Warden, and Eero Laine. "Introduction: Hamlet Doesn't Blade: Professional Wrestling, Theatre, and Performance." In *Performance and Professional Wrestling*, edited by Broderick Chow, Claire Warden, and Eero Laine, 1–6. London: Routledge, 2017.

ClickHole. "Wow: No One on 'WWE RAW' Was Mad Enough to Fight Each Other Last Night, so They Just Sent All the Fans Home." January 6, 2015. Accessed January 19, 2017. http://www .clickhole.com/article/wow-no-one-wwe-raw-was-mad-enough-fight-each-other-1648.

Coleridge, Samuel Taylor. "Chapter XIV." *Biographia Literaria, or Biographical Sketches of My Literary Life and Opinions.* 1817.

Craven, Gerald, and Richard Moseley. "Actors on a Canvas Stage: The Dramatic Conventions of Professional Wrestling." *Journal of Popular Culture* 6 (1972): 326–36.

Di Benedetto, Stephen. "Playful Engagements: Wrestling with the Attendant Masses." In *Performance and Professional Wrestling,* edited by Broderick Chow, Claire Warden, and Eero Laine, 26–35. London: Routledge, 2017.

Ezell, Jon. "The Dissipation of 'Heat': Changing Role(s) of Audience in Professional Wrestling in the United States." In *Performance and Professional Wrestling,* edited by Broderick Chow, Claire Warden, and Eero Laine, 9–16. London: Routledge, 2017.

Ferguson, LaToya. "*SmackDown* Proves the WWE Universe Really Does Matter." *A.V. Club.* January 18, 2017. Accessed April 4, 2017. http://www.avclub.com/tvclub/smackdown -proves-wwe-universe-really-does-matter-248612.

Foley, Mick. "When Smart Fans Turn Dumb." Mick Foley's Facebook page, August 22, 2016. Accessed January 19, 2017. https://www.facebook.com/RealMickFoley/posts /1383639611666173.

Ford, Sam. "Fan Studies: Grappling with an 'Undisciplined' Discipline." *Journal of Fandom Studies* 2, no. 1 (2014): 53–71.

———. "'He's a Real Man's Man': Pro Wrestling and the Negotiations of Contemporary Masculinity." In *The Routledge Companion to Media Fandom,* edited by Melissa Click and Suzanne Scott, 174–83. London: Routledge, 2017.

———. "'I Was Stabbed 21 Times by Crazy Fans': Pro Wrestling and Popular Concerns with Immersive Story Worlds." In *Seeing Fans: Representations of Fandom in Media and Popular Culture,* edited by Lucy Bennett and Paul Booth, 33–44. New York: Bloomsbury, 2016.

———. "Mick Foley: Pro Wrestling and the Contradictions of the Contemporary American Hero." In *Bodies of Discourse: Sport Stars, Media and the Global Public,* edited by Cornel Sandvoss, Michael Real, and Alina Bernstein, 89–106. New York: Peter Lang, 2012.

———. "Pinning Down Fan Involvement: An Examination of Multiple Modes of Engagement for Professional Wrestling Fans." MIT OpenCourseWare, Spring 2007. Accessed January 19, 2017. https://ocw.mit.edu/courses/comparative-media-studies-writing/cms-997 -topics-in-comparative-media-american-pro-wrestling-spring-2007/readings/ford_role _playing.pdf.

———. "Social Media Ownership." In *International Encyclopedia of Digital Communication & Society* 1, edited by Peng Hwa Ang and Robin Mansell, 1–10. Chichester, UK: Wiley, 2015.

———. "WWE's Storyworld and the Immersive Potentials of Transmedia Storytelling." In *The Rise of Transtexts: Challenges and Opportunities,* edited by Benjamin W. L. Derhy Kurtz and Mélanie Bourdaa, 169–83. New York: Routledge, 2017.

Jenkins, Henry. "*Star Trek* Rerun, Reread, Rewritten: Fan Writing as Textual Poaching." *Critical Studies in Mass Communication* 5, no. 2 (1988): 85–107.

Jenkins, Henry, Sam Ford, and Joshua Green. *Spreadable Media: Creating Value and Meaning in a Networked Culture.* New York: New York University Press, 2013.

Jenkins, Henry, and Henry Jenkins IV. "'Same Old Shit': Fan Resistance at Wrestlemania 29 (Part One)." *Confessions of an Aca/Fan,* April 16, 2013. Accessed January 19, 2017. http:// henryjenkins.org/2013/04/same-old-shit-fan-resistance-at-wrestlemania-29-part-one.html.

———. "'Same Old Shit': Fan Resistance at Wrestlemania 29 (Part Two)." *Confessions of an Aca/ Fan,* April 19, 2013. Accessed January 19, 2017. http://henryjenkins.org/2013/04/same-old -shit-fan-resistance-at-wrestlemania-29-part-two.html.

Kazi, Raza. "WWE Fans Critical of Pittsburgh Crowd during Dolph Ziggler vs. Seth Rollins." *GiveMeSport*, July 16, 2018. Accessed May 9, 2019. https://www.givemesport.com/1354270 -wwe-fans-critical-of-pittsburgh-crowd-during-dolph-ziggler-vs-seth-rollins.

Laine, Eero. "Stadium-Sized Theatre: WWE and the World of Professional Wrestling." In *Performance and Professional Wrestling*, edited by Broderick Chow, Claire Warden, and Eero Laine, 39–47. London: Routledge, 2017.

Martin, Jason. "Smart Crowds Are Often Complete Idiots." *Cageside Seats*. August 22, 2016. Accessed January 19, 2017. http://www.cagesideseats.com/wwe/2016/8/22/12582290 /smart-crowds-are-often-complete-idiots.

Mazer, Sharon. "Epilogue: The Game of Life." In *Performance and Professional Wrestling*, edited by Broderick Chow, Claire Warden, and Eero Laine, 196–206. London: Routledge, 2017.

———. *Professional Wrestling: Sport and Spectacle*. Jackson, MS: University Press of Mississippi, 1998.

———. "'Real' Wrestling/'Real' Life." In *Steel Chair to the Head: The Pleasure and Pain of Professional Wrestling*, edited by Nicholas Sammond, 67–87. Durham, NC: Duke University Press, 2005.

McBride, Lawrence B., and S. Elizabeth Bird. "From Smart Fan to Backyard Wrestler: Performance, Context, and Aesthetic Violence." In *Fandom: Identities and Communities in a Mediated World*, edited by Cornell Sandvoss, C. Lee Harrington, and Jonathan Gray, 165–76. New York: New York University Press, 2007.

McLaughlin, Thomas. *Street Smarts and Critical Theory*. Madison, WI: University of Wisconsin Press, 1996.

Morrow, Brendan. "WWE SummerSlam: Seth Rollins Criticizes Brooklyn Crowd on Twitter." *Heavy*. August 22, 2016. Accessed January 19, 2017. http://heavy.com/sports/2016/08 /wwe-summerslam-seth-rollins-finn-balor-universal-championship-belt-design-crowd -reaction-brooklyn-negative-chants-twitter-response/.

obsession_inc. "Affirmational Fandom vs. Transformative Fandom." June 1, 2009. Accessed January 19, 2017. http://obsession-inc.dreamwidth.org/82589.html.

Salmon, Catherine, and Susan Clerc. "'Ladies Love Wrestling, Too': Female Wrestling Fans Online." In *Steel Chair to the Head: Essays on Professional Wrestling*, edited by Nicholas Sammond, 167–91. Durham, NC: Duke University Press, 2005.

Shoemaker, David. "WWE SummerSlam: A Theory of Trickle-Down Thuganomics." *Grantland*. August 22, 2012. Accessed January 19, 2017. http://grantland.com/features/the-ongoing -drama-cm-punk-john-cena-wwe-summerslam/.

Thompson, E. P. "The Moral Economy of the English Crowd in the Eighteenth Century." *Past and Present* 50 (1971): 76–136.

Toepfer, Shane. "The Playful Audience: Professional Wrestling, Media Fandom, and the Omnipresence of Media Smarks." PhD diss., Georgia State University, 2011.

Warden, Claire. "Pops and Promos: Speech and Silence in Professional Wrestling." In *Performance and Professional Wrestling*, edited by Broderick Chow, Claire Warden, and Eero Laine, 17–25. London: Routledge, 2017.

Ware, Nicholas. "Wrestling's Not Real, It's Hyperreal: Professional Wrestling Video Games." In *Performance and Professional Wrestling*, edited by Broderick Chow, Claire Warden, and Eero Laine, 48–56. London: Routledge, 2017.

SAM FORD is Director of Cultural Intelligence for Simon & Schuster, a CBS company. He is coauthor of *Spreadable Media*.

chapter seven

BOTCHAMANIA AND THE ACOUSTICS OF PROFESSIONAL WRESTLING

Christian B. Long

Professional wrestling on television is, like professional sports on television, a physical, visual spectacle.[1] And professional wrestlers, like other professional athletes, are in the main imposing, heavily muscled people who constitute a central feature of that spectacle. World Wrestling Entertainment (WWE) pays close attention to the setting of its spectacle, creating distinct sets for its television series—including *Raw*, *SmackDown Live*, and other special events—down to the colors of the ropes that encase the ring. Sound also features in this spectacle. Most main event–level professional wrestlers—those even nonfans might recognize—have a repeatable catchphrase (or several): "Hulkamania's runnin' wild, brother!"; "If you smell what The Rock is cooking!"; "And that's the bottom line, cuz Stone Cold said so!"; "You can't see me!"; "Yes! Yes! Yes!" What professional wrestlers say to each other and the audience during interview and promo segments on shows like *Raw* and *SmackDown* can simultaneously advance the performer's character, a feud with another wrestler, and the overall narrative. During matches, wrestlers cry out in pain or even improvise sayings like "Suplex City, bitch!"—as Brock Lesnar did at *WrestleMania 31*—that can advance the match's narrative and contribute to the show's fictional world. In addition to sounds coming from the wrestlers themselves, the sound of the live crowd also factors into the spectacle that is professional wrestling, perhaps most noticeably with the audible explosion of joy when a match finishes, which is comparable to when sports crowds cheer a home run, a touchdown, or a goal.

But sound matters in professional wrestling beyond the ways in which it resembles legitimate sport, beyond what wrestlers say to the audience, and beyond even how the live audience responds to the wrestlers' actions and speech. Fans watching at home pay close attention to the sounds of professional wrestling, including the sounds of wrestlers wrestling. It is precisely these sounds, among other gaffes from both inside and outside the wrestling ring, that have become the subject of critique in a popular series of online fan videos known as Botchamania. Produced by English wrestling fan Matthew Gregg (screen name "Maffew") beginning in 2007, Botchamania videos feature poorly executed wrestling maneuvers and other kinds of obvious in-ring mistakes, as well as moments when wrestlers audibly tell the other wrestler what to do next. This kind of speech, known in the industry as "calling spots," is not intended to be picked up by television microphones. As Sharon Mazer notes, "Beyond the spectacular elements, many of which are now common in many other sports as well, professional wrestling is an athletic performance practice that is constructed around the display of the male body and a tradition of *cooperative* rather than competitive exchanges of apparent power between men."[2] It is precisely this hidden truth of professional wrestling that audible called spots inadvertly reveal. The recurring "Everyone Talks Too Much" segments of Botchamania videos, which are dedicated to calling spots, can thus be read as a critical fan practice that demonstrates the importance of acoustics to professional wrestling. Revealing these hard-to-hear sounds and then reading the gestures and actions that follow opens up televised professional wrestling to a new sort of analysis based on an aesthetic theory that positions sound as essential to understanding this intensely physical undertaking. In this chapter, I argue that paying close attention to sound in televised professional wrestling can create a critical space in which the sounds of a match provide access to the true craft of wrestling; as a result, matches become narratively heterogeneous, simultaneously telling the intended fictional story—a fiction based on in-ring competition—and a truer documentary story based on the semi-improvisatory collaboration at the heart of professional wrestling practice.

In what follows, I will describe how the two broad categories of professional wrestling fans, marks and smarts, navigate the soundscape of televised professional wrestling. I will then relate Botchamania videos and their recurring segments to fan practices like vidding. Subsequently, I will analyze the critical sound practices in five exemplary "Everyone Talks Too Much" segments, demonstrating the extent to which careful and critical attention to sound in professional wrestling introduces productive ambiguities. Finally, I will conclude by linking the practices found in Botchamania videos to other televised events and the ways that those events are analyzed and understood by their fans.

I Hear Wrestling Is Fake: Sound and Televised Professional Wrestling

Dedicated wrestling fans, and "smart" fans in particular, are the intended audience for Botchamania videos. Such fans think of themselves as smart because of their increased awareness of the stories *behind* the stories that take place on the show, approaching "the genre of wrestling as would-be insiders."[3] While marks respond only to the transparent narrative dynamics of wrestling, smarts tend to read the matches intertextually: in conversation with previous matches, both on the card and in wrestlers' performance histories, and even as evidence of commercial, professional, and sometimes interpersonal dynamics. Additionally, the most heavily invested fans don't just attend live events and watch television but also create their own wrestling-related work. In one of the earliest academic engagements with professional wrestling and its fandom, Mazer argues that "professional wrestling fans are always in a process of becoming insiders. . . . They don't so much suspend disbelief as they sustain it while looking for moments in which to believe. They look to see the fake and to see through the fake to the real."[4] This complex process often takes the form of carefully rewatching matches and taking part in online wrestling communities that spread and cultivate insider knowledge (or some facsimile thereof). In online forums, smart fans rarely read matches literally as athletic contests; more often, they look for ways in which a match may suggest or reveal something true.

Henry Jenkins IV's contribution to *Steel Chair to the Head: The Pleasure and Pain of Professional Wrestling* explains this version of smart fandom. "When I watched *RAW*," he writes, "I'd find myself more captivated by the implied real-life dynamics . . . than by the televised feuds. I'd try to imagine the backroom deals and grow heated over the hirings and firings."[5] Such an approach to reading the show swaps the traditional good-against-bad morality plays (or shades-of-gray morality plays) for a kind of corporate allegory whereby what happens in the ring may represent a coded description of WWE's business practices and writing room meetings. However, Jenkins eventually left smartdom, arguing that "to some degree this so-called aesthetic revolt was all posturing, a way for a self-selected few to separate themselves from the crowd as the newsgroup's too-cool-for-the-mainstream elite. . . . But now I'd rather keep wrestling at more of a distance."[6] In other words, Jenkins gave up on being a smart for the comfort and pleasure of being a mark. Mazer anticipates the smart readings that Jenkins first loves and then leaves behind. She writes, "The more insistent fans become in their exposés of wrestling's fakery, the more they look to experience the real. As they expose the con artistry of the game, they revel in it and, on some level, seek to be conned."[7] However, whether he is indulging in or disavowing allegorical readings of matches, Jenkins—and the smart or mark approaches he oscillates between—treats wrestling as an ersatz version of a sporting event that stages morality plays. Such an approach, be it naive or too cool for the mainstream, privileges narrative and visual concerns. The ways in which sound functions in the improvised construction remains critically unengaged for the most part.

Professional wrestling is fake, at least insofar as the outcomes of matches are predetermined as part of a larger semiscripted, serialized narrative. When wrestling is considered in this way, botches come to represent the visible seams of the fiction, moments through which viewers can glimpse the underlying reality of performers collaborating in real time to create a narrative product. Seeing a visible botch is easy: a wrestler drops her opponent on her head; a wrestler jumps too far and lands not on his opponent but on the floor; the table doesn't break. But *hearing* a botch is harder; it demands a higher level of attention. For example, *Uproxx* contributor Brandon Stroud's *Monday Night Raw* review for July 27, 2015, makes two very specific complaints about *Raw*'s sound mixing. He first jokes about how even he, a nonexpert, notices that Sasha Banks's entrance music doesn't sound right: "Turn up Sasha Banks' entrance music, would you? In Raw arenas (and on TV) you can barely hear it. A lot of the NXT themes seem muted. I'm not a sound engineer or whatever so I don't know if they just recorded them at a lower volume so they wouldn't deafen people at Full Sail, but I do know how much I want that intro blaring, so do me a favor."[8]

Stroud's second complaint moves past entrance music and into the ring itself: "While you're at it, turn DOWN the ring mics. You can hear everything the wrestlers say, especially the louder ones like Cena and Paige. My only real problem with Sasha vs. Paige on Raw is that I could hear them working it out. I know Maffew needs an easy five minutes in the middle of Botchamania, but you guys are running HD Everything. Turn down the ring mic a little and get the camera out of their faces for a second. I could see Paige's tonsils."[9]

Both complaints speak to issues with the televised show's sound mix: a deficit of entrance music means that part of the show is missing, while a surfeit of audible sound from the ring—in the form of the wrestlers communicating with each other—is not supposed to be part of the show at all. As Stroud notes in his allusion to Maffew, the sound of wrestlers like Banks and Paige talking creates a sonic surplus that Botchamania videos turn to critical use. Sound theorist Michel Chion's consideration of the ambiguous nature of sound in televised tennis offers an effective way to understand how sound creates and explains ambiguity in televised professional wrestling. In narrative terms, professional wrestling resembles soap opera, but formally, the audiovisual aesthetics of wrestling more closely resemble televised sporting events than *Days of Our Lives*.[10] It may seem like a strange comparison, but much of the in-match portions of WWE shows like *Raw* formally resemble a tennis match, not only in terms of shot composition (static master shots featuring the entire ring or court are interspersed with traveling ringside or courtside close-ups) but also in terms of audio presentation. As Chion describes it in *Audio-Vision: Sound on Screen*, televised tennis is the "acoustic sport par excellence."[11] In Chion's description, "the sonic signature" of tennis includes "the thump with a dry echo, by which the ear can gauge the spatial limits of the court or arena. In addition to the racquet strokes we now hear a number of small, finely delineated sound events, very well reproduced on the televised soundtrack: subtle hisses and squeaks created by the opponents' legs and feet moving across the court; panting, breathing, and sometimes grunts or shouts when the players are fatigued and playing ever harder."[12] This combination of strikes, squeaks, and grunts creates "an entire acoustic narrative, but with the characteristic narrative ambiguity of the universe of sounds; we hear precisely what is happening, yet we don't *know* what is happening. There is not a different impact sound for each racquet or each player."[13]

The sound of racquets hitting the ball back and forth in a rally works together with the sounds of bodies playing tennis—running, slipping, grunting—and the sounds of the crowd in response to shots—oohs, aahs, and explosions of cheering—to create a fairly clear acoustic narrative. When a player wins a point, the audience cheers and the chair umpire updates the score. Leaving aside how easy it is to tell tennis players' grunts apart—players almost always have an idiosyncratic grunt style—the sonic signature of the televised event works in concert with the visual narrative to produce an unambiguous narrative. Professional wrestling has a similar sonic signature: the dry snare of the mat when a body hits it, the squeaks when a wrestler runs into the ropes, the wet slap of bodies colliding. A wrestling match usually features recognizable stages—opening, heel heat, babyface comeback, finish—each of which has its own recognizable sounds and typical audience reactions.

Sound works with images to reduce the ambiguity of professional wrestling matches in two ways: one verbal and one more abstract. Verbal clarification comes in the form of the announcers or commentators, who narrate the action for television viewers. The decorum particular to tennis—silence when a player is serving, for instance—means that, as Chion notes, "the commentators agree to curb their prattling so as to let us hear ten, twenty, sometimes thirty seconds of volleys without a peep out of them."[14] Professional wrestling very rarely observes such niceties. WWE commentators are particularly rigorous in their enforcement of the narrative and the clarification of its meaning, on the level not only of the match itself but of the larger show as a whole. The face-heel announce team WWE typically uses, whereby one announcer celebrates moral victories and decries injustices while the other sympathizes with the villains, provides explicit verbal clarification of both sides of the bout.[15] During the 1990s' "attitude era," for example, Jim Ross would frequently use phrases like "goofy as a pet coon" to describe a lovable babyface, while he would also indignantly yell "Stop the damn match!" or "That man's got a family!" to signal that the heel had crossed some moral line.[16] Thus, the moral didacticism of WWE announcers reflects and reinforces the narrative dynamics of the matches and allows the larger narrative to be advanced as unambiguously as possible.

In a more abstract sense, the incongruity between the distance of the sound and that of the image helps maintain the illusion of a competitive sporting event. Here, Chion's description of tennis again parallels professional wrestling. In televised tennis and WWE alike, "the *image* selected by the editing crew alternates distanced perspectives (high-angle views of the whole arena) with close views (faces or feet of the players, via telephoto lenses)."[17] However, for most televised sporting events, Chion notes, "This differential treatment, especially in moments when one of the players is grumbling or ranting and raving, produces a type of sound-image relation that is common to televised sports broadcasts yet completely unknown to cinema: faces of men or women in closeup, via telephoto lens, superimposed on their faraway and indistinct voices. In short, it gives us a symmetrical 'close-far' in contrast to the 'far-close' more characteristic in fiction films, where the long shot of a character can be accompanied by his or her voice heard up close."[18]

In short, televised wrestling sounds less like a soap opera and more like a sporting event. The "close-far" image-sound relationship in televised professional wrestling is by design, as the wrestlers need to communicate with each other during the match, planning out the next move or two as they work their way to the match's conclusion. On occasion, the match's narrative will be heightened by putting both sound and image in close-up, as when a wrestler in a submission hold screams in agony. But a close-close sound-image moment can also introduce narrative contradiction, especially when it reveals the wrestlers communicating with each other, revealing the collaboration at the heart of the ostensible competition.

In simple terms, Maffew's Botchamania compilations are blooper reels, collections of mistakes drawn from various professional wrestling events, edited into twelve- to fifteen-minute-long videos. The bloopers include botched moves, clips of wrestlers stumbling over their dialogue or breaking character onscreen, illogical or particularly ridiculous narrative events (which are all too common in professional wrestling), and excerpts of wrestlers audibly calling spots. As Stroud's reference to Maffew in the aforementioned *Raw* recap indicates, Botchamania occupies a significant position in wrestling fandom. Stroud is not alone in namechecking Maffew and Botchamania. At live events, especially independent federation events, fans have been known to chant "Botchamania" when wrestlers make mistakes in the ring; in WWE, Dolph Ziggler even referred to Botchamania during a promo segment on *Raw*.[19]

In their treatment of visible botches, Botchamania videos make it clear that a well-performed match is the desired outcome. As Maffew himself tweeted in June 2016, "If someone botches I don't get my cock out and start pumping myself."[20] Nevertheless, most Botchamania videos begin with the low-hanging fruit of botched moves, many of which reveal the artifice of professional wrestling for all to see. Marion Wrenn returns to the chiasmus of the fakeness of the real and the realness of the fake that Mazer articulates: "Pro wrestling is fake, *but that's blood, a metal chair, thumbtacks in this wrestler's arm flesh, a tooth up his nose.*"[21] Leon Hunt elaborates on the effect of such imagery, arguing that "when stunts go wrong . . . their impact is especially *visible* and *tactile*. . . . Thus danger and risk take on a heightened presence, and promise a dimension that cannot be fully controlled by the participants. While the camera can just as easily be in the 'wrong' place, making a pulled punch look more fake, reminding us that 'That's not real!', certain images of televised wrestling seem to take us to the heart of the 'real.'"[22] Hunt's analysis emphasizes the importance of visible botches above all else. He describes botches as "especially *visible*" and also indicates how the show's mediation can fail to maintain the illusion of a genuine physical conflict. For instance, Hunt notes that an ill-placed camera can reveal a punch that doesn't really connect, whereas a camera shooting from a different vantage point could frame the same pulled punch in a more satisfying way, better maintaining the illusion that it actually connected.

In a piece about Botchamania in *Paste Magazine*, Jim Vorel identifies how a visual botch that results in an injury simultaneously reveals fakeness and demonstrates the importance of fakeness to professional wrestling.

"Contrary to logic," he writes, "a botch that legitimately hurts one of the performers isn't likely to make the story appear more real—rather, it inflicts a sudden break in the flow and manufactured reality of the match. It kills the willing suspension of disbelief."[23] Like Hunt, Vorel emphasizes the ways in which visuals can pull viewers into—and sometimes accidentally pull viewers out of—the wrestling match's spectacle and narrative. John Fiske writes that professional wrestling offers its audience "an exaggeration of the pleasure of looking," with the spectacle's "emphasis on excessive materiality foreground[ing] the body, not as a signifier of something else, but in its *presence*."[24] Obviously, it's better that fakeness be exposed by a pulled punch that doesn't actually hit and hurt a wrestler than by a botched move that results in injury.

In their critique of wrestling, Botchamania videos tend not to revel in dangerous and violent injury-causing botches for their own sake, though these do appear. In addition to WWE footage, Botchamania videos also include backyard wrestling clips and ultraviolent federations like Combat Zone Wrestling (CZW) and death-match tournaments, using music to offer commentary on the visceral, violent nature of such footage. Botchamania might thus be productively considered within the traditional fan practice of vidding, "the creation of interpretive media works in the form of music videos in which members of mostly female fan communities have participated since the 1970s."[25] As Francesca Coppa describes the practice, fans "use music to interpret a visual source; in other words, the song tells the spectator how to understand the montage the vidder has constructed ... [having] edited the footage to draw out a pattern or to emphasize a particular trope in the source footage, and the song will narrate and contextualize the reedited sequence, telling a new story or making an argument."[26] In a representative example, Botchamania 241 features two botches with the potential for serious injury. In the first, a wrestler puts a metal garbage can over his own head before missing a top-rope moonsault, landing on an empty patch of the mat rather than on his opponent, as intended. In the second, a wrestler tries to execute a piledriver through a ladder set up between the ring apron and security railing but manages to miss the ladder; he falls directly to the floor, endangering himself and his opponent. In this case, as in many others, Maffew scores the footage with 8-bit video game music. The 8-bit video game music underscores the cartoonish nature of ultraviolent "garbage wrestling" and implicitly poses an argument about the lack of craft on display in botch-heavy matches, as though these wrestlers are, in a sense, mindlessly mashing buttons on an imaginary video game controller rather than carefully and deliberately executing moves.[27] While equating the wrestlers in very real physical peril

145

Botchamania and the Acoustics of Professional Wrestling

with pixelated video game sprites certainly has a cruel edge, it also signals a critical stance toward the fakeness of ultraviolent wrestling (and high-spot-obsessed indie wrestling as well).[28] Botchamania videos are less interested in flagrant physical botches—head drops, face plants, and injuries—and more invested in highlighting failures of wrestling craft, including elaborate or contrived moves that detract from the pleasure of more seamless presentation of the match. One of the seams that Botchamania videos pick at is mismatched sound.

Hearing Wrestlers Botch, or "Everyone Talks Too Much"

The ambiguity produced when image and sound conflict highlights the fakeness of wrestling just as forcefully as the ill-placed camera that reveals a pulled punch. When wrestlers strike each other, they either slap their thigh (for kicks) or stomp their foot on the mat (for punches) in order to generate a sonic accompaniment to the illusory impact. The disconnection between what the camera shows and what the microphones catch in such moments demonstrates the importance of sound to wrestling. The bias toward visuality in analyses of professional wrestling not only passes over wrestlers slapping their thigh to generate the sound of a kick connecting, to use Hunt's example, but also fails to register sound's importance in general. Authentic sound—for example, the sounds of bodies colliding and screams of (simulated) pain—is part of the match's narrative. But so too are the sounds that repeated viewings of professional wrestling train the audience to expect, including these foot stomps and thigh slaps. In addition, wrestler interviews or promos, commentators' calls, and the cheers, boos, chants, or even the silence of the live audience are all part of the "realistic" sonic world of sports entertainment.

But the sound of collaborative planning—calling spots—exists outside of the match's narrative: they are essentially nondiegetic sounds. Whereas nondiegetic sound (like a musical score) is deliberately used in cinema and television to deepen or control the viewer's relationship to the diegetic world, the nondiegetic sounds of spot calling in televised wrestling are unintentional, more akin to a continuity error or the appearance of a boom mic at the top of the frame. In the documentary *Fake It So Real* (2011), there is a scene where a wrestler tells the camera: "A lot of people say jazz is the great American art form, but jazz is dead. I think wrestling is the great American art form."[29] The comparison is apt: wrestling, like jazz, is a collaborative improvisational form of performance built in part around call-and-response. A jazz combo will often agree to the general outline of a number before playing it—two choruses, trade fours, bridge, chorus out—and then handle melodic handoffs between players with nods or gestures. Miles Davis never called his spots by saying, "Herbie, you keep playing that, and I'm going to solo for sixteen bars, and then Wayne will play a reprise of the main theme" onstage. Part of a great jazz band's mystique comes from their seemingly telepathic ability to read each other clearly enough to know when something must happen. Wrestling works in much the same way, which is why sound botches have a demystifying function, exposing the collaborative and improvisatory nature of professional wrestling. By emphasizing how wrestlers communicate with each other during matches, Botchamania takes narrative and visual analysis as givens and additionally demands careful attention to the acoustics of professional wrestling. In this way, Botchamania videos establish a fan-generated discourse based, essentially, on formalist critique, with the intention of revealing the collaborative nature of wrestling's staged competitions. In what follows, I will analyze Botchamania's treatment of wrestling sound, beginning with the soundtrack produced by the live audience before moving to called spots.

Botchamania 304, which concentrates on *WrestleMania 32*, reveals one of the most obvious ways that WWE programming attempts to control the show's narrative and reception through the strategic use of sound: by raising or lowering the level of crowd noise. The show's main event pitted Roman Reigns against Triple H for the WWE World Heavyweight Championship. From Reigns's first appearance, the crowd rejected his positioning by the company as a top babyface. In this segment, Maffew makes extensive use of didactic text in the form of subtitles, prompting viewers to listen to particular moments more closely. During Reigns's entrance, captions like "sound gets muted to try and lower booing" and "booooooooooooooooo" cue viewers to pay attention to WWE's attempt to censor the crowd's negative reaction to Reigns in real time by manipulating the televised audiovisual presentation. Later, Maffew identifies six separate chants from the rebellious audience—including the anti-Reigns "Roman sucks" as well as five individual chants referring to WWE's developmental brand NXT and its Superstars ("Nakamura," "Gable & Jordan," "Sami Zayn," "Bayley," and "NXT"). Using subtitles, Maffew identifies the chant and then notes changes made to the sound mix in response. Not only does the subtitle make the sound literally visible, but the word *MUTE* slides up over the chant subtitle to block it, visually reinforcing WWE's attempt to control the narrative. In this way, Botchamania videos make their critique unambiguous by making sound and image work together: sound becomes a *visible* component of the match, in this case making clear the extent to which the live audience rejected the narrative being told in the main event of the biggest show of the year.[30]

But wrestling crowds, as contrary as they can be, do not factor as much as the wrestlers themselves in Maffew's "Everyone Talks Too Much" segments. Some wrestlers, like Sabu and John Cena, appear more often than others. Sabu's hardcore style, which often involves high-risk maneuvers executed by jumping off chairs or the top rope, leads to frequent botches. But in addition to making visible botches, he sometimes calls his spots too loudly. Botchamania 59 shows a Sabu vs. Amish Roadkill match in which Sabu clearly instructs Roadkill to "roll over!" and "keep rolling!" The two requests better position Amish Roadkill to receive a chair shot to the back instead of the chest, which makes such a blow somewhat safer. Sabu is often described as "Suicidal, Homicidal, Genocidal, Death-Defying," and his frequent physical botches affirm the madness at the root of the character. But his spot calling does the reverse, dissolving a great deal of the character's mystique. The sound ends up telling a second story that contradicts the match's main narrative: Sabu may show total disregard for his own safety, but he shows a measure of concern for his opponent's safety.

In Botchamania 241's "Everyone Talks Too Much" segment, the Big Show doesn't just call spots but repeatedly tells his opponent, Ryback, to slow down during their match. While the Sabu-Roadkill match finds Sabu calling the next spot and even doing some in-ring housekeeping, the Big Show-Ryback clip reveals the extent to which Big Show is conscious of the *pacing* of the match, encouraging his opponent to let the crowd build anticipation for moves that require picking up a five-hundred-pound man. Mind you, the match still occurs spontaneously—Big Show calls the next spot, for Ryback to take a "big block, [and] go out" of the ring, improvising based on his and Ryback's abilities and signature moves, as well as playing off things that happened earlier in the match. But Big Show is eager to make Ryback slow down, to milk the crowd so that the next move will draw a stronger reaction. Big Show's audible spots reveal how much the "winner" of the match necessarily depends on his opponent to succeed. In talking "too much," Big Show shows the double logic behind what otherwise seems like a slow, plodding match. Certainly, there is a physical reason for the match's pacing: a seven-foot-tall man in his forties with a history of knee injuries will not be especially quick in the ring. But the hidden logic of the match's slow pace shows that the Big Show, the "loser" of the match, is primarily interested in creating the best sequence of events so that his opponent wins in a satisfying manner.

John Cena, currently the biggest star in WWE, shares Sabu's habit of clearly calling his spots as well as Big Show's awareness of pacing. His loud spot calling is so obvious and frequent that Maffew has a special subsection of "Everyone Talks Too Much" called "Cena Talks Too Much," complete with its own credit sequence. In Botchamania 241, the "Cena Talks Too Much" segment is devoted to a single Cena vs. Randy Orton match, highlighting four separate spots that Cena calls: "Do something"; "Powerslam?"; "Lose the ladder"; and "Amma get up, put you through the table." As in Sabu's case, Cena's audible spot calling changes his persona. In a match without audible spot calling, the narrative would simply be that Cena finds reserves of strength and makes a comeback by putting Orton through a table, affirming his "never give up" character. But in a match where Cena audibly tells Orton to "Do something" and "Powerslam?" him, the comeback of "Amma get up, put you through the table" makes it clear that Cena is in control at all times, that Orton's advantage was merely a bit of rising action meant to make Cena's ultimate triumph all the more satisfying.

"Everyone Talks Too Much" is a great leveler: Sabu, a lower-card wrestler; Big Show, an upper-midcard wrestler; and Cena, a perennial main eventer and "the face that runs the place," all screw up in the same hilarious way. Botchamania reveals the extent to which the acoustics of professional wrestling can undermine the fiction produced in the ring: the audience can become a character in the match; wrestlers can undercut their characters by calling spots too loudly; wrestlers can expose some of the key steps in the construction of a narratively satisfying match. With all that in mind, I want to bring in one final example that ties spots, pacing, and safety together while also adding one additional element: dark humor. At the 2013 pay-per-view event *Payback*, Daniel Bryan and Randy Orton lost a tag-team match, prompting Orton to exclaim, within the storyline, that the loss was Bryan's fault, calling him the "weak link." This set up a singles match between them, which Orton won when the match was stopped for a real injury (Bryan suffered a pinched nerve). Bryan won the second match, but only by count out, and his demand that the match be restarted was ignored. This outcome led to the third match in the series, which quickly devolved into an all-out brawl that ended in a double disqualification. Finally, a fourth match, under "Street Fight" rules, would finally determine if Bryan really was the "weak link." As a Street Fight, the match turned pretty violent by television (rather than pay-per-view) standards; however, three spot-calling moments, as picked out in Botchamania 234, transform the match from the culmination of a heated rivalry to a safety-conscious, well-timed bit of violent slapstick that nevertheless still works as a high-stakes culmination to this blood feud. In the first called spot, Bryan tells Orton to "set up a table," in response to the crowd chanting "We want tables!" Bryan calls for the table, not to exact revenge on Orton—after all, he's asking for a table that he himself will be put through—but rather to take advantage of the crowd's enthusiasm. Predictably, the crowd greets Orton setting up the table with a loud cheer of approval. While Bryan's spot calling is perhaps a little loud, he does show an awareness of the camera, which comes in close to make his suffering more visible; in turn, Maffew uses subtitles to compensate for Bryan's lowered volume, making the called spot legible despite Bryan's precaution.

Later in the match, Orton twice checks on Bryan after a high-impact, dangerous move, a gesture that reinforces the ethic of care toward one's opponent even in a violent, hardcore match such as this. In so doing, Orton inadvertently demonstrates the constraints placed upon wrestlers when the level of violence is escalated in this way. After a dangerous spot, it behooves wrestlers to check on each other before continuing with the assault. Maffew punctuates these two "You alright?" moments by letting the clips run past the called spot itself: after Orton asks Bryan if he's alright a second time, he immediately returns to pasting him with a kendo stick, to which Maffew adds onomatopoeic subtitles ("*twat*"). The audible "You alright?" that Maffew highlights turns a barrage of vicious strikes into a series of slapstick punch lines. Listening to wrestlers wrestling can thus add hidden layers of unintentional storytelling to the match. The hidden narrative of Orton and Bryan's collaborative communication runs concurrently to the intended narrative of the perennial underdog Daniel Bryan expressing his frustration and proving he has what it takes by taking and inflicting ultraviolence on the third-generation, multiple-time world champion Randy Orton. Bryan and Orton's spot calling and in-ring communication, sound that is made visible by Maffew's subtitles, reveals that what looks like an eruption of fierce violence can simultaneously be read as an expression of slapstick humor.

"Everyone Talks Too Much" segments call attention to how audible spot calling can take us out of the narrative in ways that real, if botched, violence does not. Hearing Sabu or Cena call move after move is like going to the theater and repeatedly hearing an offstage prompter feed the actors their lines: it makes the craft of performance as legible as the match itself. Smarts trained in this critical reading—or, more precisely, listening—practice watch the match *and* the creation of the match simultaneously: what appears to be one kind of narrative on its surface becomes something new upon closer inspection. To hear a wrestler call spots introduces an underground narrative of craft that is only accessible to smarts, that particular kind of viewer that can simultaneously view the fictional narrative with the behind-the-scenes reality that underlies it. Such viewers are interested not just in wrestlers' ability to perform moves but in their ability to perform them *safely*; not just in who wins or loses a match but in the collaborative effort that creates narrative meaning and effective in-ring storytelling. Botchamania videos show that wrestlers create the narrative of the match through the act of wrestling, illustrating that meaning is not predetermined backstage but is rather created in the ring through improvisation, communication, and collaboration.

CONCLUSION

Focusing on audibly called spots and their effects makes Botchamania videos especially interesting and critically significant forms of fan productivity. As Matt Hills argues, one problem with academic fan studies is that "specific fan identities and communities are over-represented, or rendered canonical in academic work, whilst other fandoms remain barely present in the literature."[31] "Although academics—especially those in cultural studies—often profess an interest in 'organic intellectuals', they seem remarkably happy to ignore the prime candidates for this role within fandom."[32] Granted, some professional wrestling fans can be a little bit unsavory and reactionary, but their relative absence from academic fan studies shows that the canon of television fans worth studying excludes "a massive range of media fandoms."[33] It may be that the model of critical attention that Botchamania videos present does not transfer well to the sorts of analyses common to aca-fan and fan-scholar approaches; or it may simply be that fictional narrative television is not particularly amenable to an intense focus on interperformer communication. But live televised sport—a form that professional wrestling emulates and, as John Fiske suggests, parodies—is filled with moments of on-field communication between athletes and tends to produce the highest-rated program of the year to boot.[34]

Televised coverage of the NFL has a long tradition of analyzing the physical performance of particular plays, and announcers and analysts discuss sound as well, if less frequently. In the 2014 and 2015 seasons, for instance, Denver Broncos quarterback Peyton Manning's tendency to shout "Omaha!" before the ball was snapped became a topic of extensive discussion and analysis. Was it a code to change the play called in the huddle? Was it an indication of when the ball should be snapped? Was it a meaningless word used to confuse the defense? Manning's on-field spot calling is an audible manifestation of coaching and video sessions; it should not be surprising that coaches tend to cover their mouths when they talk to players or assistants, making such communications inaccessible to television viewers. To prematurely reveal the mechanics of how the play will unfold changes the apparently spontaneous expression of the play into a practiced set of actions by the offense in response to equally well-practiced actions by the defense (and vice versa, repeatedly). Spot calling, covered coaches' mouths, and "Omaha!" audibly direct attention away from the drama of the event as it happens and toward the importance of sound as a marker of practice, preparation, and cooperation.

Soccer also offers an ever-increasing number of fan videos that offer tactical analysis of how and why things happen on the field. For instance, Istvàn Beregi's "The Borussia Dortmund Analysis" uses text and diagrams to explain counterpressing. However, the simple communication between players that occurs—Marco Reus raises his hand to call for the ball, Nuri Sahin points to the open player who ought to receive a pass—goes unnoted. In part, this lack of notice is because the acoustics of televised soccer exclude on-field sounds and, like most vids, tactical analysis videos typically add music (quite often high-tempo dance music, although Spanish guitar music appears frequently in FC Barcelona videos). In the video "Why Is Xavi Hernandez a Great Player? Analysis," Sam Madden analyzes Xavi's body positioning and vision, using a combination of freeze-frames and text to explain the nuances of his technique. In the widest shots of the field, it is clear that Xavi, even as he scans the field, communicates to his teammates that he is ready to receive the ball. The Spanish program *El Día Después* pays particularly close attention to interactions between teammates and opponents in football matches, using the "sound" revealed by lip-reading to enrich matches with an additional behind-the-scenes narrative based on players' conversations; in turn, these dialogues demonstrate professional collaboration, the intensity of rivalries, and even the absurdity of gamesmanship. As many of these tactical analysis videos claim to have some educational value—perhaps, in part, to justify their use of copyrighted video clips under fair use—a smart fan's eye for interperformer communication could add still another dimension to these videos.

Ultimately, however, Botchamania's "Everyone Talks Too Much" segments are ambivalent in terms of what fans desire from professional wrestling. Not wanting to hear wrestlers calling spots—after all, these wrestlers talk *too much* (i.e., more than fans would like them to)—suggests that smarts would prefer a seamless narrative performance in which sound and image work together. Smarts seek out botches, not because they reveal wrestlers' lack of skill, but precisely because they reveal the incredible level of skill and training required to put on a great match. "Everyone Talks Too Much" segments foreground the transformative meaning of called spots; in this way, the smart fan becomes an insider not only in terms of the wrestling industry but also in terms of wrestling aesthetics. Watching, rewatching, and above all *listening* carefully reveals the seams in the performance.

Any viewer can see a botched move turn into an accidental injury and interrupt the match's narrative, but smart fans stake their expertise on sound: they also know how to *hear* a match. By calling attention to audibly called spots, Botchamania reveals how this subset of professional wrestling fandom gauges the aesthetic value of professional wrestling differently.

Smart fans want their wrestling to be more seamlessly fake, while also recuperating the appearance of seams as an alternative form of pleasure that adds a second layer of meaning to the match. Fans who embrace Botchamania's approach operate in a critical register that, when faced with a called spot, actively disavows involvement in the diegesis. This attention to craft is one way to assert their insider bona fides by demonstrating an awareness of how wrestlers collaborate to create a match. In addition to being smart to the business, smarts like Maffew also demonstrate an appreciation of the aesthetic and narrative experience of televised professional wrestling as both multivalent and rich. Hearing called spots is less about the business and more about the craft of wrestling—and this distinction makes Botchamania more about the wrestlers in the midst of artistic creation than about the machinations of the macronarrative scripted by WWE. The critical practice on display in "Everyone Talks Too Much" segments is arguably analogous to what Bertolt Brecht sought to create in epic theater, making Botchamania an almost Brechtian form of wrestling fandom and criticism. For Brecht, "the human being is taken for granted" in dramatic theater but is made "the object of inquiry" in epic theater.[35] To apply this schematic binary to the theatrical spectacle that is professional wrestling, dramatic theater asks its audience to keep its eyes on the finish while epic theater asks its audience to keep its eyes on the course of the match; dramatic theater is for marks, while epic theater is for smarts. The desire to unpack the collaborative construction of a match, in all its imperfect glory, exhibits what Brecht sees as the essential point of epic theater: "that it appeals less to the feelings than to the spectator's reason. Instead of sharing an experience the spectator must come to grips with things."[36] When applied to the creation, collaboration, and improvisation of wrestling as a craft, the distinction between these two modes of theatricality transforms audibly called spots from simple botches into moments that force the viewer to come to grips with the multiplicity inherent in the act of wrestling, allowing viewers to see two contradictory stories at once.

NOTES

1. In *Mythologies*, Roland Barthes writes, "Wrestling is not a sport, it is a spectacle," referring not to televised wrestling but rather to live wrestling in places like "the most squalid Parisian halls" (15).

Botchamania and the Acoustics of Professional Wrestling

2. Mazer, *Professional Wrestling*, 4 (emphasis added).

3. McBride and Bird, "From Smart Fan to Backyard Wrestler," 169.

4. Mazer, *Professional Wrestling*, 6.

5. Jenkins IV, "Afterword" 332.

6. Ibid., 336, 338.

7. Mazer, *Professional Wrestling*, 167.

8. Stroud, "Best and Worst of WWE Raw 7/27/15."

9. Ibid.

10. See Jenkins, "'Never Trust a Snake.'"

11. Chion, *Audio-Vision*, 159.

12. Ibid., 159–60.

13. Ibid., 160.

14. Ibid., 159.

15. Gorilla Monsoon and Bobby "the Brain" Heenan in the 1980s, Jim Ross and Jerry "the King" Lawler in the 1990s, and Michael Cole and JBL in the 2010s all fit this description. The three-person announce team now used on *Raw* and *SmackDown Live* follow a similar format, with one person functioning as a dedicated play-by-play announcer and the other two aligning with the babyface and heel, respectively.

16. WWE's global expansion has demonstrated how commentators for different markets read the same actions in divergent ways depending on the imagined audience. For instance, while the US commentary team treats Jinder Mahal as a heel, their Indian counterparts reacted to his unexpected WWE Championship win with unbridled babyface enthusiasm. See Hanstock, "Listen to the Indian Announcer's Team Call Jinder Mahal's Championship Win."

17. Chion, *Audio-Vision*, 160.

18. Ibid., 160–61

19. On the March 21, 2016, episode of *Raw*, Ziggler responded to Kevin Owens's description of the upcoming *WrestleMania* as KOMania by saying: "*WrestleMania*, KOMania, Beatlemania, Botchamania, Axlemania—whatever the hell you want to call it, KO" as he walked down the ramp to the ring.

20. MaffewBotchamaniaGuy, May 31, 2016 (10:50 a.m.), tweet, "Sorry to break it to you but I go to wrestling shows to have fun. If someone botches I don't get my cock out and start pumping myself," https://twitter.com/Maffewgregg/status/737672577938825216.

21. Wrenn, "Managing Doubt," 161.

22. Hunt, "Hell in a Cell and Other Stories," 119–20.

23. Vorel, "Botchamania."

24. Fiske, *Television Culture*, 243 (emphasis in original).

25. Busse and Lothian, "Scholarly Critiques and Critiques of Scholarship," 139. In their introduction to *Fan Culture: Theory/Practice*, Katherine Larsen and Lynn Zubernis note that vidding has been coded as stereotypically feminine (10), which makes Botchamania's focus on the hyperbolically masculine world of professional wrestling stand out.

26. Coppa, "Editing Room of One's Own," 123–24.

27. "Garbage wrestling" is a type of hardcore wrestling that features very few holds and throws, instead favoring brawling, extensive use of foreign objects (such as kendo sticks and fluorescent light tubes), and dangerous spots involving those weapons.

28. A high spot is a particularly dangerous (or dangerous-looking) move, often featuring one or both of the wrestlers jumping, flipping, or falling from the top rope.

29. Brody, "What to See This Weekend."

30. For a more detailed analysis of fan performativity and hostility in WWE arenas, see Sam Ford's chapter in this volume.

31. Hills, "'Proper Distance,'" 20.

32. Hills, *Fan Cultures*, 21.

33. Hills, "'Proper Distance,'" 20.

34. Fiske, *Television Culture*, 245.
35. Brecht, *Brecht on Theatre*, 37.
36. Ibid., 23.

BIBLIOGRAPHY

Barthes, Roland. *Mythologies*. Translated by Annette Lavers. St Albans: Paladin, 1973.
Beregi, Istvàn. "The Borussia Dortmund Analysis." YouTube video, 7:13. Posted November 3, 2013. https://youtu.be/iuMvLWU7SkM.
"Botchamania 59." Dailymotion video, 9:37. Posted October 11, 2014. https://www.dailymotion .com/video/x9q7tp.
"Botchamania 195." Dailymotion video, 15:03. Posted October 13, 2014. https://www.dailymotion .com/video/xn8iv6.
"Botchamania 234." Dailymotion video, 14:21. Posted July 12, 2013. http://www.dailymotion.com /video/x11toxh_botchamania-234_sport.
"Botchamania 241." Dailymotion video, 13:24. Posted October 14, 2014. http://botchamania .com/2013/12/17/botchamania241/.
Brecht, Bertolt. *Brecht on Theatre: The Development of an Aesthetic*. Translated and edited by John Willett. London: Methuen Drama, 1964.
Brody, Richard. "What to See This Weekend: 'Fake It So Real.'" *New Yorker*. June 1, 2012. http:// www.newyorker.com/culture/richard-brody/what-to-see-this-weekend-fake-it-so-real.
Busse, Kristina, and Alexis Lothian. "Scholarly Critiques and Critiques of Scholarship: The Uses of Remix Video." *Camera Obscura* 26, no. 2 (2001): 139–46.
Chion, Michel. *Audio-Vision: Sound on Screen*. Translated and edited by Claudia Gorbman. New York: Columbia University Press, 1994.
Coppa, Francesca. "An Editing Room of One's Own: Vidding as Women's Work." *Camera Obscura* 26, no. 2 (2011): 123–30.
Fiske, John. *Television Culture*. London: Methuen, 1987.
Hanstock, Bill. "Listen to the Indian Announcer's Team Call Jinder Mahal's Championship Win." *Uproxx*. May 22, 2017. Accessed July 24, 2018. https://uproxx.com/prowrestling/jinder -mahal-wwe-title-win-backlash-indian-commentary/.
Hills, Matt. *Fan Cultures*. London: Routledge, 2002.
———. "'Proper Distance' in the Ethical Positioning of Scholar-Fandoms: Between Academics' and Fans' Moral Economies?" In *Fan Culture: Theory/Practice*, edited by Katherine Larsen and Lynn Zubernis, 14–37. Newcastle upon Tyne: Cambridge Scholars, 2012.
Hunt, Leon. "Hell in a Cell and Other Stories: Violence, Endangerment and Authenticity in Professional Wrestling." In *The Spectacle of the Real: From Hollywood to Reality TV and Beyond*, edited by Geoff King, 117–28. Bristol and Portland: Intellect, 2005.
Jenkins, Henry. "'Never Trust a Snake': WWF Wrestling as Masculine Melodrama." In *Steel Chair to the Head: The Pleasure and Pain of Professional Wrestling*, edited by Nicholas Sammond, 33–66. Durham, NC: Duke University Press, 2005.
———. "Rethinking 'Rethinking Convergence/Culture.'" *Cultural Studies* 28, no. 2 (2014): 267–97.
Jenkins, Henry IV. "Afterword, Part II: Growing Up and Growing More Risqué." In *Steel Chair to the Head: The Pleasure and Pain of Professional Wrestling*, edited by Nicholas Sammond, 317–42. Durham, NC: Duke University Press, 2005.
Larsen, Katherine, and Lynn Zubernis. "Introduction." In *Fan Culture: Theory/Practice*, edited by Katherine Larsen and Lynn Zubernis, 1–13. Newcastle upon Tyne: Cambridge Scholars, 2012.
Mazer, Sharon. *Professional Wrestling: Sport and Spectacle*. Jackson, MS: University Press of Mississippi, 1998.

McBride, Lawrence B., and S. Elizabeth Bird. "From Smart Fan to Backyard Wrestler: Perform-ance, Context, and Aesthetic Violence." In *Fandom: Identities and Communities in a Mediated World*, edited by Jonathan Gray, Cornel Sandvoss, and C. Lee Harrington, 165–76. New York: New York University Press, 2007.

Stroud, Brandon. "The Best and Worst of WWE Raw 7/27/15." *Uproxx*. July 28, 2015. Accessed January 17, 2017. http://uproxx.com/prowrestling/2015/07/the-best-and-worst-of-wwe-raw-72715-take-the-fish/3/.

Vorel, Jim. "Botchamania: The Essence of Failure in Pro Wrestling." *Paste Monthly*. December 2015. http://www.pastemagazine.com/articles/2015/12/botchamania-the-essence-of-failure-in-pro-wrestlin.html.

"Why Is Xavi Hernandez a Great Player? Analysis." YouTube video, 9:01. Posted May 21, 2014. https://youtu.be/NkPXGcWg9wM.

Wrenn, Marion. "Managing Doubt: Professional Wrestling Jargon and the Making of 'Smart Fans.'" In *Practicing Culture*, edited by Craig Calhoun and Richard Sennett, 149–70. London: Routledge, 2007.

CHRISTIAN B. LONG is Honorary Research Fellow in the Graduate School at the University of Queensland. He is author of *The Imaginary Geography of Hollywood Cinema, 1960–2000*.

PART III

THEN, NOW, FOREVER: WRESTLING WITH WWE'S PAST AND TRANSMEDIA FUTURE

chapter eight

"TOUT IT OUT": WWE'S EXPERIMENTATION AND FAILURE WITH SOCIAL TV

Cory Barker

On August 20, 2012, Brock Lesnar quit WWE. Known as "the Next Big Thing" after becoming the youngest WWE champion in the company's history in 2002, Lesnar already had experience walking away from Vince McMahon's sports entertainment company. In 2004, the former NCAA wrestling champion hastily departed WWE to try his luck in the National Football League (NFL); after being cut from the Minnesota Vikings, he switched to a legitimate combat sport, mixed martial arts, and eventually became a champion of the Ultimate Fighting Championship (UFC) in 2008. But unlike Lesnar's first exit—which ended in the ring at *WrestleMania XX*—his 2012 good-bye transpired in a poorly lit backroom of a sports arena. The latter departure was also not shot by WWE's world-class production team; instead, Lesnar stood in front of a shaky camera zoomed in on his face and dryly stated: "I came here and I accomplished everything that I said I was going to do. There's nothing left for me here to conquer. I'm leaving the WWE and I'm never coming back."[1] The fourteen-second video was not first seen on pay-per-view (PPV) or television but rather on the online microvideo service Tout. Most surreal of all, Lesnar's announcement—unlike the 2004 *WrestleMania* moment—was entirely scripted. To make a scripted story beat seem less artificial and reach its savvy audience online, WWE relied on amateur video aesthetics and let social media do the heavy lifting.

WWE's plan initially worked, but not unequivocally. Thousands of viewers watched the clip on the nascent Tout, and many professional wrestling, UFC, and sports publications carried the news the next morning. Yet most people who saw the clip experienced it not on Tout but rather via WWE's flagship program, *Monday Night Raw*, or on YouTube, where it was uploaded by fans uninterested in indulging WWE's choice of video platform. By the time Lesnar announced his "retirement," WWE had spent the preceding summer promoting Tout ad nauseam, encouraging members of the WWE Universe to "Tout it out" (or share) during episodes of *Raw, SmackDown,* or PPV events to get their fifteen seconds of WWE-sponsored fame. As much as WWE promoted Tout during its programming, McMahon's company was even more invested from a financial perspective: WWE was one of the key financiers of Tout's $13.4 million Series B seed round in June 2012.[2] Recognizing the short-form video revolution on the horizon, WWE viewed their collaboration with Tout as a way to be part of the next social trend—an early adoption that contrasted with its delayed embrace of Twitter a few years prior.

WWE's Tout experiment lasted about as long as Lesnar's absence from the company. After entering into a two-year strategic partnership in 2012, WWE ceased promotion of Tout by early 2013, using it as a digital dumping ground for content more vigorously promoted on Twitter, Facebook, and Instagram; the partnership formally ended in 2014.[3] WWE's attempts to legitimize Tout—among both its talent and its fans—failed compared to similar platforms backed by more powerful companies like Vine and Instagram. However, while WWE could not be blamed for betting on the wrong start-up—in fact, it was proactively prescient regarding the potential of short-form video—its integration of Tout into its programming left much to be desired and effectively turned fans against the platform.

The failure of Tout is a particularly relevant case study for understanding WWE's role within the media industries. Though often disregarded as a producer of low culture, WWE has been at the forefront of evolutions in distribution, production, and audience engagement. Its relationship with the internet, however, has been far more complicated. This chapter concentrates on the period leading up to Tout's arrival in WWE, an era of major turmoil wherein the already blurry lines between fiction and reality began to blur even further thanks to social media and an increasingly knowledgeable fandom. I assert that, for WWE, the swift embrace of Tout served a variety of purposes: to standardize (and restrict) certain in-character practices for talent on social media; to formalize (and determine the boundaries of) a meta-storyworld beyond the confines of its weekly programming; and to discipline fans into performing approved (and pseudoscripted) behaviors under the guise of engagement. In analyzing WWE's multiplatform content, fan response, and media coverage thereof, this chapter shows how Tout's failed integration into WWE programming was a matter of execution, not concept.

WWE and the Internet

While WWE has consistently been at the vanguard of broadcasting and distribution, it has struggled to apply this innovative spirit to the internet,

in part out of fear of the web's potentially disruptive effect on their preferred storyline practices. Positioned between scripted and unscripted,
real and unreal, professional wrestling is notoriously inexplicable to nonfans. On television and at live events, performers play characters within
constructed scenarios where match outcomes are predetermined. WWE
storytelling thus functions on multiple levels: (1) the microstory of the
match in the ring; (2) the macrostory providing context to the match, typically an ongoing feud over grudges and championship opportunities; and
(3) the meta-story trying to work fans who believe they know what is and
is not scripted. Within the confines of a television series or a live event,
WWE controls all three levels of the story. On the internet, however,
where trade journalists, rumormongers, and fans share behind-the-scenes
tidbits and production leaks, WWE cedes some of that control. The web
fosters a fandom that is desperate to learn more about WWE, its backstage
politics, and the real lives of performers.

With some exceptions, WWE's engagement with the internet throughout the 1990s and 2000s merely extended kayfabe onto a different platform: events happening in and out of the ring were treated as real, unless
a performer died or got hurt, arrested, or fired. Still, WWE recognized the
value of *appearing* to allow online fans to have a voice. One of the tenets of
wrestling discourse is that fans get to have a say every night in the arena,
cheering what (and whom) they like and booing what (and whom) they
hate. In the early 2000s, WWE translated this empty axiom to the web by
encouraging fans to vote in online polls with results that would appear on
television. Writing about television and the internet, Sharon Marie Ross
argues, "Tele-participation has become an increasingly crucial element
in industrial strategies to capture the ever-splintering audience, as well as
a crucial element in viewers' expectations for television."[4] Calls for tele-
participation are also crucial to managing viewers' expectations; WWE
recognized that offering any form of participation—what Derek Johnson
refers to as "inviting audiences in"—builds goodwill.[5] Yet voting in an
internet poll is not an especially meaningful form of participation—which
is precisely why companies frame it as something more.

Nonetheless, WWE occasionally recognized the value of the internet.
In the mid-2000s, WWE enabled fans to determine what matches would
appear on the card. Initially known as *Taboo Tuesday* and later *Cyber
Sunday*, these PPV events featured the most explicit instance of fan influence on WWE programming. Though WWE stacked the options so that
fans were more likely to select results that benefited ongoing stories, by
all indications the voting was indeed legitimate.[6] By turning its programming into an *American Idol*–style project, WWE worked to "emphasize

its authenticity via its overt invitation to tele-participation—there are no 'tricks' or 'men behind the curtains' here."[7] The appearance of authenticity is doubly important for WWE, a company that trades in convincing people that scripted circumstances are, in fact, genuine. Unsurprisingly then, the company used much of its web-only content to purposefully blur the line between scripted and unscripted content throughout the early 2000s. The most notable example is *Byte This*, a live internet talk show where performers, partially in character, would take calls from fans and their peers, complete with the unpredictability of the call-in format. Crucially, WWE promoted *Byte This* as "real" so that it could later confuse even the most attentive fans when it began to integrate scripted elements into the show.

These examples demonstrate the negotiations fans encounter when responding to calls for engagement. As Mark Andrejevic argues, "the invitation to viewers is not to seize control but rather to participate in the rationalization of their own viewing experience."[8] For WWE fans, participation in online polls or self-reflexive programs provides access to a company that prides itself on disrupting the audience's grasp of the scripted and unscripted. Yet, as *Byte This* displays, WWE's awareness of fan interest in the realities of its production processes and talent allows it to leverage those "real" elements in its stories to foster even deeper investment in its product. Amid the distorted boundaries of kayfabe, WWE's treatment of the internet—and its fans on the internet—is similar to that of others working within the media industries. The knowledge community within wrestling's online fandom seeks to uncover secrets, spoil storylines, and rationalize character turns. They are, like any fandom, diverse in their perspective but capable of relying on "collective intelligence," or shared knowledge within a group that can be translated into action.[9] In response, WWE operates from a prohibitionist position, not preventing fan conversation but regularly ignoring those fans or working them into the narrative in ways that serve its vision.[10]

WWE's apprehension toward the web continued into the social media era. It did not avoid YouTube, Facebook, and Twitter but generally sought to keep content and fan engagement aligned with the television product. While official social channels disseminated PR-approved brand messaging, certain performers used social media independently to raise their own profiles. In early 2011, Zack Ryder, a performer rarely used on television, self-produced a YouTube series that regularly mocked his status within WWE and, occasionally, the rigidity of the company. Titled *Z! True Long Island Story*—a riff on the Long Island bro character portrayed by Ryder (and based on his real life) and *E! True Hollywood Story*—the web series grew in popularity online, leading Ryder to proclaim himself the "internet champion" and prompting fans to flood live shows with pro-Ryder signs.

By late 2011, grassroots support for Ryder became too loud for WWE to ignore. WWE placed him in significant onscreen stories, allowed him to reference his emergent internet popularity, and awarded him with a secondary championship. Unfortunately for Ryder—and for fans hoping to see WWE validate their online activity—his title run was short-lived, and he was regularly embarrassed as part of a regressive love triangle featuring WWE's top star John Cena and female performer Eve Torres. Speculation online suggested that WWE punished Ryder for working outside the company's normal practices to improve his standing, a theory later substantiated by fellow performers.[11] Yet, soon after the Ryder episode, WWE began utilizing YouTube less as an archive and more as a platform for original, fourth-wall-breaking content. Most notable in this regard is *The JBL and Cole Show*, a comedic behind-the-scenes look at WWE that regularly featured performers shifting in and out of character and poking fun at professional wrestling conventions.

WWE's storytelling began to change in 2011 as well. Instead of sporadically referring to the real lives of performers, WWE started to use those elements to reach the increasingly disappointed and vocal internet fans. Performers like CM Punk, an outspoken internet darling, received mainstream attention with a June 2011 promo wherein he lambasted WWE for the very things fans had been complaining about for years: stale storytelling, McMahon's stubbornness, the hypocrisy of WWE-branded antibullying campaigns, and more.[12] Punk's screed quickly morphed into a tumultuous storyline that addressed WWE's failure to adapt to the internet, as the self-appointed "Voice of the Voiceless" attacked Cena and later Triple H, who married McMahon's daughter Stephanie offscreen and thereby established himself as part of WWE's corporate hegemony. Though the angle ultimately fizzled out because of WWE's hesitation regarding how far to push the envelope, it catalyzed a more self-aware and self-reflexive moment for the company.[13] It was in this context that WWE reevaluated the worth of social media and turned to Tout to supposedly give fans what they wanted.

Reclaiming Flow and Liveness in TV's Social Era

WWE's dalliance with Tout came at the right time. Television experienced its social moment in 2010 and 2011, with networks becoming infatuated with the potential power of second screens (smartphones, tablets, and laptops) to draw viewers to the primary screen (the television). During this period, live-tweeting became a normalized industry practice, with actors and showrunners participating in the online chatter to drive interest in their projects. For the television industry, the turn toward social TV reaffirmed the power of televisual flow and liveness. Theorized by Raymond Williams, flow is the organization of television as a sequence of linked programs, advertisements, and interstitials.[14] It is both an experiential phenomenon unique to television and something planned by networks and advertisers.[15] However, the modern media ecosystem—with DVRs, streaming platforms, and social media—has destabilized our experience and providers' planning of flow. In response, companies have pushed live-tweeting and digital coviewing with stars as a way to create and control a new kind of flow—one that directs viewers from screen to screen with ancillary material and branded content.

The popularization of social media has also enabled the industry to reassert the power of liveness. Like flow, liveness is central to the viewing experience but also is managed by the industry as a programming strategy. On this subject, Jane Feuer writes, "Television's self-referential discourse plays upon the connotative richness of the term 'live,' confounding its simple or technical denotations with a wealth of allusiveness." Networks "exploit" liveness to produce a "sense of immediacy" that accentuates flow and combats the challenges of fragmentation.[16] Referred to as "pseudo-liveness" by William Uricchio, this liveness is fabricated through live chyrons in the corner of the screen or by direct address, emphasizing what is happening *right now*.[17] As Nick Couldry suggests, a sense of liveness "guarantees a potential connection to shared social realities as they are happening."[18]

Amid a sea of options and technological advancements, the media industries view social media as a way to reclaim liveness. Corporations know that viewers have no need to watch live, but hope that the allure of chatter with friends, strangers, and the cast of their favorite series will convince them to tune in. The onscreen notifications of liveness or instances of direct address now also funnel viewers toward social media through the use of hashtag chyrons and tickers highlighting posts at the bottom of the screen. Viewers are encouraged to "join the conversation" using a corporate-approved hashtag—not to further a real conversation but rather for the show to gain free publicity by trending on Twitter.

The social TV phenomenon has also helped corporations expand calls for viewer engagement. For Ross, calls for tele-participation often appear within the diegesis of programs and prompt fans to interact on the web "beyond the moment of viewing."[19] Invitations also take the form of promotional "paratexts," or the supplemental content surrounding the primary text that shapes consumer interpretation.[20] These invitations are particularly prevalent in situations where companies need something from fans—be it free labor in contests or investment in projects on Kickstarter. Whether text or paratext, promotional campaign or platform, this kind of "affective, engagement-seeking commitment" has, as Robert V. Kozinets argues, "become a desirable, if not mandatory, goal of effective marketing practice."[21] Nonetheless, despite discourses about how the internet gives consumers more power and more choice, social TV activity—including Facebook posts, tweets, GIFs, and short videos—adds up to a banal flow of content. Much of this casual activity occurs instantaneously, in response to the events on the primary screen.[22] Yet corporations attempt to find every way imaginable, on every platform imaginable, to tell consumers that their engagement is a valuable part of the media experience. The allure of real-time engagement between fans and stars is thus an "empty signifier" used to suggest a level of influence that is not present.[23]

Liveness, flow, and audience participation are core components of the contemporary WWE experience. Though a touring live show, WWE's primary mode of reaching consumers is through television. *Raw* and *Smack-Down Live* serve as the platforms for WWE's official stories, generating enough interest to inspire fans to pay for a ticket to a WWE show whenever it rolls into town, but they also function as revenue-generating programs for USA Network; as such, WWE faces the same obstacles as *Scandal* or *NCIS* insofar as it is beholden to Nielsen ratings and advertising dollars, and therefore seeks the most live viewers possible. While WWE eventually embraced Twitter to facilitate live conversation among active members of its fandom, the company saw Tout as a better way to export the in-arena experience to the home viewer.

"Join Us": WWE's Promotion of Tout

Within a week of its July 2012 investment, WWE began integrating promotions for and content from Tout into its weekly product. The press release announcing the move signaled how WWE intended to deploy Tout to create a more interactive experience: "WWE fans will have the chance to be seen and heard via Tout. . . . WWE Superstars will also interact with fans via Tout question and answer sessions leading up to the event." McMahon affirmed the value for fans, saying, "Tout's real-time video technology will become a critical component of fan interactivity in our weekly television programming and will be utilized to connect WWE directly with our fans in new ways."[24] Delivered in press release verbiage, these statements represent textbook engagement-baiting discourses. As Johnson argues, "Audiences are not just cultivated as fans, but also invited in, asked to participate in both the world of the television text and the process of its production."[25]

The invitation is explicit: fans are directly hailed, their touts are prelabeled as critical, and the experience is positioned as beneficial to WWE programming.

WWE also produced a video to explain Tout for the July 16, 2012, episode of *Raw*.[26] Featuring key performers of the era—including Cena, Punk, and Ryder—and praising a "new way to connect with WWE Superstars," the clip clearly articulates the significance of fan touts to the WWE experience. Cena describes Tout's functionality, remarking that it "allows you to tout directly to everyone—*including us*." As the video cuts between shots of the live audience and talent, presented through the frame of an iPhone, Daniel Bryan exclaims that Tout is "your ticket to be on *Raw*." Dolph Ziggler asserts, "Every Monday night on *Raw*, we may even air [fan touts] to the WWE Universe and the world." The video ends with a clear call to action: "Join us." The promotional aims are clear; Tout will make the WWE more interactive—and much better.

WWE's rollout of Tout reliably underlined the need for fan voices, even as it used the platform to further scripted storylines. In the lead-up to the thousandth episode of *Raw*, WWE led a promotional blitz for Tout across its various digital channels. WWE.com provided new Tout content daily, with Cena urging fans to "join the conversation." An archive of Cena's touts reveals that the face of WWE easily maneuvered in and out of storyline with his video content. His very first tout—posted the same day WWE announced its investment—is an archetypal example of solicitation for consumer participation. Standing backstage among production equipment and looking directly into the camera, Cena unveils his favorite moment in *Raw* history before exclaiming to viewers, "I want to know *your* favorite *Raw* moment! Reply to this or tout yourself. Let me know; I'm dying to find out!"[27] After a few posts displaying his powerlifting expertise, Cena shifts into character to tease an upcoming segment on *Raw*: "I have a huge announcement tonight on *Raw*. . . . You gotta see it!"[28] Here Cena fills three roles: (1) a brand ambassador convincing fans to use Tout; (2) a character advancing a story that would later unfold on television; and (3) a spokesperson for *Raw* and the USA Network (referenced in the accompanying caption) trying to sustain WWE's live television viewership. While Cena pushes fans to consume more content, the supposed value of their touts is marginalized within WWE's storytelling. Instead, Cena's feed is a one-way broadcast: he promotes WWE, its programming, and his other appearances, and casually solicits fan opinion. He thus embodies the hollow nature of social media engagement moderated by corporations: no legitimate dialogue, just generic promotion.

Cena's usage of Tout mirrors WWE's overall strategy in 2012. Though performers would occasionally answer questions submitted by fans, the majority of their Tout content did not directly engage with fans. WWE instituted "Tout Tuesdays" to inspire fans to post their reactions to the latest episode of *Raw*. The first Tout Tuesday came on July 24 and was promoted not with Cena but rather with another face familiar to online fans: Ryder. As the main page stated, "Zack Ryder Touted his reaction to WWE's historic 1,000th episode of *Raw*, and you can get in on the conversation right here! Click to find out how to respond to The Long Island Iced-Z's Tout and add your opinions to the Raw 1,000 discussion!"[29] As in touts from Lesnar and Cena, Ryder delivered his recap backstage, in a dimly lit hallway with the camera close to his face. And as in Cena's limp calls for fan engagement, Ryder offered only a basic plea: "*Raw* 1,000 was sick— even though I didn't have a match. Hey broskis, what did *you* think of *Raw* 1,000?" The text accompanying Ryder's tout was equally rudimentary: "Want to get in on the conversation? Watch the Ultimate Broski's Tout here and reply with your own message using the hashtag, #Raw1000!"[30] WWE falsely framed this exchange as a conversation; people were talking *at* one another but not to each other. The hashtag was symbolic, a way to imply the potential for conversation, but not one in which Ryder or WWE would directly participate. For WWE fans, the only real acknowledgment came via the broadcasting of their touts on television.

The integration of Tout into WWE television began immediately, with the July 16, 2012, episode of *Raw* featuring a collection of answers to Cena's question about favorite *Raw* moments. Welcomed by announcers Michael Cole and Jerry Lawler as "cool," the montage of fan touts illustrated the simplicity of the form. Four WWE fans recapped their favorite moments in a confessional mode; all spoke directly into their webcams, illuminated by the brightness emitting from their computer monitors. As with other promotions for Tout, WWE presented the clips within a video frame that was itself embedded into a web browser.[31] Although the videos aired in high definition across the world, WWE accentuated that looking at Tout meant literally looking at the internet. WWE's visual positioning of Tout segments as happening *online*, in a web browser as part of a real-time stream of content, highlighted the perceived liveness of Tout and, by proxy, *Raw*. Feuer asserts that television "*is* live in a way that film never can be. Events *can* be transmitted as they occur; television (and video-tape) look more 'real' to us than does film."[32] John Ellis argues that the "live" image produces an "effect of immediacy . . . as though the TV image is . . . transmitted and received in the same moment that it is produced."[33]

Within the context of the highly produced *Raw*, low-definition video clips with mediocre audio transmission appear even more live and immediate; these clips are decidedly *not produced*.

Similarly, the framing of touts as a real-time stream—rather than something curated by WWE producers—is not unlike the use of "live" chyrons. With this approach, WWE tapped into what Couldry calls the myth of "a 'shared' ritual center," where viewers are trained by television to feel connected to one another.[34] The shared ritual center is not entirely false; social platforms like Tout allow fans to connect with one another and to potentially feel involved in the televisual experience. Yet this ritual center is perpetuated by corporations to keep viewers attentive. Tout thus served two functions related to liveness: making its programs appear more live and convincing fans to use the platform and watch to see if their tout made it onto the televised broadcast.

WWE's incorporation of fan touts also aided its attempts to capitalize on the new social flow. The visual presentation of touts—complete with webcam aesthetics, web browsers, and smartphones—explicitly referenced the growing social experience of consuming television in the twenty-first century. As Max Dawson asserts, most digital content produced by the media industries tries to embrace viewers' desire to migrate between screens and platforms.[35] Despite the disruptive nature of new technology and consumer habits, corporations plan and extend flow in ways that are both financially viable and meaningful to viewers. With Tout, WWE channeled the emerging consumption habits of its fans into the promotion of a new social platform. Tout segments concede that content is being produced, consumed, and shared by fans on handheld devices. For WWE, this tactic was not just to persuade fans to integrate Tout into their social flow but more specifically to redirect them back to the live television broadcast.

Placement of touts within the broadcast also framed WWE as more willing than ever to listen to fans. However, as with most companies' dalliances with social media, WWE did not offer a platform for true engagement, let alone critique. Televised touts were uniformly safe and celebratory of WWE's product. In the segment about favorite *Raw* moments, fans recapped four moments that any casual viewer of WWE would remember, with two fans highlighting the work of "Stone Cold" Steve Austin, the company's biggest star. In another Tout segment before April 2013's *WrestleMania 29*, fans were asked to predict the winner of the main event between

Cena and The Rock. In this instance, fans played along with WWE's storytelling reality, treating the match as if it were real. Many participants even delivered their predictions in the form of promos, mimicking the verbal styles of Cena or The Rock.[36] Consequently, this alleged fan engagement primarily played as promotion for an upcoming PPV. WWE saw immediate results of its Tout partnership: during the first night of promotion on *Raw*, more than four hundred thousand users logged in to the platform and more than one million touts were viewed during *Raw*.[37] However, WWE quickly encountered obstacles with the platform, primarily regarding its integration into storylines. It was in this context that professional wrestling's version of reality and performance clashed with the engagement promised by Tout.

"So Brock Lesnar Touts?": Tout and WWE Storylines

While Tout had minimal influence over fan participation, it produced more curious results for WWE storylines. WWE constructs an intricate storyworld where events are more or less "real" depending on what it wants the audience to feel. Social media, however, has given performers more autonomy over the manner in which their onscreen personae translate to the web. Each performer uses services like Twitter differently: while company man Cena mostly tweets to promote upcoming events, aspiring stand-up comedian Dolph Ziggler tweets jokes at the expense of everyone from WWE writers to his own character. As the touts from Cena and Ryder demonstrate, this inconsistent posting style translated to the video platform as well. Many of Cena's posts were delivered in his typical performance voice, counseling fans to watch *Raw* or to participate in WWE promotions. Ryder, by contrast, attempted to replicate the self-aware sadsack persona cultivated in his popular YouTube series.

The visual nature of Tout made the disparity between these styles clearer. The formal characteristics of touts are familiar to viewers of amateur YouTube productions or fans of "lifecasters" like JenniCam who broadcast their everyday experiences.[38] Fan touts were defined by their low resolution, sharp light from the computer screen, choppy sound, and unintentional shaky-cam effect brought on by simultaneously holding a device and talking into its camera. Writing of lifecasting, Sarah Banet-Weiser notes, "This kind of transparency and disclosure blurs traditional divisions between public and private, so that one's private life is a central feature of popular entertainment."[39] Though Tout only unveiled the lives of users in fifteen-second bursts, it continued the trend of asking "normal" people to make their private lives more public in the name of connectivity and engagement. WWE's shunning of normal production practices was intended to make touts seem as real as possible: personal, confessional, and unscripted. Banet-Weiser argues that, in modern culture, "the authentic and the commodity self are intertwined within brand culture, where authenticity is itself a brand."[40] By stripping away high-definition camera equipment, WWE presented the aura of an authentic expression. The wrinkle is that the authentic and the real are purposefully inaccessible in the realm of professional wrestling. For instance, on July 25, 2012, Cena touted himself *really* completing a snatch-grip deadlift.[41] However, he captioned it with a reference to a loss he had recently experienced in the ring. The post is thus a palimpsest, offering a sneak peek at Cena's life outside the ring, a furthering of a fictional story, and a pitch for Cena's signature motivational messaging.

Viewed through the prism of brands, WWE's strategy makes sense. However performers choose to use social media, the goal is to generate interest. If fans buy into Cena's inspirational touts and then buy his new shirt, it is a victory for WWE. If fans follow Ryder or Ziggler on social media because they deliver self-aware deconstructions of the conventions of professional wrestling, and then buy their new shirts, the result is the same. Performers are real people, but they are indeed playing characters, and characters are brands. As Banet-Weiser asserts, "authenticity is not only understood and experienced as the pure inner self of the individual, it is also a relationship between individuals and commodity culture that is constructed as 'authentic.'"[42] WWE used Tout to develop such authentic relationships between performers and fans.

The first months of the partnership generated great interest in Tout and contributed to WWE's growing digital profile. While the broadcasting of fan touts was unpopular among the most vocal online fans, the segments were also brief enough to easily ignore. It was the Lesnar incident in August 2012 that ultimately turned the tide against Tout. In storyline, Lesnar had been running wild since his return in the spring, holding the company hostage with his sheer star power. After defeating real-life *and* storyline boss Triple H, Lesnar claimed he had nothing left to accomplish. In the middle of *Raw*, he left the ring and made the announcement of his exodus via Tout. Like Cena before him, Lesnar effectively blurred the lines between kayfabe and reality with his tout, purposefully referencing his rocky relationship with WWE and playing on fans' real anxieties that he could leave at any time, as he had done previously in 2004. Unlike Cena, however, Lesnar lacked the acting skills to make even a brief clip seem authentic. Lesnar's performance in the video is stilted, his eye line suggests the use of cue cards, and his body appears uncomfortably rigid. That

WWE aired this clip repeatedly amid its normal high-definition production to illustrate its story significance only served to underline its shortcomings. Throughout his tenure in WWE, Lesnar has not so much played a character as he has played himself. In this instance, WWE's decision to have him act out an evidently real scenario only pushed him to deliver a performance that was as unreal as ever. The authenticity of Lesnar—his most attractive quality in a world of scripted combat—was suddenly compromised.

Lesnar would leave WWE, albeit only in storyline, for a few months. In the aftermath, WWE faced harsh criticism for its use of Tout to further a major storyline when an in-ring segment with Lesnar would have sufficed. Before the Lesnar segment, many fans viewed Tout as WWE's latest corporate obsession—something it would ruin with incessant promotion until even the most sympathetic fans would grow to hate it. After the segment, fans and reporters alike were frustrated by the decision to make a promotional tool part of the story. Fans on message boards were not kind; one noted, "So Brock Lesnar Touts? That in itself kills his character worse than anything he actually said. . . . that's gotta be the most humiliating thing possible."[43] In December 2012, a website that parodies rumormongering professional wrestling news sources posted an "article" with the following headline: "Michael Cole Replaced by Robot That Mentions Tout a Million Times per Second."[44] By early 2013, touts were only promoted online, linked to more popular platforms like Facebook, Twitter, and YouTube, and went unmentioned on any television broadcasts.

WWE's decreasing interest in Tout can be seen in the activity of Cena and Ryder. Between July 11 and August 31, 2012, Cena and Ryder sent more than seventy-five touts combined. From September 1, 2012, to early 2014, the duo barely equaled that figure. During that stretch, similar platforms—Vine and Instagram video—grew in popularity, boasting growing user bases in the hundreds of millions. By mid-2014, WWE quietly announced that its two-year partnership with Tout had come to an end. While WWE has embraced other platforms, Tout pivoted away from social networking, becoming a video service for publishers and brands. At this point, Tout is but a joke among fans and for Daniel Bryan, who repeatedly mocked the platform on *Talking Smack*, WWE Network's short-lived *SmackDown Live* after-show.

CONCLUSION

WWE's deployment of Tout failed for many reasons. WWE tried to use the platform to convince fans to watch live programming as often as possible, as if it were a dangling carrot promising potential engagement. Though it was a sound strategy in response to emergent social media, second screen activity, and declining Nielsen ratings, the specific features of Tout and WWE's sales pitch did not appeal to a majority of fans. The conversation promised by WWE and Tout in that opening press release was pushed aside for generic, celebratory responses from a small subset of fans. WWE's incessant promotion of facile fan touts also damaged its sales pitch. Perhaps most importantly, however, Tout's influence on performance, characterization, and storytelling further disrupted WWE's already convoluted and confusing mélange of the scripted and the real. The partnership between WWE and Tout was a victim of its own hype, it provided little of substance for fans hoping to participate, and it had a limited impact on WWE storylines.

While Tout demonstrated how quickly promising ideas can turn sour, it also enabled WWE to recalibrate its approach to fan engagement. After Tout, WWE normalized its social media practices to mirror those of most of the rest of the media industries: YouTube for video, Twitter for live engagement, Facebook for news, and more personalized platforms like Instagram and Snapchat for the extension of performers' personae. While WWE still integrates fan voices into their television broadcasts, such elements have been reduced to basic polls and a curated selection of tweets scrolling at the bottom of the screen. Likewise, Superstars continue to use their Twitter or Instagram accounts to blur the lines between their characters and their real lives, but WWE does not integrate such posts into stories with any regularity. All this extra content deepens the fan experience, building stronger ties between fans and WWE and its performers, but consumption of this material is not needed to follow WWE's ongoing serialized narrative.

WWE's experiment with Tout reinforces that the media industries' adoption of new technology is never simple, immediate, or purely successful. While WWE would prefer that fans and business partners forget that Tout was ever part of the WWE experience, such failures can nevertheless be as instructive as successes. WWE's dalliance with Tout demonstrates that even the most responsive, fan-oriented media companies struggle with how to let fans become part of the story. This case study also shows that fans will generally not respond positively when a new platform or tool is forced upon them, particularly when there are so few real benefits to engagement. Finally, it shows that companies will listen and pivot in the face of fan complaints, but only when more popular alternatives present themselves.

The failures of Tout notwithstanding, WWE has been tremendously successful in expanding its social footprint. Further research could consider how WWE manages to inspire fan engagement without enabling direct participation, or how fans more actively resist WWE's social and televisual narratives through their own tactics. For instance, the ongoing controversy surrounding audience dislike of their latest appointed hero, Roman Reigns, would provide a fascinating case study for how the company attempts to manipulate fan opinions across platforms. At worst, WWE's experiment with Tout signals that the company is continuously seeking new strategies to execute its core storytelling vision.

Notes

1. ConfoHD, "Brock Lesnar Leaves the WWE."
2. Dave Meltzer, "WWE Financials Announced, What Was Up and Down Plus a Guidance of an Increase in the Next Month," *Wrestling Observer*, August 2, 2012, accessed October 20, 2012, http://www.f4wonline.com/more/more-top-stories/118-daily-updates/26844-wwe-financials-announced-what-was-up-and-down-plus-a-guidance-of-an-increase-in-the-next-five-month.
3. WWE, "Tout Tag Teams with WWE."
4. Ross, *Beyond the Box*, 18.
5. Johnson, "Inviting Audiences In."
6. Chris Jericho explains his *Taboo Tuesday* experience as if the voting was legitimate. See Jericho and Fornatale, *Undisputed*, 293–95.
7. Ross, *Beyond the Box*, 115.
8. Andrejevic, *Reality TV*, 152.
9. Lévy, *Collective Intelligence*.
10. Jenkins, *Convergence Culture*, 134–45.
11. For more on the Ryder saga, see Rueter, "Curt Hawkins Says."
12. For more on Punk's promo, see Shoemaker, "Introducing the Worked-Shoot Era," and Dru Jeffries's introduction to this volume.
13. Shoemaker, "Brief History of Wrestling Fakery."
14. Williams, *Television*, 79.
15. Ibid., 84–85.
16. Feuer, "Live Television," 13.
17. Uricchio, "Television's Next Great Generation," 182.
18. Couldry, "Liveness, 'Reality,' and the Mediated Habitus," 356.
19. Ross, *Beyond the Box*, 4–10.
20. Gray, *Show Sold Separately*, 4–8; Murray, "'Celebrating the Story the Way It Is.'"
21. Kozinets, "Fan Creep," 162.
22. Brooker, "Going Pro," 76.
23. Jenkins and Carpentier, "Theorizing Participatory Intensities," 266.
24. WWE, "Tout Tag Teams with WWE."
25. Johnson, "Inviting Audiences In," 63.
26. WWE, "Get Tout and Connect with the WWE Universe like Never Before."
27. UltimateWWENet, "What's Your Favorite."
28. Unfortunately, Tout's archives have disappeared from the internet between the initial drafting of this chapter and its publication. Though the tout itself is unplayable, the webpage containing the video can still be accessed via the Wayback Machine: @JohnCena, Tout, July 11, 2012. https://web.archive.org/web/20120724115222/http://www.tout.com/m/apgqq6.
29. WWE, "Home."
30. WWE, "Tout Your Reactions to *Raw* 1,000 with Zack Ryder."
31. WWE, "WWE Universe Touts Their Favorite Raw Memories: Raw, July 16, 2012."

32. Feuer, "Live Television," 13.

33. Ellis, *Visible Fictions*, 127–42.

34. Couldry, *Media Rituals*, 97.

35. Dawson, "Television's Aesthetic of Efficiency."

36. WWE, "WWE Universe Touts Who They Want to Win between John Cena and The Rock at WrestleMania: Raw, Apr."

37. Laird, "How the WWE Blew Up Tout."

38. For more on Jennicam, see Knibbs, "Jennicam."

39. Banet-Weiser, *Authentic (TM)*, 60.

40. Ibid., 5.

41. @JohnCena, *Tout*, July 25, 2012, accessed May 10, 2019, https://web.archive.org/web
/20120818095004/http://www.tout.com/u/johncena.

42. Banet-Weiser, *Authentic (TM)*, 14.

43. *PW Scene* Staff, "Brock Lesnar Is Leaving WWE For Good."

44. Kayfabe Staff, "Michael Cole Replaced by Robot That Mentions Tout a Million Times per Second."

Bibliography

Andrejevic, Mark. *Reality TV: The Work of Being Watched*. Lanham, MD: Rowan and Littlefield, 2004.

Banet-Weiser, Sarah. *Authentic (TM): The Politics of Ambivalence in a Brand Culture*. New York: New York University Press, 2012.

Brooker, Will. "Going Pro: Gendered Responses to the Incorporation of Fan Labor as User-Generated Content." In *Wired TV: Laboring Over an Interactive Future*, edited by Denise Mann, 72–97. New Brunswick: Rutgers University Press, 2014.

ConfoHD. "Brock Lesnar Leaves the WWE—WWE Official TOUT." YouTube video, 0:14. Posted August 20, 2012. Accessed October 20, 2016. https://www.youtube.com/watch?v=82bfkvmsnvg.

Couldry, Nick. "Liveness, 'Reality,' and the Mediated Habitus from Television to the Mobile Phone." *Communication Review* 7, no. 4 (2004): 353–61.

———. *Media Rituals: A Critical Approach*. London: Routledge, 2003.

Dawson, Max. "Television's Aesthetic of Efficiency: Convergence Television and the Digital Short." In *Television as Digital Media*, edited by James Bennett and Niki Strange, 204–29. Durham, NC: Duke University Press, 2011.

Ellis, John. *Visible Fictions: Cinema, Television, Video*. New York: Routledge, 1982.

Feuer, Jane. "Live Television: The Concept of Ontology as Ideology." In *Regarding Television: Critical Approaches*, edited by E. Ann Kaplan, 12–22. New York: University Publications of America, 1983.

Gray, Jonathan. *Show Sold Separately: Promos, Spoilers, and Other Media Paratexts*. New York: New York University Press, 2010.

Jenkins, Henry. *Convergence Culture: Where Old and New Media Collide*. New York: New York University Press, 2008.

Jenkins, Henry, and Nico Carpentier. "Theorizing Participatory Intensities: A Conversation about Participation and Politics." *Convergence: The International Journal of Research into New Media Technologies* 19, no. 3 (2013): 265–86.

Jericho, Chris, and Peter Thomas Fornatale. *Undisputed: How to Become the World Champion in 1,372 Easy Steps*. New York: Grand Central Publishing, 2011.

Johnson, Derek. "Inviting Audiences In: The Spatial Reorganization of Production and Consumption in 'TVIII.'" *New Review of Film and Television Studies* 5, no. 1 (2007): 61–80.

Kayfabe Staff. "Michael Cole Replaced by Robot That Mentions Tout a Million Times per Second." *Kayfabe News.* December 29, 2012. Accessed October 23, 2016, http://www .kayfabenews.com/michael-cole-replaced-by-robot-that-mentions-twitter-a-billion-times -per-second/.

Knibbs, Katie. "Jennicam: Why the First Lifecaster Disappeared from the Internet." *Gizmodo.* April 14, 2015. Accessed October 22, 2016. http://gizmodo.com/jennicam-why-the-first -lifecaster-disappeared-from-the-1697712996.

Kozinets, Robert V. "Fan Creep: Why Brands Suddenly Need 'Fans.'" In *Wired TV: Laboring Over an Interactive Future,* edited by Denise Mann, 161–75. New Brunswick: Rutgers University Press, 2014.

Laird, Sam. "How the WWE Blew Up Tout." *Mashable.* July 17, 2012. Accessed October 20, 2016. http://mashable.com/2012/07/17/wwe-tout/#lSbGHMoTikqK.

Lévy, Pierre. *Collective Intelligence: Mankind's Emerging World in Cyberspace,* translated by Robert Bononno. New York: Plenum, 1997.

Murray, Simone. "'Celebrating the Story the Way It Is': Cultural Studies, Corporate Media, and the Contested Utility of Fandom." *Continuum: The Journal of Media and Cultural Studies* 18, no. 1 (2004): 7–25.

PW Scene Staff. "Brock Lesnar Is Leaving WWE For Good." *PW Scene.* August 21, 2012. Accessed October 23, 2016. http://www.pwscene.com/viewtopic.php?nomobile=1&f= 2&t=18303.

Ross, Sharon Marie. *Beyond the Box: Television and the Internet.* Malden, MA: Blackwell, 2009.

Rueter, Sean. "Curt Hawkins Says That WWE Treatment of Zack Ryder 'Broke the Spirit of the Locker Room.'" *Cageside Seats.* June 26, 2014. Accessed October 2016. http://www .cagesideseats.com/2014/6/26/5845664/curt-hawkins-says-that-wwe-treatment-of-zack -ryder-broke-the-spirit.

Shoemaker, David. "A Brief History of Wrestling Fakery." *Grantland.* June 15, 2012. Accessed October 20, 2016. http://grantland.com/features/john-cena-big-show-how-century -pretend-fighting-led-wwe-reality-era/.

———. "Introducing the Worked-Shoot Era." *Grantland.* August 1, 2011. Accessed October 20, 2016. http://grantland.com/features/introducing-worked-shoot-era/.

UltimateWWENet. "What's Your Favorite Monday Night Raw Memory? Tout Your Video Reply Now Using #Raw!" YouTube video, 0:15. Posted July 16, 2012. https://www.youtube.com /watch?v=dbbOMfyMWyo.

Uricchio, William. "Television's Next Great Generation: Technology/Interface Culture/Flow." In *Television After TV: Essays on a Medium in Transition,* edited by Lynn Spigel and Jan Olsson, 163–82. Durham, NC: Duke University Press, 2005.

Williams, Raymond. *Television: Technology and Cultural Form.* London: Routledge, 1990.

WWE. "Get Tout and Connect with the WWE Universe like Never Before." YouTube video, 0:57. Posted July 15, 2012. https://www.youtube.com/watch?v=3uMsbRldmKs.

———. "Home." July 24, 2012. WWE. Accessed via the Wayback Machine. Accessed October 20, 2016. https://web.archive.org/web/20120724030641/http://www.wwe.com/.

———. "Tout Tag Teams with WWE." WWE Corporate. July 11, 2012. Accessed October 20, 2012. http://corporate.wwe.com/news/company-news/2012/07-11-2012.

———. "Tout Your Reactions to Raw 1,000 with Zack Ryder." WWE. July 24, 2012. Accessed October 20, 2016. http://www.wwe.com/shows/raw/2012-07-23/tout-reactions-zack -ryder.

———. "The WWE Universe Touts Their Favorite Raw Memories: Raw, July 16, 2012." YouTube video, 1:03. Posted July 16, 2012. Accessed October 20, 2016. https://www.youtube.com /watch?v=QECyBd9xbwQ.

———. "The WWE Universe Touts Who They Want to Win between John Cena and the Rock at WrestleMania: Raw, Apr." YouTube video, 0:51. Posted April 1, 2013. Accessed October 21, 2016. https://www.youtube.com/watch?v=HDqZiW3KKKA.

CORY BARKER is Assistant Professor in Residence in the Department of Communication at Bradley University. He is coeditor of *The Age of Netflix: Critical Essays on Streaming Media, Digital Delivery, and Instant Access.*

chapter nine

"WE'RE NOT JUST CHEERLEADERS": READING THE POSTFEMINIST POLYSEMY OF *TOTAL DIVAS*

Anna F. Peppard

Total Divas is a behind-the-scenes reality show featuring members of WWE's Divas Division. Jointly produced by WWE and the E! network, the show began airing in 2013 and, as of this writing, has completed its eighth season. The show's first episode, "Welcome to the WWE," introduces the cast via their ranks within a competitive hierarchy. Nattie, ring name Natalya, is a veteran; Nikki and Brie, ring names Nikki and Brie Bella/the Bella Twins, are former champions returning after a yearlong hiatus; relative newcomers Ariane and Trinity, ring names Cameron and Naomi/the Funkadactyls, are midcard, fan-favorite wrestlers; and finally, Eva Marie and JoJo, fresh out of training camp, are the newbies. Within this episode, the professional and interpersonal conflicts that have become the stock-in-trade of countless reality shows are focused on the yearly megaspectacle of *WrestleMania*. For the Divas, this event demands peak physicality as well as glamour; throughout the episode, training sessions in which the Divas wear yoga pants and sports bras are juxtaposed against dinners and galas in which they try to outshine each other in ball gowns and sequined cocktail dresses. Nattie explains that for the Divas, competition for a spot on the *WrestleMania* card is especially intense: "*WrestleMania* is the biggest event of the year for the WWE. And if there are eight or ten guys' matches on the show, there's only one girls' match. So, that leaves ten Divas in the locker room, clawing and fighting for that one spot." Ariane and Brie, preparing to be featured at *WrestleMania* for the first time, reiterate the life-altering importance of the event. Ariane describes *WrestleMania* as "like a dream come true," while Brie states that it is not only "the *biggest* event in our careers" but also "one of the biggest events that happens in the world."

As the scheduled *WrestleMania 29* match between the Bella Twins and the Funkadactyls approaches, competitive tensions intensify; a perfectly coiffed Nikki and Brie mock Ariane and Trinity's last-minute costume crisis while Nattie, Eva Marie, and JoJo huddle together in the broadcast booth, counting down the minutes to the match. Moments after Ariane and Trinity sprint for the stage, Nattie realizes something is wrong: the final match has started, but the Divas are nowhere to be seen. Nattie, Eva Marie, and JoJo leave the broadcast booth to find Nikki, Brie, Ariane, and Trinity slumped on a set of plain black couches in a stark white dressing room, sharing a graven silence. Amid a series of cuts and close-ups in which tears can be seen misting each woman's eyes, Ariane and Brie say together, "We got cut." For a show that opens with a rousing, techno-beat theme song in which a female voice declares "Ain't gonna stop me now" over the white and hot-pink letters of the show's title surrounded by glittering flashbulbs, this is an unexpectedly dour climax. It is also, however, an unexpectedly feminist climax; in these final moments, the sometimes-petty competition that dominates the rest of the episode all but dissolves as the Divas are forced to confront their shared marginalization within a patriarchal and frequently misogynist industry in which female labor is always the most disposable.

The contradictory depiction of the Divas within this episode, which is typical of the show as a whole, is cultivated rather than naive. As John Fiske describes, all popular texts deliberately incorporate multiple, often contradictory interpretative possibilities. According to Fiske, "An essential characteristic of television is its polysemy, or multiplicity of meanings. A program provides a potential of meanings which may be realized, or made into actually experienced meanings, by socially situated viewers in the process of reading."[1] As the first reality television show to focus on the personal lives of WWE performers, *Total Divas* generates additional polysemy—and additional pleasure—through the highly ambiguous relationship between the real and the fake.[2] Brenda R. Weber argues that reality television generates meaning and pleasure in part through "the fluidity of the real and the constructed."[3] This fluidity "fosters and demands a splitting of one's critical consciousness into an insistent hybridity so that texts, events, people, and moments can be simultaneously and legitimately real and fake, actual and artifice, performed and natural."[4] Similarly, Sharon Mazer argues that the world of professional wrestling is "a form of imaginative empowerment" that is "imbued with essential contradictions within and between the fiction of the play and the fact of the business."[5]

Total Divas' representations of gender contribute additional polysemy. The show attempts to marry the "catfights and confessionals" format made popular by other loosely scripted reality shows featuring groups of women—such as the *Next Top Model* (US version 2003–) and *The Real Housewives* (2006–) franchises—to women in an unusual professional context that requires stereotypical performances of female beauty and sexuality as well as connotatively male physical labor. Significantly, *Total Divas* also represents perhaps the first time that WWE's female performers have been marketed to a primarily female audience.[6] The series therefore offers an opportunity to address an aspect of the WWE Universe that has been seriously neglected by existing scholarship.[7] A vast majority of the scholarship that has considered representations of gender in professional wrestling has focused on its appeal as "masculine melodrama," characterizing wrestling as "always a performance by men, for men, about men."[8] This neglect is unfortunate, especially because it risks replicating WWE's own historical marginalization of its female performers.

The stars of *Total Divas* are far more than simple sex objects (if such a thing as a "simple" sex object even exists). Like all professional wrestlers, these women are "part of larger commodity packages," selling multiple possibilities at once.[9] Analyzing *Total Divas* has the potential to inform both the nature of WWE's storytelling practices within the transmedia era and the construction and marketing of female strength within our postfeminist society. Because female wrestlers, similarly to the female superheroes and action heroes analyzed by Dawn Heinecken in her book *The Warrior Women of Television*, "so visibly [assume] a role defined as masculine and powerful," they are "a great place to investigate the meanings of female power circulating in society."[10] Weber further argues that "reality TV is the perfect contemporary testing ground on which to assess gender politics and what it means to be 'real' in an age of the manufactured image."[11] In this chapter, I examine the political implications of the ways in which *Total Divas*—on its own and through its interactions with in-ring storylines and other official and unofficial intertexts—promotes and manipulates the polysemy of its strong, sexy, and scripted (but potentially real) female wrestlers. Ultimately, I argue that although *Total Divas* addresses WWE's institutionalized sexism in some interesting and potentially critical ways, aspects of its cultivated polysemy also deflect and limit its critique of WWE and the postfeminist society that informs its recent representations of female strength.

A Brief History of Women's Wrestling

To properly understand the place of *Total Divas* within the WWE Universe, it is necessary to know something of the history of women's professional wrestling. Before the twenty-first century, female wrestlers were only sporadically present within the organization now known as WWE, with the company's Women's Championship often being left vacant for years at a time. Beginning in the early 2000s, WWE's contingent of female wrestlers expanded significantly, as evinced by the promotion of female performers in reality show competitions such as *WWE Diva Search* (2004–2007) and *WWE Tough Enough* (2001–2004, 2011–2015), the latter of which featured a mix of male and female contestants. Yet these competitions, all of which targeted WWE's traditionally male audience, often replicated the typical sexism of the "attitude era."[12] As Christiana Molldrem Harkulich describes, throughout WWE's history but especially during the attitude era, "The majority of women have been portrayed as sexually available heel characters who are manipulative or morally loose."[13] In addition, "Women's wrestling during this period often featured 'matches' that did not occur in the ring but rather in pudding, gravy, and other wet substances or, alternatively, bikini, lingerie, and evening gown competitions. On rare occasions, Women's breasts were 'accidently' [*sic*] exposed."[14] *WWE Diva Search* featured similarly sexist narratives, including challenges wherein aspiring female wrestlers were required to seduce male wrestlers. *WWE Diva Search* also joined the attitude era's other programming and publishing endeavors in cross promoting the Playboy brand: *Diva Search* featured Playboy playmates as contestants, seven WWE Women's Championship holders appeared on *Playboy* covers between 1999 and 2008, and provocative photo spreads featuring seminude female wrestlers were a common feature of WWE's *RAW Magazine*. In general, concurrent with what Sarah Projansky describes as the rise of "do me postfeminism" and what Carla Rice calls "the 'pornification' of popular culture—the blurring of boundaries between porn and pop culture," the intense sexualization of female wrestlers that began in the 1990s and continued into the early 2000s guaranteed that they would "continue to enter the public world on male terms and be subject to its sexism."[15]

WWE began referring to its female performers as Divas in 1999, and the 2008 decision to retire the Women's Championship and replace it with a Divas Championship solidified this rebranding. This name change can be read as sexist and misogynist. As Harkulich notes, "The Divas Championship belt featured a large pink butterfly that looks more like a Barbie accessory than a professional wrestling title, and it mirrored the trivial way that the Divas matches were treated on television."[16] And yet, on its own, *diva* is a complex term. Within what Susan J. Leonardi and Rebecca A. Pope call the "masculinist tradition" of opera, the stereotypical diva is a "seducing siren and whore," a femme fatale whose "vanity, competitiveness, and self-absorption" presents female power as manipulative, deceitful, and ultimately ruinous.[17] More recently, though, the meaning of the term has expanded. Female, feminist, and queer writers and critics have reclaimed the figure of the diva as a "political force" whose (literally or metaphorically) powerful voice "asserts equality and earns authority in the public, masculine world."[18] While it is beyond the scope of this chapter to comprehensively debate the validity of these competing meanings, these readings all acknowledge that the role of the diva has always been performative, embodying, enacting, and giving voice to gendered fears and desires. As Leonardi and Pope put it, the diva is "not so much a person as a position, a condition, a situation."[19] On the one hand, then, replacing the Women's Championship with the Divas Championship signaled that WWE's female wrestlers were different from its male performers in terms of gender as well as sex, which served to overload them with multiple levels of cultural baggage before they ever stepped into the ring. On the other hand, this name change also ensured their complexity, signaling their potential to eventually move beyond limited gender stereotypes.

This complexity is evident in the fact that the rebranding of the Women's Division as the Divas Division coincided with female wrestlers being increasingly linked to feminism. Throughout much of 2015 and 2016, WWE claimed to be in the midst of a "Divas Revolution," whose promotional materials directly evoked female empowerment. Perhaps the clearest example of this promotion is a video that aired before the Divas match at *SummerSlam* 2015, in which Stephanie McMahon, WWE's chief brand officer and onscreen commissioner of *Raw*, delivered a speech beginning with the words, "There is a revolution with women in sports," accompanied by a video montage that included images of Ronda Rousey, Serena Williams, the World Cup–winning US women's soccer team, and Captain Kristen Griest and First Lieutenant Shaye Haver, the first women to graduate from the US Army's Ranger School.[20] The recent discontinuation of the Divas branding in favor of a new Women's Championship—a change that coincided with a rebranding of the Divas Revolution as the Women's Evolution—arguably relieves some of the cultural baggage that came with the Divas label. Yet this re-rebranding also reaffirms the especially complex polysemy of WWE's female performers, emphasizing as it does the particularly fraught politics of naming where female wrestlers are concerned.[21]

REPRESENTING EMPOWERMENT IN *TOTAL DIVAS*

Total Divas represents a bridge between the attitude era and the PG era. While the Bella Twins are models-turned-wrestlers who got their start on *Diva Search*, a close reading of the show proves that it was and remains an integral part of WWE's efforts to promote its female wrestlers as icons of empowerment. The aforementioned final moments of the show's first episode attest to this fact; in this series-establishing episode, the decision to show the pain and injustice of cutting the Divas from *WrestleMania* represents a significant acknowledgment of the institutional marginalization of female performers by and within WWE. *Total Divas'* first episode also initiates a narrative trajectory in which the Divas' interpersonal battles are contained within an overarching quest to redeem and reclaim the Divas Division, a quest that has supposedly been realized with the Divas Revolution/Women's Evolution. Some of the feminist aspirations of *Total Divas* are not completely unjustified. Though *Total Divas* is not completely dissimilar to such obviously sexist reality television shows as *The Bachelor* (2002–) and *Wife Swap* (US version 2004–2010, 2013), in which, as Su Holmes and Deborah Jermyn describe, "women are frequently figured as hostile and competitive with one another," *Total Divas'* behind-the-scenes format also allows it to show comparatively nuanced examples of female community.[22] In an October 8, 2015, editorial for Forbes.com about the trend of female performers congratulating each other after matches within WWE's developmental division NXT, Alfred Konuwa inadvertently highlights the ways in which the requirements of kayfabe tend to limit WWE's ability to represent genuine (or even just genuine-seeming) female friendships. Konuwa observes that "women crying and hugging after great matches has become an increasingly uncomfortable staple at NXT Takeover events" and claims that such displays are "redundant if not demeaning." According to Konuwa, such breaks with kayfabe diminish female wrestling: "For fans to be interested in the type of main event that would headline WWE's biggest pay-per-view, they need to be invested in the storyline rather than individual matches. If WWE Superstars and Divas constantly break character after these matches, it will be tough to believe the characters dislike each other and need to settle the score in a major main event."[23] Konuwa's viewpoint illustrates a powerful double bind: in order to be respected (read: empowered) within the world of professional wrestling, women must deny the female community that has always been so essential to female empowerment in the real world.

In contrast, *Total Divas* largely eschews the narrative logic of in-ring storylines and is thus (relatively) free of the burden of kayfabe.[24] The female wrestlers who appear on the show are situated in the "real world"; they use their real names and are filmed at their real homes alongside real family members in the context of real relationships, which are often with fellow WWE performers. Hence, Divas who are rivals in the ring on *Raw* or *SmackDown* are often shown to be friends on *Total Divas*—training together, eating together, traveling together, shopping together, and congratulating each other after matches that pit them against each other in supposedly bitter feuds. In *Total Divas*, the Divas' need and desire to stick together and support each other are given greater emphasis than petty catfights or physical confrontations. For instance, the show depicts several *Sex in the City*–style brunch dates and yearly vacations that, in a textbook example of the show's polysemy, allow for both bikini-clad debauchery and moments of intense female bonding in which personal secrets and fears are revealed, discussed, and "healed"—usually through the aid of alcohol and shopping.[25]

Interestingly, the show's most sustained rivalries and confrontations result from threats to the Divas' unity, which is located primarily in their shared quest to redeem women's wrestling. As a case in point, Eva Marie becomes the main villain of the show's fourth season as a result of WWE's efforts to, in the words of director of talent relations Mark Carrano in the season 4 opener, "Diva Divide," "move her up the chain as quick as we can." As part of this push, Eva Marie is separated from the other Divas to train with a personal coach near her home in Los Angeles. The other Divas view Eva Marie's preferential treatment as profoundly unfair. In "Diva Divide," Nattie complains that "None of us got private coaches." Brie similarly highlights the difference between Eva Marie's experience and her own, saying, "I trained at a batting cage, I trained at canned food buildings." Eva Marie's privileges are additionally situated as a threat to the authenticity of the Divas Division, with the other Divas characterizing Eva Marie as lacking skill and dedication to the craft of wrestling. Following the revelation of Eva Marie's private coach, Paige, a mainstay on the cast since midway through season 3, declares in a confessional, "I spent nearly ten years to try and get where I am today. You [Eva Marie] get to be *home*, every single day, and train there? Talk about silver spoon—you've had the *easiest* Diva career I have ever witnessed." Nikki, also in a confessional, expresses a similar outrage: "Out of all girls that have worked so damn hard in the past eight years, you're going to give special treatment to a girl who doesn't even really want to wrestle? Do you want to go back to having matches where people want to take a snack break? It makes me sad. And it almost makes me want to stay, because it's almost like—you're not going to destroy the Divas Division."[26] Eva Marie's inadequacy and inauthenticity are specifically situated within a supposed overreliance on beauty and sex appeal. Says Brie, "She should thank God that she has a pretty face, because other than that she would have nothing." Paige similarly declares, "We always put wrestling first, and she doesn't—she puts her red hair first." While the framing of these objections to Eva Marie's priorities and preferential treatment as motivated by a desire to legitimize female wrestling gives them a feminist bent, Eva Marie also invokes feminism to fire back at her critics. Near the end of "Diva Divide," in her first face-to-face confrontation with the other Divas since beginning her private training, Eva Marie asserts, "When I came on to be a WWE Diva, it's all about empowering women," then suggests that this message is contradicted by the other Divas' determination to "cut [her] down." Brie, however, interrupts Eva Marie's pleas for mercy with another authenticity claim, stating, "*You* are tearing down our division because you absolutely suck at wrestling."

In this episode, the repeated claims that Eva Marie's feminine narcissism and unfair promotion interfere with her ability to be a good wrestler invoke the cooperative nature of professional wrestling. As Mazer observes, "Professional wrestling is an athletic performance practice that is constructed around . . . a tradition of cooperative rather than competitive exchanges of apparent power."[27] However, the suggestion that Eva Marie is compromising the Divas Division by prioritizing her beauty and sex appeal is undercut by the fact that virtually all female wrestlers, including all of the other *Total Divas* cast members, are also required to prioritize these things. Most of the *Total Divas* cast members have had breast augmentations, and they are often shown pursuing other cosmetic surgery procedures, such as Botox. In addition, whether they are in the ring, out on the town, or relaxing at home, all of the cast members are almost invariably shown wearing heavy makeup, fake eyelashes, and hair extensions, as well as highly sexualized clothing and costumes. Even Paige, who calls herself an "anti-Diva" and who is the only member of the cast to eschew spray tans, customarily wears fake eyelashes and hair extensions; Paige's studded leather in-ring costume is also highly sexualized, evoking the aesthetics of both punk and bondage. Of course, professional wrestling is, in general, "a bodily performance of myth-making," in which male professional wrestlers are often pressured to risk their long-term health in the pursuit of muscular physiques and are, in their own ways, objectified.[28] As Lucia Rahilly observes, there is an obvious eroticism to the male wrestler's "sensationally muscle-bound, bronzed, and cleanly waxed body."[29] Yet for male wrestlers, eroticism is not generally highlighted in the same way or to the same degree as it is for female wrestlers.[30] Common trends in ringside commentary confirm this fact. As Nicholas Sammond observes, "While the ringside patter may sometimes refer to [female wrestlers'] strength and agility, announcers rarely forget to mention the female wrestler's body as a sexual object, a formidable assembly of tits and ass that also happens to be able to kick butt."[31] The filming techniques of *Total Divas* substantiate these trends. In any given episode, the camera will linger on the Divas' taut butt cheeks inside their revealing in-ring costumes, string bikinis, and bodycon dresses, and confessionals are always framed to include views of the Divas' amply displayed cleavage.

Despite these filming techniques, many of the storylines in *Total Divas* highlight and critique the politics of objectification. The season 1 episode "The Fat Twin" features two storylines that function as a case in point. In the first storyline, Nikki is shamed about her weight by commenters on Instagram as well as by her sister Brie, who challenges her to a twenty-one-day juice cleanse so that she and Nikki can look as identical as possible for a bikini photo shoot advertising *SummerSlam*. The Nikki storyline is clearly critical of fat shaming; when Nikki sees an Instagram comment that says, "Nikki is SOOO the FAT twin," she is visibly upset and has tears in eyes as she declares, "Now you know why there are so many insecure women in entertainment." The episode's second storyline involves Ariane deciding whether to get breast implants. In a confessional, Ariane directly addresses the professional pressure to get implants. She says, "WWE has merchandise, so the more fans you have, the more money you make. . . . And, I hate to say it, but sex sells, baby." Though Ariane seems initially enthusiastic about the prospect of implants, the episode presents her set of temporary silicone inserts as ridiculous and even somewhat monstrous. At the surgeon's office, Ariane slides the implants into her sports bra and tries to dance, only to have the inserts fly out, landing on the floor with an audible splat. Later in the episode, one of the implants falls out while Ariane is swimming, causing Trinity to exclaim, "They float! . . . They look like little jellyfish." Among the Divas, opinions vary about whether Ariane should get implants, with Trinity coming out strongly against the procedure while Nikki vocally encourages it.

Both storylines conclude with feel-good messages about the importance of being yourself; Nikki claims to have learned to "embrace" her "curves," while Ariane decides implants would convey the "wrong impression." In a confessional, Ariane states, "I've decided that right now is not the time for me to get a boob job, because I want to be a role model. By doing something that alters my body, I don't want to send the wrong impression to the fans that I love and care about. This is the way I am and I embrace that, and I want my fans to feel the same exact way." Both storylines also, however, substantiate the reasonableness of fan and industry demands related to slimness and breast size. For instance, Nikki's repeated protestations that she is not fat are countered by scenes highlighting her excessive consumption. During a scene in which Nikki dines at a restaurant with Brie and her fiancé Bryan (ring name Daniel Bryan), Brie's assertion within a confessional that she is *always* healthy" while Nikki eats "whatever she wants" is intercut with shots of Nikki drinking red wine, perusing the dessert menu, and finally ordering and savoring a vanilla ice cream–topped chocolate lava cake, which is shown in close-up on Nikki's plate, spoon, and bright red lips.[32] By making a spectacle of Nikki's consumption, this scene suggests that she is actually gluttonous, which in turn suggests that she is not only actually fat but also, in contrast to her twin sister, Brie, actually unhealthy. This presentation of Nikki as gluttonous, fat, and unhealthy undercuts her professed empowerment at the end of the episode, making it less about recognizing the arbitrary and unrealistic nature of female beauty norms and more about learning to embrace a personal decision to be fat. Certainly, for women in particular, it can be extremely empowering to pursue one's pleasures in contravention of beauty norms. Yet Nikki does not, by any reasonable measure, truly contravene such norms; in addition to her perfectly coiffed long hair, elaborate makeup, and sexy, luxury brand-name fashions, Nikki possesses both much larger breasts and a much smaller waist than the average American woman. In order to view Nikki's supposed rejection of beauty norms as empowering, one must a view a conventionally attractive woman—one who clearly works very hard to achieve and maintain her attractiveness— as not attractive enough. Similarly, in order to view Ariane's decision not to get implants as empowering, one must view breast augmentation—an invasive, costly procedure with a high risk of complications—as normal and reasonable, a view that is supported, interestingly, by Nikki's pride in her implants, which apparently help her navigate and overcome her own bodily insecurities.

As Kathy Davis observes, there is a problematic tendency in some feminist criticism of cosmetic surgery to erase women's agency; at worst, such criticism presents women who pursue cosmetic surgery as "frivolous, mistaken, or manipulated" by a "feminine beauty system" that turns them into "dopes."[33] To its credit, "The Fat Twin" does emphasize the Divas' critical agency through their conflicting opinions about breast augmentation. Yet the episode's ultimate emphasis on implants as a personal choice also elides, or at the very least diminishes, the existence of institutional pressures. As Susan Bordo describes, within the postfeminist era, cosmetic surgery is "continually described . . . by patients, surgeons, and even by some feminist theorists—as *an act* of 'taking control,' 'taking one's life into one's own hands'"; yet these advocates of "taking control" rarely acknowledge the ways in which a woman's choices tend to be circumscribed by patriarchal and racist beauty ideals.[34] Tellingly, in "The Fat Twin," Ariane's observation that "sex sells" highlights the fact that a female wrestler's choice not to get implants may be less available than the choice to get implants. History confirms this circumscription of choice; as Catherine Salmon and Susan Clerc observe, many of WWE's most successful female wrestlers, including Lita and Chyna, were promoted far more vigorously after receiving breast augmentations.[35]

Regardless of whether one views *Total Divas'* presentation of cosmetic surgery as positive or negative, it inevitably situates the female wrestling body as an ideological problem, whose contours and borders must be routinely questioned and policed. This theme is taken up even more directly through the show's routine attempts to generate drama by highlighting the Divas' affliction with various female medical issues. For instance, in the season 1 episode "No Longer the Bridesmaid," Ariane is rushed to the hospital with stomach cramps, which are diagnosed as a possible case of endometriosis. This storyline is followed up later in the season in the episode "Seeing Red," in which Ariane initially attributes experiencing pain during intercourse to her endometriosis; when a gynecologist declares her uterus and vagina medically normal, Ariane visits a sex therapist with her partner, Vinny. In the season 2 episode "For Better or for Worse," Eva visits the emergency room with stomach pain, bloating, and blood in her urine and is diagnosed with a ruptured ovarian cyst; this episode generates considerable drama through the possibility that the cyst may affect Eva Marie's ability to have children. In the season 3 episode "Twin Leaks," Eva Marie faces another medical emergency when a leak in her breast implants results in silicone seeping into her bloodstream; once again, the possibility that this condition might interfere with Eva Marie's ability to bear children is a central dramatic focus. In the season 3 episode "Divas Unchained," Trinity faces her own reproductive crisis. Experiencing faintness and abnormal bleeding after the removal of a birth control implant she received in the season 2 episode "Flirting with Fandango," Trinity is revealed to have uterine polyps that may need to be surgically removed and that might affect her ability to have children. In the season 5 episode "Baby Talk," Paige reveals that her ability to have children is similarly uncertain; in this episode, Paige tearfully confesses to having had a past miscarriage and an unnamed surgery that may make it difficult for her to become pregnant.

In part, the prominence of these female medical issues reflects an impulse to interrogate the female wrestling body. The same impulse is evident in other WWE programming. According to Douglas Battema

and Philip Sewell, WWE tends to inspect the bodies of its female wrestlers in different and more extreme ways than it does the bodies of its male
wrestlers: "While announcers and performers may allude to female breast
enhancement, any discussion of steroid use and cosmetic surgery for men
is silenced."[36] This different emphasis suggests that female wrestlers are
somehow faker than male wrestlers, their contours shaped by scalpels and
silicone as much (or more) than reps. In a related vein, the seeming realness of the Divas' female medical issues might be read as emphasizing the
fakeness of their connotatively masculine physical strength. As Misha
Kavka observes, "the emergence of the 'true' from the 'performed' self
underlies the aesthetics as well as the authenticity effects of Reality TV."[37]
In other words, in much the same way that fans know wrestling is worked
but are nonetheless seduced by the possibility of witnessing a shoot, viewers of reality television know it is fake but are nonetheless seduced by the
possibility of reality. Because they rupture the veil of performance to afflict
the physical body, illnesses and injuries are especially tantalizing signs of
reality. As such, beyond the fact of their dramatic prominence, the female
medical issues in *Total Divas* can take on an outsize importance as sign-
posts of the real amid the fake. Although *Total Divas* does shine a light on
certain taboo women's health issues—including contraception as well as
the sometimes-messy complications of breast augmentation—the prominence and specific presentation of these issues suggests that the Divas'
narrative of redemption includes a struggle to gain and maintain control
over bodies that are resistant to becoming strong and powerful and whose
reproductive features—uterus, ovaries, and breasts—are a constant
threat.

  Total Divas' emphasis on ideal heterosexual relationships similarly
substantiates sex and gender norms. Virtually all of the main stars of *Total
Divas* are in long-term heterosexual relationships, and relationship dynamics are central to almost every episode of the show. There is one wedding
per season, which typically ropes in several additional episodes depicting
the proposal, bachelorette parties, and other aspects of wedding planning.
On the one hand, *Total Divas'* focus on ideal (i.e., romantically and personally fulfilling) heterosexual relationships functions as a counterpoint
to WWE's typical presentation of strength and heroism as defined primarily (or exclusively) through masculine competition that often includes the
subjugation of women. *Total Divas* depicts male wrestlers who are sensitive, caring, and invested in long-term relationships that frequently require
them to adjust their own behavior to better suit the needs and desires of
their female partners. John Cena is presented throughout the series in a

particularly romantic light. In the series' first episode, Cena and Nikki act out a scene from the film *The Notebook* (2004) that involves Nikki jumping into Cena's arms and kissing him in the rain. In future episodes, Cena, a fierce individualist who is initially resistant to commitment, is gradually changed by Nikki's love; in season 1, Cena invites Nikki to move in with him and redecorate his home, and in season 5, he finally agrees to marry her.[38] In addition, the fact that so many of the *Total Divas* cast members are in long-term relationships with other WWE performers suggests a measure of gender equality; in a direct contrast to the reality show *WAGS* (2015), which aired directly after *Total Divas* during the second half of its fourth season, *Total Divas* depicts men and women who are partners in life as well as work.

However, the show's decision to showcase female wrestlers within the context of ideal heterosexual relationships can also be read as a denial that the Divas' gender deviance, which is implicit in their connotatively masculine profession, might be coupled with sexual deviance. The only Diva to express same-sex desire is Rosa Mendes, who joins the cast in the first episode of season 3, "Eggs Over Freezing," following a year-and-a-half hiatus from WWE to deal with substance abuse issues. Rosa's same-sex desire showcases the PG-era WWE's deliberate but thoroughly problematic efforts to be more diverse and inclusive.[39] In the season 3 episode "Divas Unchained," Rosa flirts with Nattie, buys her lingerie for her birthday, and tries to kiss her on the lips at a bar. Nattie is outraged by Rosa's attempted kiss, but her outrage is not, the show is careful to emphasize, due to homophobia; instead, Nattie is outraged because she is married. "I'm married," Nattie tells Trinity in the bathroom, following the attempted kiss. "I mean, just because I'm having issues with TJ doesn't mean I want Rosa's tongue down my throat." Later, Rosa insists that her kiss was meant as a gesture of friendship rather than romance. Rosa tells Nattie: "I wanted to make you feel pretty, and I wanted to make you feel confident. And I mean if girls hit on you, then you're hot as [censored]. . . . My intentions were not to have you as my lover, or girlfriend, or anything like that."

In the later season 3 episode "Cross Country Catastrophe," Rosa's same-sex desire emerges again. In this episode, Rosa, following several failed dates with men, takes Nattie to a lesbian bar. The scene at the lesbian bar is carefully controlled; the Divas do not actually enter the bar, but rather stay on the patio out front, only interacting with a single patron, whom Rosa kisses chastely—and rather awkwardly—on the lips. The supposed escalation of this encounter happens off camera; according to an onscreen caption, Rosa returns to the hotel room she shares with Nattie sometime "after 5 am." Following this incident, Rosa confesses to a "history with women" but claims that this history is the result of a fear of men. Says Rosa: "I associate love with pain, Nattie. Every time that I've fallen in love, I've been hurt. Girls are just easier. I'm like, scared of men. I'm like, freaked out of men, because I'm scared of a relapse." Nattie reassures her: "I think the most important thing in life is a human connection. And it's more important than championships, it's more important than money. So if you enjoyed kissing that girl, then, so be it. . . . If that makes you happy, you know you have a little glow about you. . . . If it makes her feel good, it makes you feel good, then you guys can get your rocks off together." Despite what may be good intentions, this storyline features a decidedly tentative intersectionality, wherein homosexuality is okay only as a last resort, and only because love can, occasionally, exceed gender. Even more problematic, though, is the fact that this storyline confirms the stereotype that lesbians are spurned heterosexuals.

Where race is concerned, *Total Divas*' approach to intersectionality is similarly tentative and problematic. The cast of *Total Divas* is more racially and ethnically diverse than the vast majority of American media. Nikki, Brie, and Eva Marie identify themselves as Mexican and Italian; JoJo identifies herself as Dominican and Mexican; Rosa identifies herself as Czech, Puerto Rican, and Costa Rican; Trinity identifies herself as African American. Yet besides being noted by the characters in their self-descriptions, race and ethnicity are rarely discussed in the show; instead, racial inclusion is taken as a given through the example of the Divas' friendship. This postracial inclusiveness is admirably idealistic but comes at the expense of necessary critique. *Total Divas* presents a rosy vision of racial equality that glosses over WWE's long and continuing history of racial stereotyping. As Justin G. García observes, "The use of racial and ethnic gimmicks and angles has been a major staple of wrestling since the 1920s and 1930s."[40] Such stereotypes are very much on display in the literal ghettoization of Trinity and Ariane's tag team within the Blaxploitation-inspired group Planet Funk. In the ring entrance of the Planet Funk team, which is frequently shown on *Total Divas*, the much smaller, scantily clad, and darker-skinned Trinity and Ariane dance with pom-poms beside the much lighter-skinned, much larger male wrestlers Brodus and Tensai, who are fully clothed in hats, tracksuits, and large gold chains. The depiction of Trinity and Ariane within this entrance is both sexist and racist, inasmuch as the different status or authority of the men and the women is signaled by their graphically different sizes, roles, clothing, and skin tones. At best, the Planet Funk entrance situates Trinity and Ariane as cheerleaders for Brodus and Tensai; at worst, it situates them as prostitutes, with Brodus and Tensai as pimps.[41] *Total Divas'* silence on racial politics is typical of WWE as a whole. While WWE has mobilized racial and ethnic stereotypes in different ways at different times, and while it is possible, as Battema and Sewell argue, "to read [black] characters such as D'Lo Brown, The Godfather, or Mark 'Sexual Chocolate' Henry as ironic critiques of racist stereotypes," WWE programming does not, as a rule, "encourage viewers to engage seriously in a critique of this form of racism."[42]

INTERSECTIONS WITH IN-RING STORYLINES

While a comprehensive analysis of *Total Divas* in conversation with contemporaneous in-ring storylines is beyond the scope of this chapter, it is worth discussing a few of the most significant intersections between the show and the ring, as these moments do much to inform the operation and implications of *Total Divas'* polysemy. One of the most prominent intersections was the long-term feud between three-time Divas champion AJ Lee and the *Total Divas* cast.[43] This feud was ignited shortly after *Total Divas* began airing, on the August 26, 2013, episode of *Monday Night Raw*. Following a match that included all the stars of *Total Divas* as either performers or valets, Lee—who, in real life, declined to participate in the show—lambasts the *Total Divas* cast as shallow, shameless celebrity seekers. Lee's opposition to *Total Divas* is cast in highly gendered terms. In the August 26 *Raw* segment, Lee wears jeans, sneakers, and a cropped T-shirt with the Divas Championship belt draped over her shoulder while the *Total Divas* cast wear ring costumes adorned with sequins and an assortment of 1950s pinup–inspired outfits; Brie, for instance, wears a polka dot bra and high-waisted sailor shorts, while Nikki wears a strapless, flared, polka dot dress. Standing on the entrance platform looking down at the ring, Lee begins her critique of the *Total Divas* cast speaking in a "ditzy" voice, performing a stereotype of a female (or feminized) fan of reality television: "OMG you guys. I just watched last night's episode of *Total Divas*, and it was *insane*. Oh my gosh—I mean, the Bellas were dealing with their obvious Daddy issues, the Funkadactyls broke up and then got back together again, Natayla's fiancé isn't much of a man . . ." Lee switches to a bolder tone for the remainder of her long speech, which is worth quoting at length because of how comprehensively it outlines her character's opposition to the show and its cast:

> Do you want to know what I see when I look in that ring, honestly? A bunch of cheap, interchangeable, expendable, useless women. Women who have turned to reality television because they just weren't gifted enough to be actresses. And that just weren't *talented* enough to be champions. I have done

more, in one year, than all of you have done in your entire collective careers. I have *saved* your Divas Division. I have shattered glass ceilings. I have broken down doors. Why? So a bunch of ungrateful, stiff, plastic mannequins can waltz on through without even so much as a thank you? . . . I gave my *life* to this, and you were just *handed* fifteen minutes of fame. I didn't get here because I was cute, or because I came from some famous wrestling family, or because I *sucked* up to the right people. I got here because I was *good*. I *earned* this championship. And no matter how many red carpets you guys want to walk in your $4000 ridiculous heels, you will *never* be able to lace up my Chuck Taylors. You are all worthless excuses for women, and you will *never* be able to touch me. And that—is reality.[44]

Lee would continue to play this antagonistic anti-Diva role throughout the remainder of her career, with many of the same phrases from the above speech repeated in subsequent performances and promotional materials.

The preceding analysis of *Total Divas* should make it clear that not all of Lee's complaints are unjustified. And yet, within Lee's speech, each potential subversion of WWE's institutionalized sexism mentioned is coupled with an opposing possibility. Although Lee presents herself as a feminist and supporter of the Divas Division, she is notably masculine coded, both by virtue of her tomboy aesthetic and by her position as an advocate for "authentic" wrestling (i.e., stereotypically masculine programming), which she situates in opposition to the inauthenticity of a certain brand of reality television (i.e., stereotypically feminine programming). In part, then, Lee's speech can be read as reassuring *Raw*'s primarily male audience that the more feminine pleasures of *Total Divas* will not infect in-ring matches or storylines. Lee's authenticity is, however, challenged by her character's history of female-coded mental instability, manifesting most often in hysterical jealousy within the context of various staged relationships with male wrestlers.[45] Lee's ability to threaten the status quo is also limited by the fact that she is only one woman facing both a male-dominated crowd and the rest of the Divas Division. In addition, the feminist implications of Lee's speech are undercut by the fact that she divides the Divas Division and invites fans to take a stand with or against certain versions of female strength; in this way, Lee evokes female empowerment while also policing it, diminishing the complexity of female desires and experiences. Consequently, although the feud between Lee and the *Total Divas* cast brings some important issues regarding WWE's treatment of its female performers to the fore, its ability to truly challenge WWE's sexism is threatened by its multiplicity of meanings.

The legacy of the #GiveDivasAChance Twitter campaign further evinces how difficult it can be to hold WWE properly accountable for its politics of representation. This hashtag trended on Twitter for two days following a widely criticized thirty-second match on February 23, 2015, between the Bella Twins and the team of Paige and Emma. Although the hashtag was started by fans in response to WWE's marginalization of its female performers, it was quickly picked up by WWE and worked into an existing feud between the Bella Twins and AJ Lee (sometimes paired with fellow anti-Diva Paige). In a sidebar promo that played before a championship match between Nikki and AJ on the March 16, 2015, episode of *Monday Night Raw*, the hashtag was ridiculed by Nikki and Brie as a means of asserting their identity as heels versus AJ's identity as a face. In this video, Nikki poses the question, "Give Divas a Chance?" to which she and Brie respond in unison, "Give us a break." On the one hand, the #GiveDivasAChance campaign is a hopeful example of fan activism, suggesting that WWE is not always totally in control of its narratives and can, on occasion, be challenged by fans newly empowered by social media. On the other hand, WWE's ability to quickly appropriate and exploit #GiveDivasAChance to promote preexisting storylines suggests that its control was never really in jeopardy.

CONCLUSION

It is convenient but not coincidental that the climax of the first episode of *Total Divas* so perfectly presages the Divas Revolution and Women's Evolution. This chapter's close reading of the polysemy built into *Total Divas*' every storyline, episode, and image demonstrates WWE's sophisticated ability to adapt to changing social mores and fan desires, as well as its equally sophisticated ability to recuperate critique. As discussed throughout this chapter, *Total Divas* is both sexist and feminist, both stereotypical and surprising. This polysemy ensures that embracing the Divas Revolution/Women's Evolution makes as much sense as not embracing it; depending on how one parses the show's multiplicity of meanings, both possibilities are equally available. Furthermore, within both *Total Divas* and WWE as a whole, the highly uncertain, continually flexible relationship between the real and the fake means that different moments and gestures can be retrospectively reframed as either real or fake, legitimate or illegitimate, depending on the storytelling needs of the present and future. While WWE's adoption of #GiveDivasAChance and its embrace of the resulting Divas Revolution/Women's Evolution might at first glance seem like a hopeful (or dangerous) example of WWE admitting its own flaws, this admission is also an incredibly useful marketing tool; in effect, this example shows WWE authenticating the effectiveness and prescience of its preexisting narratives by incorporating legitimate fan anger at those same narratives.

Moving forward, the political efficacy of the ongoing Women's Evolution—as it manifests within in-ring storylines, *Total Divas*, and its spinoffs, *Total Bellas* (2016–) and *Miz & Mrs.* (2018–)—will depend on whether meaningful dissent, including meaningful feminist critique, can exist within a transmedia empire that is so skilled at commodifying it.[46] What is fairly certain, though, is that rebranding the Divas Division into a new Women's Division is unlikely to offer much in the way of resolution. This change, which takes a step forward by resurrecting the past, is yet another instance of polysemy, open to competing interpretations: Does it celebrate a feminist future or disguise a sexist past (and present)? The smart money says that where WWE's female wrestlers are concerned, feminism and sexism will continue to coexist, at least until one or the other no longer sells.

Notes

1. Fiske, *Television Culture*, 16.
2. While WWE has produced other behind-the-scenes shows and web series starring male wrestlers, none of this programming focuses on the personal lives of the performers to the same degree as *Total Divas*.
3. Weber, "Trash Talk," 5.
4. Ibid., 20.
5. Mazer, *Professional Wrestling*, 163, 153.
6. WWE mainstays *Raw* and *SmackDown* have an estimated 68% male viewership. See Harris, "WWE Viewing Demographics Breakdown Released."
7. Where there have been some excellent analyses of female wrestling fans, this scholarship has typically focused on such fans' devotion to male wrestlers. See Dell, *Revenge of Hatpin Mary*; Salmon and Clerc, "'Ladies Love Wrestling, Too.'"
8. Jenkins, "'Never Trust a Snake,'" 77; Mazer, *Professional Wrestling*, 100.
9. Sammond, "Introduction," 7.
10. Heinecken, *Warrior Women of Television*, 21.
11. Weber, "Trash Talk," 14.
12. *WWE Diva Search* originally aired on Spike TV, which was marketed as "the first television channel for men."
13. Harkulich, "Sasha Banks," 150.
14. Ibid., 154.
15. Projansky, *Watching Rape*, 82; Rice, *Becoming Women*, 204; Whelehan, *Overloaded*, 63.
16. Harkulich, "Sasha Banks," 157.
17. Leonardi and Pope, *Diva's Mouth*, 12, 17.
18. Ibid., 19.
19. Ibid., 9.
20. Ronda Rousey has since signed with WWE, making her first appearance at the *Royal Rumble* in 2018.
21. This change was implemented in the *WrestleMania 32* preshow in 2016. Officially, WWE has ceased referring to its female performers as Divas, now using the gender-neutral term *Superstars*.
22. Holmes and Jermyn, "'Pig,' the 'Older Woman,' and the 'Catfight,'" 46.

23. Konuwa, "WWE's Future Is Gender-Neutral."

24. There are some notable exceptions to this rule. For instance, Nattie's season 2 feud with Summer Rae does intersect with an in-ring feud. In general, though, staggered scheduling makes narrative synergy difficult; *Total Divas* typically airs several months after the timeline of events it depicts.

25. This is not to suggest that stereotypical reality show catfights do not exist on *Total Divas*; certainly, there are episodes in which the Divas fight over men and succumb to jealousy, sometimes to the point of slapping each other and pulling each other's hair. However, these types of conflicts are rare in season 1 and become even rarer in subsequent seasons.

26. Nikki's invocation of "a snack break" refers to an oft-voiced criticism among fans—that Divas matches are so underwhelming or unimportant that they are effectively intermissions between the other (male) matches. In other words, Divas matches are an ideal time to visit the concession stand.

27. Mazer, *Professional Wrestling*, 4.

28. Castleberry, "Squared Circle Intentionalities," 105.

29. Rahilly, "Is RAW War?," 227.

30. As a rule, the copious muscles of male wrestlers signal activity and power, guarding against the passivity generally associated with objectification. In addition, the sexual characteristics of male wrestlers are rarely (if ever) emphasized to the same degree as the sexual characteristics of female wrestlers; although male wrestlers often display their "packages" within spandex pants and tiny trunks, their costumes are not specifically designed to highlight the penis, whereas the costumes of female wrestlers are often designed to highlight or expose breasts and buttocks. Those male wrestlers who are presented in a blatantly erotic context are clearly meant to be read as gender deviant (e.g., Goldust).

31. Sammond, "Introduction," 4.

32. For analyses of Daniel Bryan's in-ring career, see Christian Norman's and Sean Desilets's chapters within this volume.

33. Davis, "Revisiting Feminist Debates on Cosmetic Surgery," 35–36.

34. Bordo, *Twilight Zones*, 49–50.

35. Notably, it was only following her breast augmentation that Nikki was significantly promoted as a solo performer, eventually becoming the longest-reigning Divas champion of all time. During Nikki's reign, Brie, who does not have breast implants, continued to wrestle in solo matches but was most prominently featured as Nikki's valet. Salmon and Clerc, "'Ladies Love Wrestling, Too,'" 174.

36. Battema and Sewell, "Trading in Masculinity," 266.

37. Kavka, "Reality TV and the Gendered Politics of Flaunting," 56.

38. A preview of *Total Divas'* eighth season suggests that Nikki may be breaking up with John. Depending on how it is depicted, this storyline might be read within the context of WWE's continued promotion of female empowerment as a rejection of romantic clichés.

39. Various episodes of *Total Divas* also highlight the Divas' involvement in the NOH8 campaign in support of marriage equality and the antibullying Be a STAR Alliance, while the season 6 episode "Orlando Strong" features Trinity returning home to Orlando to host a memorial for the victims of the Pulse nightclub shooting.

40. García, "Latin Lords of the Ring," 38.

41. Trinity's most common finishing move, the "rear view," which is shown multiple times on *Total Divas*, is also very problematically racialized. In this move, Trinity, in her own words, must "jump up and do a toe touch while hitting the girl with my behind" (Season 1, "Welcome to the WWE"). To what extent Trinity had input in the development of this move is not made clear within the context of the show.

42. Battema and Sewell, "Trading in Masculinity," 268. As García observes, "At different times wrestling has used racial and ethnic angles for two very different purposes: either to build positive fan support among co-ethnics or, conversely, to generate negative reactions and hostility

from the crowd and enhance the wrestler's status as a heel (villain)" ("Latin Lords of the Ring," 38). Although Planet Funk could generate both types of responses, this does not negate or excuse the fact that Trinity and Ariane are clearly marginalized in gendered and racialized ways relative to Brodus and Tensai, nor does it address the discrepancy in which *Total Divas* discusses gender politics but not racial politics.

43. At one time, AJ Lee was the longest-running Divas champion of all time, reigning for approximately seven months. This record was broken by Nikki Bella following Lee's retirement from in-ring competition in 2015.

44. In this passage, I have used italics to try and replicate the points of emphasis in Lee's delivery of this speech.

45. It is worth noting that despite evoking stereotypes about mental illness within the ring, Lee, who in real life has bipolar disorder, has become an advocate for mental health awareness beyond the ring. For a fuller discussion of Lee's activities in this area, see Morales and Dozal, "'I Learned Most of My Anatomy from WWE,'" 165.

46. *Total Bellas*, which focuses on Brie and Nikki Bella and their immediate friends and family, began airing in 2016; it recently completed its fourth season as of this writing. *Miz & Mrs.*— which focuses on Michael Gregory Mizanin (ring name the Miz) and his wife, former Diva Maryse Mizanin—premiered on July 24, 2018.

Bibliography

Battema, Douglas, and Philip Sewell. "Trading in Masculinity: Muscles, Money, and Market Discourse in the WWF." In *Steel Chair to the Head: The Pleasure and Pain of Professional Wrestling*, edited by Nicholas Sammond, 260–94. Durham, NC: Duke University Press, 2005.

Bordo, Susan. *Twilight Zones: The Hidden Life of Cultural Images from Plato to O.J.* Berkeley: University of California Press, 1997.

Castleberry, Garrett L. "Squared Circle Intentionalities: What a Framework for 'Wrestling Studies' Can Look Like." *Popular Culture Studies Journal* 6, no. 1 (2018): 100–120.

Davis, Kathy. "Revisiting Feminist Debates on Cosmetic Surgery: Some Reflections on Suffering, Agency, and Embodied Difference." In *Cosmetic Surgery: A Feminist Primer*, edited by Creddisa J. Heyes and Meredith Jones, 35–48. Burlington, VT: Ashgate, 2009.

Dell, Chad. *The Revenge of Hatpin Mary: Women, Professional Wrestling and Fan Culture in the 1950s.* New York: Peter Lang, 2006.

Fiske, John. *Television Culture.* New York: Routledge, 1989.

García, Justin G. "Latin Lords of the Ring: Politics, Nativism and Mexican/Chicano Identity Through Professional Wrestling." In *Identity in Professional Wrestling: Essays on Nationality, Race, and Gender*, edited by Aaron D. Horton, 37–55. Jefferson, NC: McFarland & Company, 2018.

Harris, Jeffrey. "WWE Viewing Demographics Breakdown Released." *411Mania.* November 12, 2014. Accessed May 30, 2016. http://411mania.com/wrestling/wwe-viewing -demographics-breakdown-released/.

Harkulich, Christiana Molldrem. "Sasha Banks, the Boss of NXT: Media, Gender and the Evolution of Women's Wrestling in WWE." In *Identity in Professional Wrestling: Essays on Nationality, Race and Gender*, edited by Aaron D. Horton, 148–61. Jefferson, NC: McFarland & Company, 2018.

Heinecken, Dawn. *The Warrior Women of Television: A Feminist Cultural Analysis of the New Female Body in Popular Media.* New York: Peter Lang, 2003.

Holmes, Su, and Deborah Jermyn. "The 'Pig,' the 'Older Woman,' and the 'Catfight': Gender, Celebrity, and Controversy in a Decade of British Reality TV." In *Reality Gendervision: Sexuality and Gender on Transatlantic Reality Television*, edited by Brenda R. Weber, 37–53. Durham, NC: Duke University Press, 2014.

Jenkins, Henry. "'Never Trust a Snake': WWF Wrestling as Masculine Melodrama." In *The Wow Climax: Tracing the Emotional Impact of Popular Culture*, edited by Henry Jenkins, 76–102. New York: New York University Press, 2007.

Kavka, Misha. "Reality TV and the Gendered Politics of Flaunting." In *Reality Gendervision: Sexuality and Gender on Transatlantic Reality Television*, edited by Brenda R. Weber, 54–75. Durham, NC: Duke University Press, 2014.

Konuwa, Alfred. "The WWE's Future Is Gender-Neutral and Filled with Tears." *Forbes*. October 8, 2015. Accessed May 27, 2016. http://www.forbes.com/sites/alfredkonuwa/2015/10/08 /wwes-future-is-gender-neutral-and-filled-with-tears/#ec15476b5c93.

Leonardi, Susan J., and Rebecca A. Pope. *The Diva's Mouth: Body, Voice, Prima Donna Politics.* New Brunswick: Rutgers University Press, 1996.

Mazer, Sharon. *Professional Wrestling: Sport and Spectacle.* Jackson, MS: University Press of Mississippi, 1998.

Morales, Gabriela I., and Mario A. Dozal. "'I Learned Most of My Anatomy from WWE': A Health Communication Argument for Health-Related Studies of Professional Wrestling." *Popular Culture Studies Journal* 6, no. 1 (2018): 155–72.

Projansky, Sarah. *Watching Rape: Film and Television in Postfeminist Culture.* New York: New York University Press, 2001.

Rahilly, Lucia. "Is RAW War? Professional Wrestling as Popular S/M Narrative." In *Steel Chair to the Head: The Pleasure and Pain of Professional Wrestling*, edited by Nicholas Sammond, 211–31. Durham, NC: Duke University Press, 2005.

Rice, Carla. *Becoming Women: The Embodied Self in Image Culture.* Toronto: University of Toronto Press, 2014.

Salmon, Catherine, and Susan Clerc. "'Ladies Love Wrestling, Too': Female Wrestling Fans Online." In *Steel Chair to the Head: The Pleasure and Pain of Professional Wrestling*, edited by Nicholas Sammond, 167–91. Durham, NC: Duke University Press, 2005.

Sammond, Nicholas. "Introduction: A Brief and Unnecessary Defense of Professional Wrestling." In *Steel Chair to the Head: The Pleasure and Pain of Professional Wrestling*, edited by Nicholas Sammond, 1–22. Durham, NC: Duke University Press, 2005.

Total Divas. Produced by Bunim/Murray Productions and WWE. E! Network, 2013–present. USA.

Weber, Brenda R. "Trash Talk: Gender as an Analytic on Reality Television." In *Reality Gendervision: Sexuality and Gender on Transatlantic Reality Television*, edited by Brenda R. Weber, 1–36. Durham, NC: Duke University Press, 2014.

Whelehan, Imelda. *Overloaded: Popular Culture and the Future of Feminism.* London: Women's Press, 2000.

ANNA F. PEPPARD is SSHRC Postdoctoral Fellow at Brock University.

chapter ten

DANIEL'S SPECTER: DANIEL BRYAN, CHRIS BENOIT, AND THE WORK OF MOURNING

Sean Desilets

In his book *Specters of Marx*, Jacques Derrida makes this distinction between a specter and a spirit: "What distinguishes the specter or the *revenant* from the *spirit*, including the spirit in the sense of the ghost in general, is doubtless a supernatural and paradoxical phenomenality, the furtive and ungraspable visibility of the invisible, or an invisibility of a visible X, that *non-sensuous sensuous* of which *Capital* speaks ... with regard to a certain exchange value; it is also, no doubt, the tangible intangibility of a proper body without flesh, but still the body of some*one* or some*one* other."[1] The commodity's (surplus) value, its "paradoxical phenomenality," derives, of course, from work, whose value must disappear (along with the worker's body) to endow the commodity with its fetishistic value. Derrida's commentary documents the persistence of the spectral in Marx, excavating Marx's failure to disentangle the materiality of work from "the spectral logic that also governs the effects of virtuality, of simulacrum, of 'mourning work,' of ghost, *revenant*, and so forth."[2] The result of Derrida's exploration of Marx is what he calls a "hauntology," an alternative to ontology that stresses "the *affectivity* or the *presence* of a specter, that is, of what seems to remain ineffective, virtual, insubstantial as a simulacrum."[3]

Professional wrestling provides an especially powerful instantiation of the persistence of the spectral in the function of labor. In fact, the parlance of the industry infuses the very word *work* with spectrality. Among the many suggestive linguistic turns that have developed among professional wrestlers (and now, thanks to the internet, among its "smart" fans), the term *work* holds a special place in wrestling jargon. It refers both to the actual aesthetic/industrial practice of wrestling itself (one *works* a match) and also to the logic of deception that runs through the professional wrestling world (when an injury is not real but rather part of a storyline, for example, it is referred to as a *work* or as *worked*). For professional wrestlers, then, *work* always includes not only the generation of value through productive labor but also, and as an inseparable aspect of that labor, as the very *essence* of that labor, the production simultaneously of the spectral—of spectral combat among bodies whose doubled interrelation makes work into a collaborative deception. Professional wrestlers' bodies appear in the ring as agents of antipathy and violence, but they generate that image collaboratively. Universal among wrestlers is the understanding that their first responsibility is to protect themselves and their opponents from injury.[4] This ethic of care undergirds another ethic, which has to do with generating the illusion of violence using an ever-evolving and highly ritualized repertoire of techniques and movements. The spectacle of violence is what we might call the commodity form of the professional wrestling match. Of course, the picture is much more complicated. The packaging of professional wrestling—the theatrical props, the management of storylines—is in part authored by the managerial apparatus that surrounds wrestlers (road agents, writers, directors, and, above all in WWE, its CEO and booker, Vince McMahon). Without wrestling matches, however, none of this would matter. And the wrestling match is, in the final analysis, the work of wrestlers. It is their work in the sense that it is what their labor makes into a saleable commodity and also their work in the sense of their generation of a simulacrum.

If a wrestling *match* itself always displays a doubled and ambivalent mode of performance, in which the most successful collaboration gives the most convincing appearance of genuine conflict within the fanciful conventions of the form, the body of the professional wrestling worker—like the bodies of all workers—represents the conduit through which the materiality of labor passes into the spectral value of the commodity. The difference is that the wrestler's body does not disappear, as do the bodies of typical working-class laborers. On the contrary, it constitutes the decisive element of the commodity. Derrida sees Marx holding out the hope that, with an analysis that belies the commodity's mystified glamour and recognizes the work hidden beneath it, "Nothing there will be any longer an affected mannerism, giving itself airs."[5] The work of the professional wrestler, though, *is* "affected mannerism," albeit an affected mannerism that puts the body at stake. Wrestling thus represents a striking instance of Derrida's embodied spectrality, particularly in its mixture of embodiment with illusion.

The body of the professional wrestler recalls questions that Derrida associates with the ghost of Hamlet's father. Derrida suggests that the ghost's armor "may be but the body of a real artifact, a kind of technical prosthesis, a body foreign to the spectral body that it dresses, dissimulates, and protects, masking even its identity."[6] This carapace conceals the spectral body that may hide beneath it, but at the same time it highlights the threat of inauthenticity that the specter always presents. These questions of authenticity always bear stakes that derive from the "play of theatricality." For wrestlers, they directly affect the real world of life and death, labor and exploitation. Professional wrestlers' bodies function like the ghost's armor: they are aesthetic objects, meant to display a martial impenetrability that plays a crucial role in the cat-and-mouse game of deception that characterizes contemporary professional wrestling. All fans know wrestling combat is simulated, but verisimilitude is nonetheless a central value. The appearance of strength that wrestlers gain from size and muscularity plays a crucial role in this illusion. But as I explain in greater detail below, the conditions under which wrestlers work often force them to maintain their physiques using steroids, growth hormone, or, at best, the unhealthy quantities of painkillers that are required to maintain a workout regimen while injured. Understanding the extraordinary stresses that professional wrestlers' bodies endure at the nexus of theatricality and athleticism, and situating that experience politically, requires a Derridean spectral analysis.[7]

The term *mourning* occurs often in Derrida's account of hauntology because the specter signifies something apparently lost but nonetheless paradoxically present. Two sites of mourning predominate in *Specters of Marx*: the persistence of Hamlet's father in the form of his ghost (and the actions it motivates) and the "death" of the Marxist dream in the ascendancy of neoliberal economic and social policy. In both cases, the figure to be mourned remains *active* and powerful. Mourning is a kind of accounting or responsibility, and "the ghost would be the deferred spirit, the promise or calculation of an expiation."[8] The specter thus has three closely related features: it is linked to a loss, it *embodies* that loss, and in so embodying it, it *activates* it and motivates a move toward justice.

Leveraging Derrida's spectral economy, this chapter argues that the body of one professional wrestler, Daniel Bryan, has done "mourning work" for another, Chris Benoit, and that Benoit's spectral infusion into Bryan's body and career provides a counternarrative to efforts on the part of WWE to efface the responsibility it bears for crimes that Benoit committed. The chapter begins by reviewing the details of Benoit's actions and explaining how Benoit's legacy inflected Bryan's career. It then turns its attention to the industrial conditions that have governed the labor experiences of professional wrestlers in the period that spans both wrestlers' careers, approximately 1990 to the present, attending especially to the maintenance and deployments of professional wrestlers' bodies. These reflections will serve as a backdrop for my analysis of first Benoit's, and then WWE's, efforts to narrativize Benoit's behavior. Finally, I will consider the uncanny echoes of Benoit's actions that haunt Bryan's WWE run, ultimately arguing that Bryan himself serves as a memorial for Benoit, whose memory WWE has attempted to efface. I will suggest that Bryan's immense popularity with WWE fans arises in part from his functioning as a place of mourning and remembrance for Benoit. Here, far from *effacing* the function of work in generating value, spectrality, which reflects the means of production, militates against forgetting and mystification.

CHRIS BENOIT AND DANIEL BRYAN

On the weekend of June 22–24, 2007, WWE wrestler Chris Benoit killed his wife, Nancy; his seven-year-old son, Daniel; and himself in his home in Fayetteville, Georgia. Forensic evidence suggests he asphyxiated Nancy first, sometime on Friday, June 22. He killed Daniel very shortly after Nancy. Daniel had Xanax in his system and was likely unconscious when Benoit attacked him. Bruises to Daniel's face suggest that Benoit killed him with a variant of the "crippler crossface" hold, one of Benoit's signature finishing moves in WWE.

Assessing the causes of events like this is next to impossible, but some clues have emerged. A postmortem investigation of Benoit's brain revealed that the countless head traumas Benoit endured during his wrestling career had left his brain profoundly damaged; specifically, the damage was consistent with chronic traumatic encephalopathy (CTE), which has been blamed for violent and self-destructive behavior in several professional football players.[9] Other work-related factors may also have helped motivate Benoit's actions. Benoit's best friend in the wrestling industry, Eddie Guerrero, had himself died of a heart attack in 2005, at age thirty-eight. Heart attacks are common in long-term steroid abusers, and the list of professional wrestlers who have died of heart attacks before reaching fifty is shocking.[10] In fact, Benoit himself had an enlarged heart, though it is unlikely he knew that.[11] Friends report that Benoit never recovered emotionally from Guerrero's death.[12] Benoit made a series of telephone calls and text messages over the weekend of the murders, including several to Eddie's brother, Chavo Guerrero, also a professional wrestler employed at the time by WWE.[13] Like Eddie Guerrero, Benoit suffered from severe and chronic pain and had a long history of drug use and, probably, abuse. The drugs he took included painkillers, steroids, and antianxiety medication.[14]

All these factors, every one of which probably contributed in some way to Benoit's breakdown, resulted from his career in professional wrestling, much of it in WWE's employ.[15]

WWE preempted the June 25 episode of its flagship television show *Raw* with a series of testimonials on Benoit's life and career, but once the details of the murder-suicide became clear, the company attempted to erase Benoit from its history. His matches were removed from DVD releases, and his name was scrubbed from WWE.com. His actions motivated a whole series of new restrictions on WWE wrestlers, who were banned from using moves associated with Benoit or reminiscent of his actions. Performances of choking, for example, were banned. Nearly ten years later, his matches do appear on the WWE Network, but a search for his name yields no results, and the matches are not indexed in the way other matches are. The streaming service includes cue points that mark the beginnings and conclusions for most matches on its archived shows, Benoit's being a notable exception. Benoit is a metadata ghost, a hole in the net of information that facilitates fans' interaction with WWE history. In short, though the rigor of WWE's efforts to make Benoit disappear has relaxed over time, the company still tries to efface his memory.

Over that same weekend in June, Bryan Danielson was on tour with Ring of Honor Wrestling (ROH), one of the largest independent promotions in the United States.[16] On the night of June 22 in Dayton, Ohio, Danielson wrestled in a tag-team match with Nigel McGuinness against Takeshi Morishima and Naomichi Marufuji. On June 23 in Chicago Ridge, Illinois, Danielson lost to KENTA in the evening's main event. Morishima, Marufuji, and KENTA were all under contract with the Japanese promotion New Japan Pro Wrestling, which has a long-standing working relationship with ROH. These were probably among the best wrestling matches worked anywhere in the world on those dates. With the exception of McGuinness, who was also no slouch, the wrestlers mentioned here all ranked among the ten most skilled wrestlers active at the time. Benoit would have been on that list, too. The connections between Danielson and Benoit are more extensive than that, though. Benoit helped to import Japanese wrestling styles into America over the course of the 1990s, and it is unlikely that ROH would have been pushing all these Japanese wrestlers in 2007 if not for his influence. Further, Benoit's devotion to the "strong" or hard-hitting style then prominent in Japanese professional wrestling probably contributed to the state of his brain. His concussions resulted, of course, from his willingness to take real blows to the head instead of simulating them. Realism of this sort was also a signature element of Japanese strong style, with which KENTA and Marufuji in particular are deeply associated.[17] But if the Japanese wrestlers with whom Danielson worked over this terrible weekend belong—perhaps—to the aesthetic history of the weekend's events, Danielson himself bears the most intimate (and strangest) relation to their afterlife.

Two years after Benoit's death, WWE hired Danielson and changed his ring name to Daniel Bryan. Such name changes are common for wrestlers entering WWE; they constitute one of WWE's techniques for maintaining control over the intellectual property that wrestlers' bodies represent to the company. A wrestler whose name is trademarked by WWE cannot use that name outside of WWE without permission, so these name changes make it more difficult for a wrestler who has established a reputation in WWE to leverage that reputation while working for other wrestling promotions (or anyone else).[18]

WWE never promoted (or pushed) Bryan as vigorously as his skills and steadily growing popularity seemed to suggest they should. It is possible that Bryan's weak push resulted in part from his similarities to Benoit. More likely, neither was the sort of wrestler WWE was likely to push; neither was particularly big, and WWE does not have a history of valuing the artisanal working ability (or workrate, in wrestling jargon) that both wrestlers displayed.[19] The national expansion that won WWE a near monopoly in the American wrestling marketplace was fueled by the popularity of Hulk Hogan, who was a brilliant showman but not a particularly graceful or creative wrestler. His success fortified a tendency already present in WWE to value size over workrate. To some extent, Benoit overcame these limitations. He had his initial US success in a rival national promotion that valued workrate somewhat more highly, and his steroid use gave him a bodybuilder's physique. Bryan probably enjoyed neither of these dubious advantages, but, like many independent wrestlers of his generation, he was heavily influenced by Benoit. He used several of Benoit's recognizable moves and showed Benoit's influence in his interest in strong style. So incidental factors (size) and volitional ones (aesthetic influence) linked Bryan and Benoit, and their shared characteristics made them both unlikely main eventers in WWE.

Thus, although his similarities to Benoit probably boosted Bryan's popularity with fans, they also hurt his push. In June 2010, Bryan, then playing an increasingly unhinged heel character, was apparently fired by WWE when he choked an announcer during an episode of *Raw*. As part of a somewhat leaky embargo against wrestlers using moves and mannerisms associated with Benoit and his crimes, WWE had genuinely banned performances of choking. So the firing looked like a real rather than a storyline event—a shoot rather than a work.[20] But by August Bryan had returned, and soon thereafter he began using two moves that were reminiscent of Benoit: the flying headbutt (which probably earned Benoit some of his concussions) and a variation of the crossface submission hold. Prestigious wrestlers had been able to get away with using some of Benoit's moves, but no one in Bryan's precarious situation would have done so without explicit permission. With its economies of deception and allusion, wrestling tends to incite paranoid thinking, and I will not guess at how self-conscious these echoes were on the part of WWE or Bryan. The symbolic associations, however, are undeniable: Bryan's depiction as an agent of uncontrollable violence, his "firing" under a post-Benoit code of behavior, and his use of Benoit-associated moves upon his return all link the rocky trajectory of his career with Benoit's.

In one of the strangest echoes between the two wrestlers, in 2013 Bryan apprehended a burglar who had broken into his home, using a wrestling move (the rear naked choke, also a standard MMA hold and a distant relative to Benoit's crippler crossface) to keep the burglar restrained until police arrived.[21] He thereby performed an act of domestic heroism that in some ways produced a positively valorized reflection of Benoit's actions. But Bryan did not escape all the hazards that brought Benoit down. Just as he *was* finally getting a serious push, Bryan was plagued by a series of injuries—including at least one concussion. In 2016, at age thirty-four, he retired from the ring, taking on an onscreen role as one of the commissioners on *SmackDown Live*, WWE's B television show. At that point, he had been kept out of the ring for nearly a year by WWE doctors, who would not clear him to wrestle because of his long history of concussions (he had suffered several, it seems, without reporting them). WWE had become much more sensitive to the deleterious effects of multiple concussions since the Benoit murder-suicide, and until very recently it seemed unlikely that Bryan would ever wrestle again for WWE.[22] A significant campaign by Bryan himself, though, along (one suspects) with the prospect that Bryan would leave WWE to wrestle elsewhere, convinced the company to bring Bryan out of retirement.[23] In his first match back, at *WrestleMania 34* in April 2018, Bryan integrated a simulated neck injury into his match. One hopes that Bryan has a long late-phase career ahead of him. He seems to genuinely enjoy wrestling, and his matches are consistently exciting. But, despite some striking exceptions, the career outcomes for wrestlers who sustain serious head and neck injuries are not usually good.

WRESTLING, WORK, EXPLOITATION

As Andrew Zolides's contribution to this volume demonstrates, the labor conditions of professional wrestlers are unenviable. WWE wrestlers work relentless schedules, are constantly on the road (where, in many cases, they pay for their own hotel rooms and travel), and wrestle in a physically demanding style.[24] Nagging injuries have no time to heal, and injured wrestlers lose money when they take time off. (WWE wrestlers are paid a downside guarantee, which varies considerably but may be quite small, and make most of their money on a match-by-match basis and on merchandise sales, the latter of which also depend on wrestlers' presence at shows.) Few wrestlers who have been working full-time in the business for a sustained period escape chronic pain of some kind. Benoit's circumstances were certainly worsened, as I have mentioned, by steroid abuse. Though WWE has now cracked down (to some extent) on the use of performance-enhancing drugs, instituted responsible concussion protocols, and taken steps to minimize the head traumas wrestlers necessarily endure, it is unclear whether the underlying conditions that contributed to Benoit's actions have been substantially alleviated. Wrestlers still work a physically grueling schedule, still depend on remaining active (even when injured) to sustain their incomes, and are still held to dangerously unrealistic aesthetic and performance expectations that are hard to maintain without resorting to performance-enhancing drugs (and it is clear that some wrestlers still use either steroids or growth hormone, despite WWE's drug-testing policy).[25]

A careful look at the business of wrestling, however, reveals how "spectral" effects permeate even these baseline economic factors. WWE has a grossly lopsided pay structure for wrestlers and thus underpays the majority of its performers given the profitability of the company and the brevity of most wrestlers' careers.[26] And WWE's recent switch from monthly pay-per-view events to an over-the-top streaming subscription service model seems to have enabled the company to grab back even more of the revenue from its most significant events.[27] Though the exploitative nature of these practices is undeniable, they result in part from ideologically inflected marketplace conditions. One reason WWE pays out so little of its gross income to performers is that certain of its revenue streams are less robust than those of other sports franchises. For instance, television networks are willing to pay much more for other sports programs even when those programs draw significantly fewer viewers than wrestling; the perception that wrestling fans are economically marginal means that the networks draw lower advertising rates on wrestling shows. A wrestling viewer is worth a lot less to advertisers than, for example, a soccer viewer, though the difference in ad rates probably exaggerates the actual economic difference between the two, as wrestling's value is also diminished by some advertisers' queasiness about associating themselves with a culturally denigrated form of entertainment.[28] There is, therefore, a vital link between the exploitation of professional wrestlers and the exploitation of their fans. If, as I will argue, Daniel Bryan memorializes Chris Benoit against WWE's efforts to forget him, then he can also serve to underscore the political urgency of recognizing these economic connections between professional wrestlers and their largely working-class fans.

TELLING BENOIT'S STORY

WWE sought vigorously to evade any responsibility for Benoit's actions. They deployed their most articulate wrestlers in the media to claim that steroid use was not widespread among wrestlers (a blatant lie) and that Benoit's actions ought to be viewed as aberrant acts by a "monster" (Vince McMahon's own word).[29] I have mentioned WWE's effort to scrub Benoit from its history, which is certainly the most elaborate and ambitious of the corporation's many attempts at historical revision. Though WWE has always underplayed the role of steroids in wrestlers' deaths, they have never worked so hard to erase a wrestler from its history as they have in Benoit's case. By contrast, WWE took a more familiar line in its handling of the death of Benoit's best friend, Eddie Guerrero. The signal characteristic of WWE's telling of Guerrero's story is sentimentality, and the friendship between Benoit and Guerrero played a crucial role in that narrative before Benoit had to be scrubbed from WWE's official line. Guerrero's successful recovery from drug addiction, the underdog narratives that always accompanied both him and Benoit, and the very public (and widely endorsed) memorializing gestures that Eddie's friends, relatives, and fans continue to use in the ring—Rey Mysterio Jr. still points to the heavens from the top rope before using one of Eddie's signature moves, and Sasha Banks's ring gear at *WrestleMania 32* was an explicit tribute to him—all make Eddie Guerrero a highly sentimentalized figure. The scene between Guerrero and Benoit in the ring at *WrestleMania XX* after Benoit won WWE's second most prestigious championship was one of the most operatic in professional wrestling history. As confetti poured over them, the two men wept and embraced in the ring. This was that rare professional wrestling event that functioned equally well as a work and as a genuine, unaffected phenomenon. It really *was* moving to both Benoit and Guerrero that they had managed to succeed in WWE despite the challenges presented by their sizes, wrestling styles, and, in Guerrero's case, race. But the endless repetitions of Guerrero's story served to obscure the extent to which the problems he overcame were *caused* in part by his involvement in professional wrestling. Recall that, like many wrestlers of his era, Guerrero died of a heart attack brought on by steroid abuse. That abuse was a direct effect of WWE's fetishistic investment in immense male bodies and its willingness to condone the use of dangerous drugs to produce those bodies and to maintain them through a full-time wrestler's relentless schedule.

The horrible nature of Benoit's crimes put this kind of sentimentalizing narrative out of reach—hence WWE's clumsier efforts at simple erasure. The signifying network that Benoit himself constructed around his actions produces two counternarratives against WWE's efforts to decontextualize Benoit's breakdown. First, he deployed several signs that claim for himself the sentimentalizing narrative that WWE provided for Eddie Guerrero. It was clear to everyone around Benoit that Guerrero's death affected him powerfully. The investigation of Benoit's crimes turned up a diary of Benoit's that contained entries addressed to Eddie. One of the diary entries promised that Benoit would "join [Guerrero] soon." This gesture was not a purely private one: Benoit had told professional wrestling journalist Bryan Alvarez that he was keeping a diary with entries addressed to Eddie.[30] Benoit also produced other sentimentalizing gestures. He placed Bibles next to each of his victims, meaning, I think, to indicate that his wife and son were of exalted value to him.[31] As if in anticipation of WWE's decision to deny him the narrative position that the company generally reserves for dead wrestlers, then, Benoit himself presented a series of sentimentalizing signs both in the staging of the murders and for some time beforehand, particularly in his way of mourning Eddie.

Even more strikingly, though, Benoit coded his actions to defy WWE's cowardly efforts to treat his breakdown as an isolated act of evil. Several of his most obviously meaningful actions pointed directly to his work as a professional wrestler. As I have noted, forensic evidence suggests that Benoit killed Daniel with his signature submission hold, the crippler crossface (one of the moves that Bryan has used in his own career).[32] Benoit also hanged himself from a piece of weightlifting equipment, linking his death to the body obsession that motivated his steroid abuse. Steroids probably worsened Benoit's depression. They certainly contributed to Eddie Guerrero's death. So Benoit's weightlifting equipment was by no means a politically neutral furnishing; it was, rather, an element of his economically mandated efforts to alter his body in accordance with WWE's expectations. Finally, it seems that most, if not all, of Benoit's contacts with the outside world during the weekend were with wrestling colleagues. Chris Benoit had given his entire life to professional wrestling. Despite WWE's best efforts, there is no denying that he also gave it his death and the deaths of those closest to him.

Benoit himself, therefore, provides resources for counteracting WWE's repudiation of him. But Benoit's spectral persistence in the professional wrestling world does not halt with the immediate aftermath of his rampage. To hear other echoes of Benoit's life and death, I turn now to the haunted WWE career of Bryan Danielson. Danielson had a brief run in WWE from 2000 to 2001, but his first consequential run with the company began in 2009, two years after the Benoit murder-suicide. Given WWE's well-established tradition of tasteless (and clueless) decisions, it may not be surprising that the new name the company gave to Danielson should produce such striking resonances with the Benoit events. Danielson's new name was Daniel Bryan. This name change both denies and recalls the nearly genetic connection between Benoit and Danielson. Removing the *son* from *Daniel's* name and swapping the positions of his patronymic and given names both seem calculated to disassociate Bryan from Benoit's son and victim Daniel, but of course the changes also mean that they are now two Daniels, each of them strangely entangled with Benoit. Juggling the morphemes *Daniel* and *son* opens up the spectral possibility that Bryan might be Benoit's son. And indeed the Benoit events would shadow Bryan throughout his WWE career, shaping his fate like a ghostly inheritance.

Two Daniels, then, one living and one dead: one the son of a man who stands, in some ways, also in a relation of paternity to the second, the first haunting the second, twinned together with him by a name and a history. That history itself includes an act of renaming, the reappropriation and redistribution of a name to mark one kind of ownership (in renaming him, WWE stakes a legal and financial claim to Bryan) and to disavow another (the severing of *son* from *Daniel*). For when Daniel lost his *son*, the loss also made another son named Daniel present again. The double denial of patrimony at play here—the displacement of the patronymic to the site of the given name, coupled with the removal of the signifier of patrimony itself (*son*)—can only make the second, older Daniel into another son for Benoit. Both Daniel's son and Benoit's, his rebirth as a WWE performer accomplished by way of a double sleight of hand that effaced the younger Daniel's sonhood and infused the new Daniel with the ghost of the son. These spectral siblings also find themselves linked to WWE, the corporate parent that helped to produce their common father. Given the role of Benoit's actions in WWE's subsequent carefulness around concussions, the younger Daniel's fate might also have served to prophesy the happier fate (for now) of the elder. Daniel's death might have determined Daniel's life—interrupting his career, putting the writing on the wall to his ambitions, frustrating him, but sending him out into the larger world less cataclysmically damaged than the father who found no other recourse during that disastrous weekend than to send his own Daniel *out* of the world. When Benoit placed Bibles near the bodies of his wife and son, he invited us to read the scene he staged as a set of signs. One way to satisfy that request is to imitate the Daniels' biblical counterpart, who knew how to read the writing on the wall as an answer—and a threat—to unaccountable power (Daniel 5:13–20).[33]

Benoit's experience has functioned like a site of trauma for WWE discourse. The silence around Benoit and the distortions that affect every effort to address him—the unsearchability of his name; the unmarked quality of his performances; the haunting, uncertain effect he seems to have had on Bryan's career—these effects communicate their urgency precisely in their spectrality, their incomplete silence. That the ghosts of Benoit's presence should take uncertain and elliptical forms is not surprising. I am not arguing that Bryan self-consciously imitated Benoit's style wholesale or that WWE's reservations about him were directly or persistently linked to Benoit. Many spectral encounters are a matter of chance, taking on meaning only retroactively and haphazardly. Bryan seems haunted by Benoit (and Daniel) on the basis of such chance encounters—the effects of Bryan's naming, the coincidence that Bryan subdued an intruder using his wrestling skills, and finally, painfully, the fact that Bryan's career was interrupted by concussions (as Benoit's certainly should have been long before June 2007). It is these coincidences, more even than the similarities between the two workers, that place them in spectral relation to one another.

FANWORK

As I have established above, the work of professional wrestling responds to Derrida's reading of Marx, illustrating the persistence of the spectral even in the midst of the process—labor—whose visibility is supposed to exorcise it. Placed in relation to my earlier discussion of the conditions under which wrestlers do their labor, though, wrestling also promises to conjure forth some new implications for Derridean "hauntology"—the dynamic under which any claim to stable ontology will prove itself haunted by the specter of its own conceptual instability.[34] Antonio Negri has noted that among the words associated with Marxism, the one that appears least often in Derrida's book is *exploitation*, even though exploitation is the basis of Marx's ontology. Conceding that Marx's account of exploitation is—predictably—insufficient for present conditions, Negri nonetheless asserts that "in the ghostly production of postindustrial capitalism, [the mechanisms that produce exploitation] remain intact and become even more powerful."[35] WWE wrestlers are certainly not typical exploited workers, and the conditions they encounter will not translate to the experiences of today's technological working class. Just as their conception of work offers an opportunity to reflect on the spectral quality of labor as the origin point of the commodity in *all* capitalism, though, some particular echoes of wrestlers' exploitation promise to reveal how the hauntology of contemporary capitalist production can take on a political urgency. Even as the younger, lost Daniel has haunted the older Daniel's career, that career has itself, in its ghostly reflection of *Benoit*'s career, served to animate Benoit's specter and mobilize it against WWE's efforts to consign Benoit to oblivion. Bryan has given WWE fans a chance to assert the value of their own emotional labor as consumers in a way that was facilitated by Benoit's memory.[36]

The fan responses that have punctuated Daniel Bryan's career in WWE may serve to memorialize Benoit more vividly than any officially sanctioned monument could. The stylistic similarities between Benoit and Bryan would be clear to any schooled observer of their work. In fact, in a strange coincidence, one of the leading professional wrestling newsletters published an article in February 2007—just four months before the Benoit murder-suicide—debating whether Benoit or Bryan was the best wrestler in the world.[37] Partly because Bryan located himself so clearly in the aesthetic tradition occupied by Benoit, the vehemence of fan support for Bryan has been genuinely remarkable. It has become increasingly common for a certain class of fans to resist the narratives presented by WWE—to boo people who are presented as faces and cheer those presented as heels, for example—but the affection fans evince for Bryan is not mere contrarianism, and it goes beyond the usual cohort of cynical fans. In fact, the almost absurdly affirmative nature of this reaction found perfect illustration in the chant that Bryan began using early in his WWE career. He simply threw both arms into the air and chanted "Yes!" In the early part of Bryan's run, this was a feature of the loveable goof/good guy persona that was assigned to him, which itself may have functioned to disassociate Bryan from Benoit (who was generally characterized as a dour sadist). When Bryan turned heel, he replaced his "Yes!" chant with "No!"—thus a paradoxical structure developed under which fans would show their hostility to Bryan using the very same "Yes!" chant that they also used to celebrate him when he was a (comical and ineffectual) face. Throughout this entire period, it must be stressed, Bryan's actual work in the ring was excellent, and serious fans were frustrated by the comical depiction of his character (not necessarily because they objected to comedy figures but because such figures do not often compete in long or important matches). In the period prior to Bryan's temporary retirement, fans became more vociferous. They began to use the "Yes!" chant in upper-card matches not involving Bryan to protest his exclusion for these matches. They booed other wrestlers who were receiving major pushes instead of Bryan— especially large bodybuilder types whose pushes were perceived to derive primarily from their physiques rather than from their abilities in the ring.[38] In short, fans rejected WWE's efforts to belittle Bryan, and they did so in a way that was willfully affirmative. Though the motivations of wrestling fans are never unmixed or uncomplicated, I see their resistance to WWE narratives as an indirect answer to the narrative silence that the company maintains around Benoit. The relationship here is not direct, but there is a metonymic link between the Benoit and Bryan stories. And absent any productive way for fans to insist on Benoit as an element of WWE's history, I see their celebration of Bryan as an act of public performed memory and Bryan himself as a key monument to Benoit's role in wrestling history. The overwhelming success of the "Yes!" chant, which also appeared in other professional sports venues and persists to this day, is an act of mourning and of memory.[39]

Chris Benoit. Daniel Benoit. Daniel Bryan. This chiasmic chain of names gives name to the spectral work that binds these people together genetically, economically, and politically. Against a forgetting that would efface the mourning that Benoit earned through decades of spectral (by which I mean real) violence, the "Yes!" chant holds both Daniels together, lets us recognize them as common inheritors of Benoit's work, and makes the ghostly work of mourning into an assertion of the spectral quality of *all* work without denying what that work does to us.

Conclusion

Early in *Specters of Marx*, Derrida asserts that "there has never been a scholar, who, as such, does not believe in the sharp distinction between the real and unreal, the actual and the inactual, the living and the non-living, being and non-being."[40] He says this in reference to the scene in *Hamlet* in which Marcellus, the soldier, suggested that Horatio, whom he calls a "scholar," address the king's ghost. As a scholar, Horatio is supposed to be able to determine what the ghost wants. But, says Derrida, "Marcellus did not know what the singularity of a position is, let's not call it a class position as one used to say long ago, but the singularity of a place of speech, of a part of experience, and of a link of filiation, places and links from which alone one may address oneself to the ghost."[41] Marcellus errs in assuming that Horatio, as a scholar, can speak to the ghost, when in fact only the son, Hamlet, can do so. Hamlet's filial association suits him uniquely to speak with his father's ghost. For Derrida's "part of experience," we might read Hamlet's passionate attachment to his father, which is so ostentatiously on display in the following scene of Hamlet's insistent mourning. Hamlet's filial qualification comes along with a deep affective connection. Marcellus assumes that a scholar is "a spectator who better understands how to establish the necessary distance or how to find the appropriate words for observing, better yet, for apostrophizing the ghost, which is to say for speaking the language of kings or of the dead."[42] But in the play, links of filiation and affection are the true qualifications for speaking to ghosts. The "necessary distance" and linguistic aptitude that serve the scholar will not help when confronted with the dead king, but the soldier cannot see the difference.

I want to draw two lessons from this Derridean parable. The first has to do with Daniel Bryan, who occupies all three positions in this triangle. I have argued here for the link of filiation and affection that connects him to Chris Benoit. But Bryan is also, to invoke a familiar wrestling cliché, a "student of the game." He forged his similarity with Benoit by means of careful attention to Benoit's ringwork, which includes not only the immediate physical performance of certain moves but also—a Bryan specialty—the placement of these moves in the melodramatic context of a wrestling match. Bryan's resemblance to Benoit is as much a matter of study as it is of training. On the other hand, it is still a matter of training. Bryan's corporeal presence is not armored the way Benoit's was, but he still presents himself as a combatant, a soldier, in WWE narratives. His desire to return to the field of battle has been his story for the last three years. He has returned now. Let us hope that this unique confluence of perspectives protects the prince/scholar/soldier Daniel Bryan from the worst consequences associated with each of those three positions, which are complacency, delusion, and injury.

The second lesson is for scholars of wrestling. Most of us are also fans, connected to wrestling by affinities that stretch back into our life histories and entangle themselves with our most intimate fantasies. We have outgrown the notion that scholarship is a matter of establishing the necessary distance of objectivity. Our affective engagements with our objects of study need to be understood and confronted rather than made to disappear. Derrida's Marcellus also believes that the scholar is good at "speaking the language of kings or of the dead." Here, too, imagines Derrida, the future has come to the rescue. Calling on the scholar Horatio to speak to the ghost, "Marcellus was perhaps anticipating the coming, one day, one night, several centuries later, of another 'scholar.' The latter would finally be capable, beyond the opposition between presence and non-presence, actuality and inactuality, life and non-life, of thinking the possibility of the specter, the specter of possibility."[43] The messianic language here is deliberate, of course. There is a necessary link between this capacity to think "beyond the opposition between presence and non-presence" and the advent of true justice. Marx is the scholar that Derrida finds at that intersection. He is still, perhaps, a scholar yet to come, or to return. For Chris Benoit, we can be sure that any justice to come will have come too late. But his spectral return encoded in the body of Daniel Bryan, in all its ambiguity and halting uncertainty, ought to teach us that we scholars can choose between speaking "the language of kings *or* of the dead." Instead of bowing down to the king, we can choose to remember the feared and reviled dead, to contest the opposition between "life and non-life," and thereby to help turn the strange theatrical enterprise we've chosen to love toward exalting bodies rather than destroying them.

Notes

1. Derrida, *Specters of Marx*, 7.
2. Ibid., 75.
3. Ibid., 10.
4. Chow, "Work and Shoot," 79–80.
5. Derrida, *Specters of Marx*, 115.
6. Ibid., 8.
7. Several of the contributors to *Ghostly Demarcations*, an edited volume produced in response to *Specters of Marx*, accuse Derrida of robbing Marx of his political urgency. In response, Derrida argues that, on the contrary, *Specters* emphasizes the unrelenting demand for justice that runs throughout Marx's work. This essay is intended in part as a defense of Derrida's position. See Derrida, "Marx & Sons," 221–24.
8. Derrida, *Specters of Marx*, 136.
9. Alvarez, "Benoit Brain Massively Damaged," 1–7; Omalu et al., "Chronic Traumatic Encephalopathy."
10. Skipper, "Hard Drugs, Heart Attacks, and Chris Benoit."
11. Omalu, "Chronic Traumatic Encephalopathy," 131.
12. Alvarez, "Benoit Kills Family, Self," 1.
13. Lewis, "Last Days of Chris Benoit."
14. Omalu, "Chronic Traumatic Encephalopathy," 131.
15. It is also important to note that Benoit probably had a history of domestic violence, which may not have been linked to his work. See "Benoit's History of Domestic Violence Exposed."
16. ROH still exists, but it is no longer an independent promotion. It is owned by Sinclair Broadcasting, now better known as a purveyor of extreme right-wing news.
17. KENTA went on to work in WWE's Cruiserweight division under the name Hideo Itami. He left the company in early 2019. He, too, has suffered from career-threatening injuries.

18. This is hardly an ironclad rule. CM Punk, for example, was allowed to keep the name he used in the indies—on the condition that he let WWE trademark the name for merchandising purposes. See "Tuesday's Ask PWTorch," as well as Andrew Zolides's chapter in this volume.

19. Neither Bryan nor Benoit was small by normal human standards. According to Omalu ("Chronic Traumatic Encephalopathy," 131), Benoit was six feet one at his death, but WWE (which often exaggerates the size of its wrestlers) lists him at five feet eleven. Speculation on wrestling discussion boards places him under that, closer to five feet ten. At the height of his career, he was *extremely* muscular. Bryan is substantially smaller, apparently around five feet eight, and is also muscular, but he does not have the bodybuilder's physique that Benoit had. Given that the poststeroid era has generated smaller wrestlers overall in the decade that separates the two wrestlers' WWE careers, I suspect they are probably similarly undersized relative to their cohorts in WWE. Both wrestlers got their starts among physically smaller colleagues and in contexts where agility was more highly valued than it ever has been in WWE—Benoit in Japan, Bryan (then Danielson) in US independent promotions like ROH.

20. Keller, "WWE Releases Bryan Danielson," 1.

21. Simpson, "WWE Wrestler Daniel Bryan Apprehends Burglar."

22. This sensitivity is further highlighted by the presentation of Bryan's mental health in multiple episodes of the reality show *Total Divas*, in which Bryan is a recurring supporting character, as well as its spinoff *Total Bellas*, in which Bryan is a central character. In both shows, Bryan is shown manifesting symptoms of anxiety and depression related to his forced retirement and his quest to return to the ring. While these portrayals of Bryan's mental health struggles can be read as critiquing WWE's treatment of Bryan, they also justify his retirement and promote WWE as a responsible, caring employer that prioritizes the health of its wrestlers. Bryan's return to the ring is preceded by his decision, in the *Total Bellas* season 1 episode "Bella Family Secrets," to receive mental health therapy.

23. Until quite recently, it was unthinkable for a wrestler to leave WWE voluntarily for the prospect of better pay and treatment elsewhere. But Cody Rhodes's post-WWE career has demonstrated that a well-known, savvy businessperson can prosper outside WWE. See Castleberry, "Squared Circle Intentionalities," 110–13.

24. Corteen and Corteen, "Dying to Entertain?," 50–52.

25. For a useful thorough discussion of WWE's testing policies, see "Does WWE's Wellness Policy Work." After Brock Lesnar failed a 2016 United States Anti-Doping Agency test necessitated by his return to MMA fighting, WWE admitted that their contract with Lesnar expressly stipulated that the company would not punish Lesnar for test failures. In other words, WWE granted Lesnar a license to use steroids. See Mitchell, "Chris Benoit," 11. WWE has been placing female wrestlers in more prominent positions over the last few years. As Anna F. Peppard's chapter in this volume suggests, the aesthetic standards may be even less realistic for them. As WWE's female Superstars push themselves to work a more athletically demanding style while maintaining their bodies as required, we can probably expect to see a pattern of serious injuries emerge soon: Paige's recent injury-related retirement at age twenty-five may be the first of many. (Like Bryan, Paige has since taken on the role of *SmackDown Live* general manager.)

26. Smith, "WWE's Highest-Paid Wrestlers."

27. Keller and Caldwell, "WWE Network," 2.

28. Kline, "Inside the WWE Raw and Smackdown Deals."

29. Lewis, "Last Days of Chris Benoit"; Keller, "Statute of Limitations," 1.

30. Alvarez, "Benoit Brain Massively Damaged," 1.

31. Ibid.

32. Alvarez, "Benoit Fallout," 2.

33. Summoned by King Belshazzar to interpret words written on the wall of his palace by a spectral hand, the prophet Daniel explains that the writing refers to the life of Belshazzar's father Nebuchadnezzar, who "killed those he wanted to kill, kept alive those he wanted to keep alive, honored those he wanted to honor, and degraded those he wanted to degrade. But when his

heart was lifted up and his spirit was hardened so that he acted proudly, he was deposed from his kingly crown, and his glory was stripped from him."

34. Jameson, "Marx's Purloined Letter," 37.

35. Negri, "Specter's Smile," 10. See also Derrida's response to Negri in "Marx & Sons," 260.

36. For an account of the affective labor done by wrestling fans, see Smith, "Passion Work."

37. McNeill, "Best Wrestler in the World," 11.

38. See Christian Norman's chapter in this volume for an extended reading of the storytelling surrounding this phase of Bryan's career.

39. For instance, the "dream match" at WWE NXT *TakeOver: Dallas* between Sami Zayn and Shinsuke Nakamura ("the king of strong style") provoked a vociferous "Yes!" chant.

40. Derrida, *Specters of Marx*, 12

41. Ibid.

42. Ibid.

43. Ibid., 13.

Bibliography

Alvarez, Bryan. "Benoit Brain Massively Damaged." *Figure Four Weekly.* September 17, 2007.

———. "Benoit Fallout: Doctor Busted." *Figure Four Weekly.* July 9, 2007.

———. "Benoit Kills Family, Self." *Figure Four Weekly.* July 7, 2007.

"Benoit's History of Domestic Violence Exposed." *TMZ.* July 26, 2007. http://www.tmz.com /2007/06/26/benoits-history-of-domestic-violence-exposed/.

Castleberry, Garret L. "Squared Circle Intentionalities: What a Framework for 'Wrestling Studies' Can Look Like." *Popular Culture Studies Journal* 6, no. 1: 100–120.

Chow, Broderick D. V. "Work and Shoot: Professional Wrestling as Embodied Politics." *TDR: The Drama Review* 58, no. 2 (Summer 2014): 72–86.

Corteen, Karen, and Ajay Corteen. "Dying to Entertain? The Victimization of Professional Wrestlers in the USA." *International Perspectives in Victimology* 7, no. 1: 47–53.

Derrida, Jacques. "Marx & Sons." In *Ghostly Demarcations: A Symposium in Response to Jacques Derrida's Specters of Marx,* edited by Michael Sprinker, 213–69. London: Verso, 1999.

———. *Specters of Marx: The State of Debt, the Work of Mourning, and the New International.* Translated by Peggy Kamuf. New York: Routledge, 1994.

"Does WWE's Wellness Policy Work: A History of Drug Testing." *Wrestlepundit.com.* June 27, 2015. http://wrestlepundit.com/wwe-news/wwe-wellness-policy-drugs-steroids/.

Jameson, Fredric. "Marx's Purloined Letter." In *Ghostly Demarcations: A Symposium on Jacques Derrida's Specters of Marx,* edited by Michael Sprinker, 26–67. London: Verso, 1999.

Keller, Wade. "Statute of Limitations." *Pro Wrestling Torch.* July 26, 2007.

———. "WWE Releases Bryan Danielson, Conduct Cited." *Pro Wrestling Torch.* June 15, 2010.

Keller, Wade, and James Caldwell. "WWE Network: Already a Success?" *Pro Wrestling Torch.* February 17, 2016.

Kline, Daniel B. "Inside the WWE Raw and Smackdown Deals." *Motley Fool.* May 17, 2014. http://www.fool.com/investing/general/2014/05/17/inside-the-wwe-raw-and-smack down-tv-deals.aspx.

Lewis, Michael. "The Last Days of Chris Benoit." *Maxim.* November 14, 2007. http://www .maxim.com/entertainment/last-days-chris-benoit.

McNeill, Pat. "Best Wrestler in the World." *Pro Wrestling Torch.* February 3, 2007.

Mitchell, Bruce. "Chris Benoit, Vince McMahon, Roman Reigns, and Brock Lesnar." *Pro Wrestling Torch.* August 4, 2016.

Negri, Antonio. "The Specter's Smile." In *Ghostly Demarcations: A Symposium on Jacques Derrida's Specters of Marx,* edited by Michael Sprinker, 5–16. London: Verso, 1999.

Omalu, Bennet I., et al. "Chronic Traumatic Encephalopathy in a Professional American Wrestler." *Journal of Forensic Nursing* 6, no. 3 (2010): 130–36.

Simpson, Jack. "WWE Wrestler Daniel Bryan Apprehends Burglar with Rear Naked Chokehold." *Independent*, July 26, 2014. http://www.independent.co.uk/news/people/wwe-star -daniel-bryan-apprehends-burglar-with-bare-naked-chokehold-9630453.html.

Skipper, Ben. "Hard Drugs, Heart Attacks, and Chris Benoit: The Tragic Deaths of WWE Legends." *International Business Times*, April 9, 2014. http://www.ibtimes.co.uk/hard-drugs -heart-attacks-chris-benoits-meltdown-tragic-deaths-wwe-legends-1444020.

Smith, Chris. "WWE's Highest-Paid Wrestlers." *Forbes*. March 31, 2016. http://www.forbes.com /sites/chrissmith/2016/03/31/wwes-highest-paid-wrestlers/#1bbff1422e00.

Smith, R. Tyson. "Passion Work: The Joint Production of Emotional Labor in Professional Wrestling." *Social Psychology Quarterly* 71, no. 2 (2008): 157–76.

"Tuesday's Ask PW Torch." *Pro Wrestling Torch*. August 13, 2013. http://www.pwtorch.com /artman2/publish/Ask_the_Editor_18/article_72676.shtml#.V3aEjzmU2MJ.

SEAN DESILETS is Senior Lecturer in the Arts and Sciences Writing Program at Boston University. He is author of *Hermeneutic Humility and the Political Theology of Cinema: Blind Paul*.

INDEX

Academy Awards, 25
Alvarez, Bryan, 104, 110, 207
Amesley, Cassandra, 124
Amish Roadkill, 148
Andre the Giant, 72
Andrejevic, Mark, 162
Angle, Kurt, 35
Ariane, 177–178, 185–187, 190, 196n42
Art of Wrestling, The (podcast), 58–60
attitude era, 6, 9, 73, 143, 180, 181
Austin, Alec, 133
Austin, Steve, 6, 9, 18n19, 19n23, 19n36, 73,
    118n19, 126, 138, 168

Bahktin, Mikhail, 57, 66
Baker, Sarah, 60–61
Bale, John, 66, 68, 75–76
Bálor, Finn, 42n55, 132
Banet-Weiser, Sarah, 169–170
Banks, Sasha, 141, 206
Barthes, Roland, 8, 79n10, 88, 104, 153n1
Batista. *See* Bautista, Dave
Battema, Douglas, 187–188, 191
Battleground (pay-per-view), 108
Bautista, Dave, 25, 28, 91–94, 130
Bayley, 147
Beck, Glenn, 39
Bella Twins (Nikki and Brie), 177–178, 181,
    183–186, 189–191, 193–194, 195n26, 195n35,
    195n38, 196n43, 196n46
Benoit, Chris, 16, 200–213, 213n15, 214n19
Benoit, Daniel, 201, 207, 208–209, 210–211
Benoit, Nancy, 201
Big Show, 34, 148–149
Bird, S. Elizabeth, 128
Bollea, Terry. *See* Hogan, Hulk
Bordo, Susan, 186
Bonner, Frances, 49–50
Booth, Wayne, 85, 86, 97n19
Botchamania, 15, 139, 141, 144–153, 154n25

boyd, danah, 56
Brecht, Bertolt, 153
Brodus, 190–191
Brooks, Phil. *See* Punk, CM
Brown, D'Lo, 191
Bryan, Daniel, 97n27, 97n32, 97n36, 97n39,
    97n41, 122, 128–129, 149–150, 166, 171,
    186, 214n22, 214n25; in relation to Chris
    Benoit, 16, 200–213; storyline
    culminating at *WrestleMania XXX*, 84–85,
    89–95, 109, 117
Bush, George W., 34
Butryn, Ted, 31, 51–52, 65–66
Byte This, 162

Cabana, Colt, 9, 30, 58–60
Caldwell, John, 50
Call, The (film), 74
Cameron. *See* Ariane
Carlson, Marvin, 27–28
Camp WWE, 74–75, 105
carnival, 1, 17n2, 28, 29, 30, 47, 53, 60, 66, 70,
    79, 120, 121, 122, 130, 133–134
Castleberry, Garrett L., 2, 29
Cena, John, 6–8, 19n25, 34, 35, 37, 74, 90–91,
    123, 127, 141, 148–150; use of Tout, 163,
    166–167, 169–171; on *Total Divas*, 188–189,
    195n38
Charleton, Chris, 109
Chatman, Seymour, 85–86
Chion, Michel, 141–142
Chow, Broderick, 28, 120
Chyna, 187
Clerc, Susan, 187
Cole, Adam, 116
Cole, Michael, 19n32, 32, 154n15, 167, 171
Combat Zone Wrestling, 145
Coppa, Francesca, 145
Couldry, Nick, 164, 168
Craven, Gerald, 120

Cruiserweight Classic, 116–117
cultural legitimacy, 5, 73
Cyber Monday (pay-per-view), 161

D-Generation X, 6
Davis, Kathy, 186
Dawson, Max, 168
DC Comics, 25
Danielson, Bryan. *See* Bryan, Daniel
Del Rio, Alberto, 39
Deleuze, Gilles, 66
Derrida, Jacques, 16, 198–200, 209, 211–213, 213n7
Deville, Sonya, 42n55
Di Benedetto, Stephen, 122–123
DiBiase, Ted Jr., 74
Disney, 1, 25
Dragon Gate, 116
Dudley, Bubba Ray, 133
Dyer, Richard, 49

Edge and Christian Show That Totally Reeks of Awesomeness, The, 105
El Torito, 25
Ellis, John, 168
Emma, 193
Emmy Awards, 5, 18n14
Evolution (pay-per-view), 12 , 13, 19n37
Extreme Championship Wrestling, 80n29
Extreme Rules (pay-per-view), 132–133
Ezell, Jon, 125, 128, 134n22

Facebook, 29, 30, 56, 132, 160, 162, 165, 171, 172
Fake It So Real (film), 146
Feuer, Jane, 164, 167–168
Finlay, David "Fit," 36
Fiske, John, 66–68, 145, 151, 178
Flair, Charlotte, 19n36
Flair, Ric, 19n36
Foley, Mick, 128, 132
Ford, Sam, 71, 125–126, 129, 130
Foucault, Michel, 94
Fox (television network), 3, 5, 18n10

Gable, Chad, 147
Gamson, Joshua, 49, 53–54
García, Justin G., 190, 195n42
Godfather, The, 191
Goldust, 195n30
Gray, Jonathan, 17n7, 26, 75
Great Khali, 39

Greatest Royal Rumble (pay-per-view), 38, 81n32
Green, Joshua, 71
Gregg, Matthew. *See* Maffew
Guardians of the Galaxy (film), 25, 28
Guerrero, Chavo, 201
Guerrero, Eddie, 201, 206–207
Guttmann, Allen, 104

Harkulich, Christiana Molldrem, 180
Hart, Bret "the Hitman," 73, 126–127
Harvey, David, 68, 69–70, 77–78
Havens, Timothy, 49
Heenan, Bobby "the Brain," 154n15
Heinecken, Dawn, 179
Henry, Mark, 191
Hesmondhalgh, David, 60–61
Heyman, Paul, 62n33
Hills, Matt, 26, 151
Hogan, Hulk, 8, 32, 72, 73, 77, 80n21, 86, 115, 138, 203
Hollywood, 8, 51, 54, 74
Holmes, Su, 182
Holy Foley!, 105
Hornbaker, Tim, 80n17
Hulk Hogan's Rock 'n' Wrestling, 80n24
Hunt, Leon, 144–145, 146

independent wrestling, 9, 51, 55, 60, 109, 146
Instagram, 16, 29, 160, 171, 172, 185
Iron Sheik, 33
Itami, Hideo. *See* KENTA

Jansen, Brian, 3, 8, 10
JBL, 154n15
JBL and Cole Show, The, 163
Jenkins, Henry III, 9–10, 25–26, 71, 135n49
Jenkins, Henry IV, 140
Jericho, Chris, 173n6
Jermyn, Deborah, 182
Johnson, Derek, 26, 161, 166
Johnson, Dwayne, 8–9, 54, 73, 77, 88, 138, 169
Johnson, Steve, 103
JoJo, 177–178
Jordan, Jason, 147

Kaitlyn, 34
Kavka, Misha, 188
kayfabe, 39, 62n42, 68, 90, 93, 130, 131, 133, 182;
    definitions of, 1, 17n2, 41n19, 53, 83–84, 88,
    121; in relation to social media, 29, 30, 78,
    161–162, 170; loosening of, 3, 4–7, 10–11, 16

KENTA, 202, 214n17
Kingston, Kofi, 35, 97n39
Konuwa, Alfred, 5, 182
Kozinets, Robert V., 165

Laclau, Ernesto, 94
Laine, Eero, 1, 6–7, 28, 61, 120, 129
Larsen, Katherine, 154n25
Lashley, Bobby, 133
Last Week Tonight with John Oliver, 19n39
Lawler, Jerry "the King," 77–78, 154n15, 167
Layfield, John. *See* JBL
Lee, AJ, 191–193, 196n43–45
Leonardi, Susan J., 180–181
Lesnar, Brock, 4, 97n36, 138, 159–160, 167, 170–171, 214n25
Levesque, Paul, 2, 11–12, 19n32, 31, 83, 90, 93, 96, 147, 163, 170
Lita, 187
Litherland, Benjamin, 30
Lord of the Rings, 25
Lotz, Amanda D., 17n7, 49
Lucas, George, 95
lucha libre, 61, 98n43, 103
Lucha Underground, 96, 98n43

Maffew, 139, 141, 144, 145, 147–150, 153
Mahal, Jinder, 154n16
Main Event, 126
Major League Baseball, 2, 80n29
Make-a-Wish Foundation, 37
Manning, Peyton, 151
Marella, Santino, 39
Marie, Eva, 177–178, 183–184, 187, 190
Marine, The (film franchise), 74
Marshall, P. David, 49–50
Marufuji, Noamichi, 202
Marvel Cinematic Universe, 13, 25, 28
Marvel Comics, 55
Marwick, Alice, 56
Marx, Karl, 93, 198–200, 209, 211, 213, 213n7
Mazer, Sharon, 48, 123, 128, 129, 139, 140, 144, 178, 184
McBride, Lawrence, 128
McGuinness, Nigel, 202
McMahon, Linda, 2, 14, 19n38, 34, 36, 39, 52, 61, 65
McMahon, Shane, 2
McMahon, Stephanie, 2, 11–12, 62n33, 90–91, 163, 181
McMahon, Vince, 9, 11, 36, 80n21–22, 103, 111, 115, 159, 163, 165, 199, 205; and business,

2, 13, 17n6, 52, 65–67, 72–74, 105, 107, 160; and philanthropy, 19n38, 31–32; and WWE Creative, 7–8, 19n25, 86, 90, 91, 126; onscreen appearances of, 5–7, 10, 88, 97n39
McQuarrie, Fiona, 72
Meltzer, Dave, 94, 104. *See also* Wrestling Observer Newsletter
Mendes, Rosa, 189–190
mixed martial arts, 110, 159, 204, 214n25. *See also* Ultimate Fighting Championship
Miz & Mrs., 194, 196n46
Mizanin, Maryse, 196n46
Mizanin, Mike "the Miz," 74, 88, 196n46
Monday Night Raw, 3, 18n12, 19n32, 68, 90, 116, 118n14, 126, 127, 132, 138, 140, 141–142, 144, 154n15, 154n19, 160, 165, 181, 182, 202, 203; August 20, 2012 episode of, 159, 170; August 26, 2013 episode of, 191–193; December 15, 1997 episode of, 5; July 16, 2012 episode of, 166–169; July 23, 2018 episode of, 11–12, 13; June 27, 2011 episode of, 6–9, 7, 97n26; March 10, 2014 episode of, 92–94; ratings and viewership of, 73, 95, 194n6; September 10, 2012 episode of, 77–78
Monday Nitro, 73, 105
Money in the Bank (pay-per-view), 6, 19n25
Monsoon, Gorilla, 154n15
Morishima, Takeski, 202
Morris, Jeremy, 56
Moseley, Richard, 120
Mysterio, Rey, 34, 92, 206

Nakamura, Shinsuke, 147, 215n39
Naomi. *See* Trinity
NASCAR, 35, 73
Natalya. *See* Nattie
National Football League, 2, 18n10, 35, 58–59, 151, 159
National Wrestling Alliance, 71, 72
Nattie, 177–178, 183, 189–190, 195n24
Negri, Antonio, 209–210
neoliberalism, 52, 65–67, 69, 80n22, 200
Netflix, 1, 4
New Japan Pro Wrestling, 9, 96, 98n43, 109, 116, 202
No Holds Barred (film), 73, 80n21
NXT, 96, 116, 126, 141, 147, 182

Obama, Barack, 34
Oliver, Greg, 103
Orton, Randy, 90–91, 93–94, 149–150
Owens, Kevin, 154n19

Page, "Diamond" Dallas, 73
Paige, 25, 141, 183–185, 187, 193, 214n25
paratexts, 26, 52, 165
Payback (pay-per-view), 149
Phelan, James, 87
Playboy, 180
Pope, Rebecca A.,180–181
Pro Wrestling Guerilla, 109, 114, 116
Projansky, Sarah, 180
Punk, CM, 47, 55–60, 62n33, 62n42, 97n32, 127, 166, 214n18; "pipe bomb" promo, 6–11, 7, 18n19, 19n23, 19n25, 19n36, 89, 97n26, 163

R-Truth, 6
Rabinowitz, Peter J., 87, 97n19
Rahilly, Lucia, 184
Raven, 73
Raw. See Monday Night Raw
Raw Magazine, 180
Real Americans, The, 38–39
reality era, 6, 9, 11, 14, 18n18, 19n32, 78, 83–84, 88–90, 93, 96
reality television, 3, 4, 15–16, 95, 105, 111, 177–179, 182, 188, 191–192
Reigns, Roman, 96, 127, 132–133, 147, 173
Reinhard, Carrielynn D., 29
Relph, E., 75
Rhodes, Cody, 25, 55, 214n23
Rice, Carla, 180
Ricochet, 116
Ring of Honor, 9, 109, 110, 114, 116, 131, 202, 213n16, 214n19
Rock, The. *See* Johnson, Dwayne
Rollins, Seth, 132–133
Ross, Jim, 38, 143, 154n15
Ross, Sharon Marie, 161, 164–165
Rosser, Fred. *See* Young, Darren
Rousey, Ronda, 116, 181, 194n20
Rowan, Erick, 25
Royal Rumble (match), 42n55, 91–92
Royal Rumble (pay-per-view), 18n18, 19n36, 91, 97n32, 116, 194n20
Ryback, 148
Ryder, Zack, 162–163, 166–167, 169–170, 171

Sabu, 148–150
Salmon, Catherine, 187
Sammond, Nicholas, 184
Scooby Doo! WrestleMania Mystery (film), 74–75
Scott, Michael, 56

self-reflexivity, 12, 50, 88, 90, 92–93, 97n26, 162–163
Sewell, Philip, 188, 191
Sgt. Slaughter, 32
Shoemaker, David, 10–11, 51, 58–59, 83, 88, 96n7, 128
Slam City, 74
SmackDown Live, 3, 18n10, 18n12, 33, 68, 94–95, 126, 132, 138, 154n15, 160, 165, 171, 182, 194n6, 204, 214n25
Smith, R. Tyson, 108
Snapchat, 172
social media, 1, 4, 12, 15–16, 17, 28, 29–31, 37–38, 50, 56, 60, 78, 80n23, 108, 111, 134n18, 159–160, 162, 164, 167–168, 169–172, 193. *See also specific platforms*
Solomon, Robert, 61
sports entertainment, 2, 5, 15, 29, 53, 65–68, 86, 103–117, 122, 146, 159
Stardust. *See* Rhodes, Cody
Star Trek, 25
Star Wars, 25, 95
steroids, 66, 188, 200–201, 203, 205, 206–207, 214n19, 214n25
Steve Austin Show—Unleashed!, The (podcast), 83
"Stone Cold" Steve Austin. *See* Austin, Steve
Summer Rae, 195n24
SummerSlam (pay-per-view), 89–90, 97n36, 132, 181, 185
Super Show-Down (pay-per-view), 81n32
Susan G. Komen For the Cure Foundation, 13, 37, 38–39

Taboo Tuesday (pay-per-view), 161, 173n6
Talking Smack, 171
Tensai, 190–191
territory system, 14, 66, 68, 69–73, 103, 105, 126
theater, 27–28, 36, 48, 120, 150, 153, 200, 213
30 for 30, 3
Thompson, E. P., 135n49
Tinic, Serra, 49
Toepfer, Shane, 122, 124–125, 131, 134n14
Tonight Show with Jay Leno, The, 73
Torres, Eve, 163, 183–184, 187, 190,
Total Bellas, 95, 194, 196n46, 214n22
Total Divas, 16, 177–179, 181–194, 194n2, 195n24–25, 195n38–39, 195n41, 196n42, 214n22
Tout, 16, 159–160, 163, 165–173, 173n28
transmedia, 2, 4, 11, 14, 15, 17, 61, 130, 179, 194
Tribute to the Troops, 13, 27, 32–34, 37

Trinity, 177–178, 185, 187, 189–190, 195n39, 195n41–42
Triple H. *See* Levesque, Paul
Trump, Donald, 14, 19n38, 41n40, 61, 73
Turner, Graeme, 49–50
Turner, Ted, 73, 80n22
Twitter, 11, 16, 17, 19n25, 29–30, 56–57, 62n25, 104, 128, 130, 132, 144, 160, 162, 164–165, 169, 171, 172, 192–193
205 Live, 116, 126

Ultimate Fighting Championship, 4, 18n10, 55, 116, 159
Urrichio, William, 164
USA Network, 3, 165, 166

Vine, 160, 171

Warden, Claire, 120, 125
Ware, Nicholas, 128
Weber, Brenda R., 178–179
Williams, Raymond, 164
world building, 13–14, 25–27, 77
World Championship Wrestling, 73–74, 75, 80n21–22, 105
World Class Championship Wrestling, 105
World Wildlife Fund, 17n6, 74
Wrenn, Marion, 144
WrestleMania (pay-per-view), 73, 127, 132, 154n19; *WrestleMania I* (1985), 72; *Wrestle-Mania XX* (2004), 35, 159, 206; *WrestleMa-nia XXV* (2009), 34; *WrestleMania XXVII*
(2012), 8; *WrestleMania XXIX* (2013), 168, 177–178, 182; *WrestleMania XXX* (2014), 15, 77, 84–85, 89, 91–94, 97n39, 103, 106, 108, 109–110, 117, 118n14; *WrestleMania XXXI* (2015), 138; *WrestleMania XXXII* (2016), 147, 194n21; *WrestleMania XXXIV* (2018), 42n55, 95, 204; *WrestleMania XV* (2019), 97n39
Wrestling Observer Newsletter, 51. *See also* Meltzer, Dave
WWE Diva Search, 180, 181, 194n12
WWE Hall of Fame, 38
WWE Network, 4, 11, 12, 19n34, 29, 51, 75, 80n24, 104, 105, 116, 171, 202, 205
WWE Studios, 74, 111
WWE Superstars (comic book), 74–75
WWE Tough Enough, 180
WWE Universe, 3, 13, 14, 25, 27–31, 34, 39–40, 68–69, 72, 74–78, 81n32, 114–115, 123, 126, 160, 166, 179
Wyatt, Bray, 118n12

Yeung, Stephanie M., 33
Yokozuna, 32
Young, Darren, 37–38, 42n55
YouTube, 11, 16, 56, 111, 159, 162–163, 169, 171, 172

Zayn, Sami, 38, 147, 215n39
Ziggler, Dolph, 36, 133, 144, 154n19, 166, 169–170
Zubernis, Lynn, 154n25

Lightning Source UK Ltd.
Milton Keynes UK
UKHW011320261019
352348UK00013B/289/P